Sonic Multiplicities

Sonic Multiplicities
Hong Kong Pop and the Global Circulation of Sound and Image

Yiu Fai Chow and Jeroen de Kloet

intellect Bristol, UK / Chicago, USA

First published in the UK in 2013 by
Intellect, The Mill, Parnall Road, Fishponds, Bristol, BS16 3JG, UK

First published in the USA in 2013 by
Intellect, The University of Chicago Press, 1427 E. 60th Street,
Chicago, IL 60637, USA

Copyright © 2013 Intellect Ltd

All rights reserved. No part of this publication may be reproduced,
stored in a retrieval system, or transmitted, in any form or by
any means, electronic, mechanical, photocopying, recording, or
otherwise, without written permission.

A catalogue record for this book is available from the
British Library.

Cover designer: Holly Rose
Cover photographer: Jeroen de Kloet
Copy-editor: MPS Technologies
Production manager: Bethan Ball
Typesetting: Contentra Technologies

ISBN 978-1-78320-004-7

Table of Contents

Acknowledgements — vii

List of Figures and Table — ix

INTRODUCTION: SONIC MULTIPLICITIES — 1
Sonic disappearances — 3
What is going on? — 6
Overview — 9

Chapter 1: ME AND THE DRAGON: A LYRICAL ENGAGEMENT WITH THE POLITICS OF CHINESENESS — 13
Nationalistic songs — 17
Another approach — 18
Re-nationalization I: Descendants of the dragon — 19
Re-nationalization II: Home and nation — 20
Re-nationalization III: Performing acts (i) – writing against the grain — 24
Re-nationalization IV: Performing acts (ii) – writing with a twist — 29
Shoot the dragon — 36

Chapter 2: THE PRODUCTION OF LOCALITY IN GLOBAL POP – A COMPARATIVE STUDY OF POP FANS IN THE NETHERLANDS AND HONG KONG — 39
Introduction — 41
Globalization: A sense of locality — 43
Fandom: On fans of local stars — 44
Methodology — 44
Production of locality: The linguistic and the heroic — 46
Production of locality: The social, the charitable and the personal — 49
    Community — 49
    Charity — 51
    Character — 52
Conclusion — 56

Chapter 3: BLOWING IN THE CHINA WIND: ENGAGEMENTS WITH CHINESENESS IN HONG KONG'S *ZHONGGUOFENG* MUSIC VIDEOS — 59
Destabilizing Chineseness — 65
Feminizing Chineseness — 70
Whither China Wind? — 77

Chapter 4: SEX, MORALITY AND CANTOPOP — 81
Picture Gate — 83
The Edison Chen scandal — 84
The Confucian cum Victorian ethics and the spirit of global capitalism — 88
Spectacle and image — 93
Eye see you as I see you — 95
Coda — 97

Chapter 5: BUILDING MEMORIES – A STUDY OF POP VENUES IN HONG KONG — 101
Fluid sounds — 103
Monumental buildings — 105
Building memories — 108
The Coliseum — 114
Belonging and temporality — 115

Chapter 6: OLYMPIC CELEBRATIONS AND PERFORMATIVE CONTESTATIONS — 117
The constative and the performative — 120
Welcome to Olympic Beijing — 122
Performing Olympic China from Hong Kong — 127
Shanghai also welcomes you! — 131
Criticality and popular culture — 133

Chapter 7: MUSIC, DESIRE AND THE TRANSNATIONAL POLITICS OF CHINESENESS: FOLLOWING DIANA — 137
Following Diana — 140
Diasporic hope: Rewriting migration narrative — 142
Musical hope: Rewriting modernity narrative — 144
    Language — 145
    Music — 146
    Body — 148
Methodological endnote — 150
    The flow — 151
    The bodily — 152
    The political — 152
    The personal — 153

Bibliography — 157

Index — 171

Acknowledgements

This book is not only a testament to our shared interest in Hong Kong popular music, but also to our shared sense of urgency to understand and study Hong Kong and Chinese popular music in the multiple paths and networks we have tried to track and delineate in the chapters to follow. More fundamentally, and perhaps intimately too, this book is a testament to the collaborative nature of knowledge production itself: to the possibility that academic work can be done less solitarily. The past years have seen the two of us discussing which theoretical grounding to take, how to analyse and do justice to the field data, which books to read, and who should write what – as engagingly as we discussed where to wine and dine afterwards. What we would like to say is that academic work can be done together, and with fun.

In the meantime, we are fully and happily aware that we would never have accomplished what we have without the encouragement and support of many others. In particular, we thank Ien Ang, Rey Chow, Chu Yiu Wai, John Nguyet Erni, Anthony Fung, Giselinde Kuipers, Leonie Schmidt and Liesbet van Zoonen for all our graceful discussions and lovely encounters, and for their continuous belief in our project. Then there are the friends with whom we share our collective indulgence in and mistrust of Hong Kong culture: Gladys Pak Lei Chong, Jeroen Groenewegen, Henk Hilkmann, Peter Ho, Anneke Huigen, Dineke Koerts, Kam Wai Kui, Helen Hok-sze Leung, Song Hwee Lim, Kam Wing Ling, Anne Minnema, Tak Wing Ngo, Lena Scheen, Hyunjoon Shin, Marcel Vergunst, Constance Vos, Anthony Wong and Rex Wong.

We thank Rebecca Chan, Louis Ho and Patrick Jered for helping consolidate our images and texts. We thank the Emperor Entertainment Group, East Asia Music, Warner Music and many other pop music industry people for their willingness to share. We thank the ASCA Transasia cultural studies group for their feedback. We would also like to express our gratitude to the International Association for the Study of Popular Music (IASPM) and its Inter-Asia popular music studies group for providing such wonderful moments of scholarly exchange.

We thank Intellect and our most efficient production manager Bethan Ball for their trust in us and belief in this project.

Above all, we want to thank our mothers. Yiu Fai's mother showed him the importance of popular culture by taking him to see all sorts of horror and action films when he was still a child. Jeroen's mother has continuously shown her support for all the detours and travels taken in the past and present, and it is to this unconditional encouragement that he owes his trust in writing.

Earlier versions of different chapters have been published as follows. We want to thank the journals for their permission to republish.

Chapter 1: *Inter-Asia Cultural Studies*, (2009), 10:4, pp. 544–564.
Chapter 2: *Participations*, (2008), 5:2, Available at http://www.participations.org/.
Chapter 3: *Visual Anthropology*, (2011), 24, pp. 59–76.
Chapter 5: *Berliner-China Hefte/Chinese History and Society*, (2008), 34, pp. 53–62.
Chapter 7: *Cultural Studies*, (2011), 25:6, pp. 783–808.

List of Figures and Table

Figures
Figure 1.1: Tatming Pair performing 'Don't Question the Heaven' (courtesy of People Mountain People Sea).
Figure 1.2: Nicholas Tse in MV of 'Yellow People' (courtesy of Emperor Entertainment Group).
Figure 2.1: Marco Borsato (courtesy of Loe Beerens).
Figure 2.2: Leon Lai (courtesy of Paciwood Music & Entertainment Ltd).
Figure 3.1: 'Goddess of Mercy' (Andy Lau) (courtesy of East Asia Music (Holdings) Ltd).
Figure 3.2: 'Goddess of Mercy' (Andy Lau) (courtesy of East Asia Music (Holdings) Ltd).
Figure 3.3: 'Small' (Joey Yung) (courtesy of Emperor Entertainment Group).
Figure 3.4: 'Sweet Dumplings' (Fiona Sit) (courtesy of Warner Music Hong Kong).
Figure 3.5: 'Sweet Dumplings' (Fiona Sit) (courtesy of Warner Music Hong Kong).
Figure 3.6: 'Daiyu Smiles' (Vincy) (courtesy of Emperor Entertainment Group).
Figure 3.7: 'Daiyu Smiles' (Vincy) (courtesy of Emperor Entertainment Group).
Figure 3.8: 'Sword and Snow' (Sammi Cheng and Denise Ho) (courtesy of East Asia Music (Holdings) Ltd).
Figure 3.9: 'Sword and Snow' (Sammi Cheng and Denise Ho) (courtesy of East Asia Music (Holdings) Ltd).
Figure 3.10: 'Big Red Robe' (Denise Ho) (courtesy of East Asia Music (Holdings) Ltd).
Figure 3.11: 'Big Red Robe' (Denise Ho) (courtesy of East Asia Music (Holdings) Ltd).
Figure 3.12: 'Big Red Robe' (Denise Ho) (courtesy of East Asia Music (Holdings) Ltd).
Figure 4.1: Internet circulation of the proof that these are the real celebrities being depicted.
Figure 4.2: Taken from the Internet, a timeline of Edison's sexual life.
Figure 4.3: Edison Chen in *Oriental Sunday* (Issue 599, 2 June 2009).
Figure 4.4: Edison Chen's Beijing 2011 art show.
Figure 4.5: Edison taking pictures – again.
Figure 5.1: City Hall (courtesy of Hong Kong Public Records Office).
Figure 5.2: City Hall dwarfed amidst the Hong Kong skyline.
Figure 5.3: Academic Community hall.
Figure 5.4: Queen Elizabeth Stadium.
Figure 5.5: Hong Kong Coliseum.

Figure 5.6:   Hong Kong Exhibition and Convention centre.
Figure 5.7:   West Kowloon Project.
Figure 6.1:   New Labour Art Troupe's 'Our World, Our Dream'.
Figure 7.1:   Diana Zhu.

Table
Table 3.1:   China Wind entries to Commercial Radio pop chart January 2006–October 2008.

INTRODUCTION: SONIC MULTIPLICITIES

The city is not so much a place as a space of transit. It has always been, and will perhaps always be, a port in the most literal sense – a doorway, a point in between – [... Hong Kong subjectivity is] a subjectivity constructed not narcissistically but in the very process of negotiating the mutations and permutations of colonialism, nationalism, and capitalism.

Ackbar Abbas (1997: 11)

Maybe the target nowadays is not to discover what we are but to refuse what we are. We have to imagine and to build up what we could be to get rid of this kind of political 'double bind,' which is the simultaneous individualization and totalization of modern power structures.

Michel Foucault (2000 [1982]: 336)

Sonic disappearances

Hong Kong popular music is dying, if not already dead. Ask anyone who has witnessed the heydays of Hong Kong pop, you would most likely receive this alarming reply. And you would most likely hear them hasten to add, with a mixture of pride and sadness, how different it was, how many great stars and great hits they had, then. Indeed, during the 1970s and 1980s, Hong Kong was an important producer of popular music whose appeal reached far beyond its boundaries, both regionally and globally. For a long long time, local pop delivered in the local language of Cantonese, otherwise known as Cantopop, dictated global Chinese charts; it was, simply, 'the sound of Chinese cool' (Burpee in Chu 2007: 2).

But now, chances are that participants of singing contests in Hong Kong (and the Chinese diaspora) would deliver a Mandarin song by a Taiwanese star, such as Zhou Jielun (Jay Chou). Increasingly, Hong Kong singers shift their (market) base to mainland China just as fast as the section devoted to Hong Kong singers gets downsized in music stores both online and offline. In his doctoral thesis, the veteran Cantopop lyricist and composer James Wong, pinpointed 1997 – the year Hong Kong was handed over to the Beijing authorities – as the end of the Cantopop era (Wong 2003). Figures are quoted to quantify and certify its disappearance: in 1995, Cantopop sales amounted to HK$1.853 billion, while three years later sales had dropped to HK$ 0.916 billion (Wong 2003: 169). While bad economy, over-commercialization and file-sharing technology were quoted as reasons for the disappearance of Hong Kong pop (see for instance Chu 2007; Lee, S. 2002), the death of two local superstars, Leslie Cheung and Anita Mui, in the same year, 2003, seemed to have completed the necrology.

However convincing this narrative is – and we want to make it clear that it is not our intention to undermine the harsh reality of Hong Kong's shrinking market and star share in the Greater China region – we want to contest it, to complicate it, to complement it. This book is a collection of our different ways to read Hong Kong popular music in particular and, by extension, popular music in general. Indeed, we prefer to write of Hong Kong popular music instead of Cantopop, as to steer away from defining music through language towards defining it through its locality of production. More immediately and more simply, one of the aims of this book is to (re)claim more space for Hong Kong in the field of popular music studies, which is increasingly and understandably occupied by studies privileging mainland China, reflecting and contributing to the so-called Rise of China at large. In other words, we want to address and redress the ongoing marginalization not only of Hong Kong pop music, but also of Hong Kong pop music studies itself (for a detailed discussion of the 'death of Hong Kong pop', see Chapter 5).

Take book-length treatises as an illustration. Last decade saw the publication of three English-language monographs concerning Chinese-language pop music. While the monograph *China with a Cut* (2010) written by Jeroen de Kloet, one of the authors of this book, deals predominantly with Beijing rock in the context of globalization, Nimrod Baranovich similarly situates his *China's New Voices* (2003) in mainland China, focusing more specifically on issues of ethnicity and gender during the two decades before the new millennium. Marc L. Moscowitz' work comes closer to our project, as he charts in his book *Cries of Joy, Songs of Sorrow* (2010) how Taiwan pop has become a powerful popular cultural force not only in Taiwan but also, and especially so, in mainland China. His work thus engages, like ours, with the flows of music, taking Mandopop as its focus. Yet, unlike these studies, our book takes Hong Kong as its starting point, but not by privileging Hong Kong as a unique site; rather, it corresponds with what is going on in the field of Chinese-language popular music by taking Hong Kong as its entry point. It aims to understand how the city and its popular culture is entangled in a complex transnational cultural web – a nodal point for flows of people, sounds, images, things, and ideologies, including the increasingly pervasive ideology of Chineseness – between Hong Kong, Taiwan, mainland China and the world at large.

By taking Hong Kong as one important nodal point in the global flow of culture, we also depart from available Chinese-language studies on Hong Kong pop music. Local scholar Stephen Chu is the prolific author and co-author of six books on Hong Kong pop music, all in Chinese language (Chu 2004, 2001, 2000, 1998; Chu and Leung 2011; Wong, Chu and Leung 2010). Embedded in Chinese literature studies, this impressive array of publications takes either lyrics, the textual dimension of Hong Kong popular music, or a particular period of Hong Kong pop history as its primary object of documentation and analysis. With an even stronger archival purpose, several other publications aspire to construct a historical account of how local popular music industry has originated and developed, more or less explicitly in connection with the alleged dying of Hong Kong pop (Wong 2006; Wong 2007; Fung et al. 2011). In our own inquiries we continue to draw insights from these valuable literary and historical studies. However, by situating Hong Kong and local pop in a web of flows, we are guided to look beyond the confines of lyrics to the multiplicities of popular music, and from there to contest the gloomy narrative of decline and death, to, as we said earlier, to offer different readings, ultimately to rewrite the history of Hong Kong popular music – to cite from our study of Hong Kong China Wind music, after all, the history of Chinese as well as Hong Kong pop music is yet to be written (see Chapter 3 on China Wind). In the meantime, it is also our project to rethink popular music studies through forging stronger alliances with area studies.

This book comes at a moment when narratives on the rise of China are in full swing. In the economic slipstream, numerous studies on China are currently being published, in which China generally and a bit too easily conflates with mainland China. There is a potential uncomfortable link between the economic rise of China in the context of global capitalism and the rapid expansion of studies on its culture. Indeed, in today's world, culture has become a lubricating force for the global spread of capital. As Lash and Lury write, 'culture is so ubiquitous that it, as it were, seeps out of the superstructure and comes to infiltrate, and then take over, the infrastructure itself. […] In global culture industry, production and consumption are processes of the construction of difference' (2007: 4–5). The perceived centre of the rise of China has increasingly become Beijing, as we observed earlier. Yet, Hong Kong offers possibilities to undermine or question the alleged importance of 'Chinese culture,' precisely because of its perpetual in-between position (Ma 2012). It is a city that is neither Chinese nor western, and it is precisely this cultural indeterminacy that helps to question the role of culture in today's global culture industry. Hong Kong's claim on ethnic difference is bound to be incomplete and impure, which allows a rethinking of the link between place, sound and culture in an era of intense globalization.

As Helen Hok-Sze Leung argues, 'devoid of any political possibility of an alternative nationalist claim, Hong Kong's self-narrative of difference is far more nebulous: it is often perceptible only as an undertow of unease that refuses to allow the surface calm to settle' (2008: 5). It is precisely this cultural indeterminacy that makes Hong Kong such a good case not to study but to unpack culture, to question rather than confirm Chineseness. Here we take our inspiration also from the Chinese artist Ai Weiwei, who questions, with us, the alleged importance, including its smooth transformation into capital, of 'Chinese culture'. Ai Weiwei writes, 'all our firm beliefs in culture ask the questions: Who are you? Who do you think you are? What do you want to become? Or what makes you believe you can become that? Well, what is the basis of this discourse? All we're talking about is: What has happened recently? What is happening now? What will happen in the future?' (Ai Weiwei, quoted in He 2008: 39). This book is an attempt to dig further into these questions. It inspires us to question not so much the peculiarities of Hong Kong popular music, but more the role Hong Kong plays in the global flow of sounds, images and people. In this investigation we take our inspiration in a simple, basic, yet urgent question, we want to ask ourselves: what is going on in today's global cultural industries?

What is going on?

Our contestation is not only theoretically driven but also empirically informed by our (as well as others') experience both as cultural producers and cultural consumers of Hong Kong popular music. Working in the industry for more than two decades, Yiu Fai Chow, the co-author of this book, feels not only a sense of helplessness, doom and struggle, but also a vibrancy to survive, to trick and ultimately to continue producing good music. And as we listen, we do hear more nuances than what the dwindling number of sale figures and disappearance of local superstars would invoke. Our field experience, in short, does not allow us to see Hong Kong pop music as a finished product, both in the economic and in the past sense. When we shift from economic performance – the dominant paradigm and narrative of the music industry itself, which puts forward a worrisome picture compared to the golden days of the past – when we shift to the always present, ongoing cultural circulation and flows, we encounter not death, but life; we are empirically drawn to and intrigued by the lively ways cultural producers, products, venues and consumers engage with the music-cum-meaning-making process that travels between the city, the nation, or any specific understanding of locality. To put it more straightforwardly, this book is also, and probably first and foremost, inspired by our affective investment in Hong Kong popular music over the past decades.

In his influential work *Hong Kong: Culture and Politics of Disappearance*, Ackbar Abbas argues convincingly how the city, its culture and its identity, appeared precisely at the time of its imminent disappearance with the 1997 handover to Beijing and the inevitable prospect of re-nationalization (Abbas 1997). But the postcolonial identity should never be fixed, in Abbas' words, 'it must not be another stable appearance, another stable identity. It must learn how to survive a culture of disappearance by adopting strategies of disappearance as its own, by giving disappearance itself a different inflection' (1997: 15). This book affirms empirically his belief in the resilience of Hong Kong to reinvent its culture and identity, despite, or perhaps because of, the post-1997 shadow over the city and its pop music and culture. Yet, this reinvention simultaneously undermines any possibility of having a fixed identity but is instead in a never-ending process of becoming. In a way, Abbas may even have exaggerated the importance of 1997, in particular his suggestion that only when Hong Kong was on the verge of disappearance it started to construct its identity is questionable. The rise of Cantopop in the 1970s, and even the importance of Cantonese opera, serve as indicators that Hong Kong has always already been active in producing its cultural identity, one that, as we noted earlier, is by definition impure and unfinished, given its (post)colonial condition.

Introduction

Indeed, this book concerns time as much as it does place. The studies we conducted straddle the last forty years of Hong Kong's history: from the emergence of local identity in the 70s, through the shock of Sino-British negotiations and the ultimate handover during the 80s and 90s, to the post-millennium adjustments and negotiations with the city's new power relationship with Beijing and in the Greater China region as a whole. Woven with the thread of pop, the chapters attempt a chronology of Hong Kong marked by politics of memory, of identity, of language. More specifically, we embark on a tour from the very inception of Hong Kong pop, arguably more than four decades ago, when the colonial city started building its own pop venues, and local music-makers, most notably Sam Hui, started creating songs in their native language: Cantonese. Together they invented not only a local pop tradition but also a local identity. We then retrieve experiences from the twenty years to follow, that is, from the time when Hong Kong pop continued to produce global local superstars, with such telling nicknames as the four Heavenly Kings and the two Heavenly Queens; we talk to the fans of one Heavenly King, Leon Lai. It was, on the other hand, a turbulent period for the city when its political insouciance was challenged by the imminent change from British to Chinese sovereignty scheduled for 1997, and particularly by the student demonstration and subsequent crackdown in 1989; we take pop to chart the local response during this re-nationalization process. Very quickly, the city realized its integration with mainland China was not only political, but also deeply economic and cultural. The increasing importance of the mainland market, the privileging of the 'national' tongue, and, as noted at the beginning of this introduction, the concomitant popularity of Taiwanese pop and stars not only in the mainland but also in Hong Kong itself, drove local pop to the most challenging time of its history (for a lucid and in-depth analysis of the rise of Taiwanese stars, see Moskowitz 2010). Our inquiries follow the latest vicissitudes of Hong Kong pop onto the 'China century' celebrated, for instance, by its hosting of the Olympic Games in 2008 – or troubled, for instance, by the Edison Chen scandal in the same year as the Olympics. In the current century, Hong Kong and its local pop could no longer hang on to its export dominance, and its centrality; rather, it must reckon with its positionality, with the intricate correspondences, connections and flows the city and its culture are circulating in.

By placing local pop in the context of translocal flows, we hasten to add that our concern and our politics lie in the production of the local as much as in how this production emerges, corresponds, and impacts beyond the local. Probably also inspired by an increased parochialism that sweeps currently over Europe, we basically deeply mistrust the local as a possible site of agency or politics. But we want to do more, we do not only want to insert the case of Hong Kong into popular music studies, but we want to take this opportunity to also forge alliances between the fields of popular music studies, cultural studies and area studies. Whereas the first two fields are burdened by a strong Anglo-Saxon bias, the latter is haunted by an Orientalistic paradigm in which the alleged uniqueness of other places is often overtly articulated, generally following the geopolitical ordering of the world in fixed nation-states. Musicians outside the 'West' – a discursive trope that deserves as much unpacking as its constructed and equally utterly helpless binary opposite the 'East' – often carry the geopolitical burden of representation, whereas their western counterparts are much less expected or required to produce sounds that are intimately linked to place. In other words, we want to steer away from always reading Chinese sounds as markers of some kind of Chineseness, instead we read these sounds as being part of a complex global network of actors that include imageries, media reports, websites, singers, producers, lyric writers, composers, the music industry, and so forth. This development, or shift from the local and specific to the global and interconnected, requires what Tom Solomon (2009) terms 'ethnographies of motion', in which multiple sites and multiple actors, both human and non-human, are involved. We do not claim that locality is of no importance, despite its frequent uncomfortable alignments with parochialism and nationalism. On the contrary, as our comparative study of fans in the Netherlands and Hong Kong will show (Chapter 2), place does matter at the moment of music consumption, just as the sheer solidity of music venues in Hong Kong creates affective memories to the city, as Chapter 5 shows. But we believe that there are more stories to tell, as to grasp the complexity of the transnational flow of sounds. And we hope to tell these stories in this book.

This shift in our understanding of popular music studies is at the same time our correspondence with area studies and cultural studies. As far as area studies is concerned, the inquiries we have conducted demonstrate how definite, solid, geographical boundaries normally used to demarcate the area in area studies are contested and made porous by increasing cultural flows. More specifically, the 'Hong Kong' in this book is already and always in its connections with mainland China, Taiwan and the world at large. We find it difficult, if not impossible or unproductive, to talk about Hong Kong pop music only in the context of Hong Kong. And it is not only Hong Kong; we believe the same can be said of pop music of any other areas. Popular music studies needs to move out of its Anglo-Saxon biases, by deterritorializing both its empirical focus as well as its theoretical concerns, it can overcome the danger of repeating itself.

If a certain convention in area studies still tends to privilege geographical neatness over cultural permeability, if studying China's pop music will automatically assume a different domain from that of Hong Kong or Taiwan pop, we want to suggest otherwise. Informed by how pop music flows in this globalized time, we believe it is both necessary and useful not to take, for instance, Hong Kong and China's pop music as two distinct areas of studies, but rather, as multiply and intimately connected: Hong Kong-in-China, China-in-Hong Kong (see also Groenewegen 2011). When we situate local popular music in the context of all its translocal flows, we are inevitably posing questions on boundaries, asking area studies to loosen up and rethink the boundaries they may have been guarding. What other cartographies of sound are possible? How does the mobility of music redefine political, cultural and social boundaries?

With cultural studies, our correspondence is three-fold. First, the cases of Hong Kong pop music we chose to study, as mentioned earlier, were primarily informed by what we observed in Hong Kong and the Chinese pop music world at large. Seen from this perspective, it is a response to Angela McRobbie's call for inserting the three Es – the empirical, the ethnographic and the experiential – in cultural studies (1997). As elaborated by Michael Pickering, 'If […] we can move to research and analysis in cultural studies that grows more evidence-sensitive and less theoretically presumptuous, more participant-oriented and less neurotic about its own epistemological standing, then we shall have helped the field to progress' (2008: 5). This is what we attempt to do in this book. Second, thus guided by the three Es, our collection of inquiries covers various aspects of popular music studies, including production, representation and consumption. In that sense, it supplements the bias for audience and consumption research of certain traditions of cultural studies that 'seem to assume that consumers have the vital final say in determining meaning' (Hesmondhalgh and Baker 2011: 55). Third, on a more general level, it wants to eschew the danger of theoreticism (Hall 1992; Wright 2003) by assuming a particular cultural studies strategy – simply, telling better stories about what's going on. As Larry Grossberg remarks, 'cultural studies seeks to tell better stories aimed at enabling people to imagine other – better – possibilities for the future as well as other – better – strategies to advance the struggle for such possibilities' (2010: 242). It follows that this book, taken as a whole, is theoretically eclectic, engaging with a diversity of issues and debates as warranted by the specificity of each study.

Hence our insistence on taking popular music studies in its intersections with area studies and cultural studies. Before presenting an overview of the book, we would like to insert a methodological note. Like its theorization, this book is methodologically eclectic, or promiscuous, if you like. We start with an autobiographical approach, supplemented with textual analysis. We mobilize a host of qualitative social sciences methods including interviews, focus groups and participant observation, as well as methods that are more closely connected to the humanities, such as visual analysis. We end up with following only one person on a transnational journey and to take that single 'informant' less as an object than as a subject of the research.

Overview

Following this introduction, our book begins with a study of a particular genre in the pop music tradition of Hong Kong: nationalistic songs or *minzu gequ*. For Yiu Fai Chow, a cultural studies scholar and a cultural producer (lyric writer), the power of *minzu gequ* lies precisely in its tendency to privilege a particular performance of Chineseness. In 1980 he sang one; in 2005 he penned one. Chapter 1 is an autobiographical inquiry of how he has been dealing with issues of Chineseness through the pop lyrics created during the 're-nationalization' process of Hong Kong.

From the production of nationality, Chapter 2 moves on to the production of locality in global pop. Comparing fans of local stars – the Hong Kong pop star Leon Lai and his Dutch counterpart Marco Borsato – this study finds striking differences. In general, while the Dutch fans see Marco as an ordinary human being, the Hong Kong fans characterize Leon as an extraordinary worker. Following globalization theory, we argue for the importance to include locality as an explanatory category in fan studies.

Chapter 3 investigates a relatively recent pop phenomenon: China Wind or *zhongguofeng*. In this chapter, rather than focusing on what is considered the main 'source' of China Wind songs, Taiwan, we have chosen China Wind songs originated from Hong Kong and their music videos as the primary site of enquiry. Our analyses show that while Hong Kong's China Wind pop evokes Chineseness, it also undermines Chineseness in two major ways: first, to render Chineseness as distant gaze, as ambiguous space and as ongoing struggles; and second, its feminization of Chineseness, opening up a space for questions on history and gender performance.

Our study in Chapter 4 concerns the high-profile 'Sex Photo Gate'. In early 2008, private pictures of Edison Chen, a Hong Kong-based singer-actor celebrity, with a range of famous and less famous female stars, became public after Chen brought his computer to a repair shop. Our analyses show how the scandal was mediatized with discourses of what we call the extreme moral, the extreme material and the juridical. In particular the moral as well as the material discourse, we argue, function in tandem with Cantopop's perceived lack of authenticity, turning the stars and their bodies into spectacular sites onto which capitalist dreams in conjunction with a Victorian – or Confucian – morality are mapped.

Cantopop is proclaimed to have died after the handover of Hong Kong from British to Chinese rule in 1997. Yet, simultaneously, a series of comeback concerts attests to the continuous importance of Hong Kong pop stars, apparently defying the narrative of disappearance. In Chapter 5, we propose to foreground the moment of music consumption, which may also be the moment of production. We embark on a history of music venues in Hong Kong, and analyse how they operate as emotive landmarks in a city that seems to be in constant flux. In particular, the Hong Kong Coliseum operates as an emotive landmark that transcends time and helps construct and remember the city and its citizens.

Whereas popular music is frequently linked to subversion, and music cultures are read as countercultures that help change the world, most sounds support rather than contest hegemonic identity constructions. Chapter 6 examines theme songs created in celebration of the Olympic Games in Beijing in August 2008, including those involving pop artists from Hong Kong. In this chapter, we present a close analysis of these songs and the clips. We analyse what kind of Chineseness is being celebrated and how the involvement of Hong Kong troubles any univocal celebration of Chineseness. These contestations also spilled back towards the mainland itself, where bloggers, audiences and musicians also started to poke fun at the celebration of the Olympics. We thus show how popular music simultaneously helps to celebrate the nation-state, yet at the same time offers possibilities for a creative appropriation and enables tactics of resistance.

Chapter 7 focuses on one person: Diana Zhu. Born and brought up in the Netherlands, Diana, at 15, won a Chinese singing contest in Amsterdam in 2006. Subsequently, she got a contract first from Warner Music Hong Kong, then from Warner Taiwan. Having relocated to Shanghai, her parents' 'home' city, Diana was working on her hope for a future in the

Introduction

Chinese pop market. Taking our cues from Lash and Lury's method of 'following the object', we followed Diana and started to see her entanglement – particularly over her language, music and body – not only with Warner Music, but more fundamentally with the wider dynamics that seeks to configure and maintain a sense of hopefulness in China.

At the same time, we also take this particular case study as an occasion to reflect on its wider methodological implications for conducting research on contemporary popular culture. In other words, this final chapter serves, if you like, as a general methodological endnote to the rest of the book. While our insights are drawn from this particular research narrative weaving from Hong Kong popular music, our appeal is more general: to reconfigure and study popular culture in their interface with these four dimensions – the flow, the bodily, the political and the personal.

Chapter 1

ME AND THE DRAGON: A LYRICAL ENGAGEMENT WITH THE POLITICS OF CHINESENESS

Yiu Fai Chow

It was the summer of 1980. During an orientation camp, I, together with hundreds of other University of Hong Kong freshmen, was presented with a choice violent enough to pitch affinity against affinity. We were asked: 'do you consider yourself a Hong Konger or Chinese?' It was the time when the city's political certainty as a British colony evaporated almost overnight, when London was preparing to 'revert' Hong Kong to Chinese rule. After a ritualistic show of hands, the evening ended with a collective singing of the campus hit of the year, the originally Taiwanese song 'Descendants of the Dragon/龍的傳人':

> In the ancient Orient, there is a dragon
> Its name is China
> In the ancient Orient, there are a people
> They are all descendants of the dragon
> Growing up in its giant footsteps
> I have become a descendant of the dragon
> Black eyes, black hair, yellow skin
> Forever, descendants of the dragon.
>
> ('Descendants of the Dragon/龍的傳人'[1] 1978)

While these emotional verses chanted the soundtrack for a decade that was to see the conclusion of the Sino-British talks and the preparation for the political handover of Hong Kong, I was transported to a stage where, for the first time in my life, I was summoned to perform my national and cultural identity. It was obviously not enough for me to have black eyes, black hair and yellow skin, I must say it, sing it, perform it. Chineseness, I began to understand, is not merely a biological category but a social performance.

I was born in the 1960s. I grew up in Hong Kong constantly wondering why the 'official' Chinese I learned in school was different from the Cantonese Chinese I spoke with my family; why my mother had to ask someone to write her application letter for a telephone line in English so that the application would be sped up. My first exposure to cultural studies during my university days reframed such bewilderments into more concrete notions of power and contestation.

Alongside a career in the government, I asked a friend of mine who was already releasing pop music to try my lyrical potentials. It was probably a tactical move inspired by the cultural studies belief that, perhaps, I could do something to engage with dominant versions of truth being circulated in the society, that I could give a voice to my bewilderment as an outsider. It was 1988. Four years later, I became even more of an outsider, at least geographically, by moving to the Netherlands. There, I continued my lyric writing and resumed my (academic) studies in popular culture, travelling not only between two localities, but translating between my double role as a cultural studies student and a cultural producer. As a cultural studies student, I learn how to be self-reflexive about the historical consciousness and contemporary conjuncture we inhabit. As a cultural producer, specifically as a lyric writer for commercial music, I thrive as a meaning-maker, moving between the spaces of contingencies and contradictions offered by a playful but potentially mattering site of cultural production.

This chapter is about my experience in this duality. It is, to borrow Carolyn Steedman's metaphor, a journey into the landscape to see myself (Steedman 1986). If a master may brush off ugly lines of power and contestation from a Chinese landscape painting, this journey is to close up onto the small figures spotted here and there, regaining, hopefully, 'a sense of people's complexity of relationship to the historical situations they inherit' (Steedman 1986: 19). I feel the need to ask 'What does it mean by being Chinese?' at a time when nationalistic sentiments, sustained by simple narratives such as the 'upsurge of the grand state' or the Beijing Olympic Games 2008, have been increasingly employed not only to organize national cohesion but also to feed in global diasporic longing for a perceived homeland. Such celebration of Chineseness conflates with a crucial ideological shift during the 1990s, when the Chinese Communist Party replaced its legitimizing ideology from communism to a market-driven nationalism (Barmé 1999; Gries 2004; Hughes 2006). It is this more recent, legitimizing version of Chineseness constructed during the process of China's de-imperialization, national unification and modernization that I am engaging with.[2] While contemporary popular culture is one of its major construction sites (Barmé 1999; Dai 2001), such Chineseness is historically predicated on the 'universal chauvinism' sustained by the structure of the Han-centred 'Us' versus the rest as 'Other' (Chen 2006; Gries 2004; Hughes 2006).

At the same time, popular culture offers opportunities and moments for resistance, subversion and critique (Fiske 1989). A central theme of this chapter is to resist simplicity, to resist certain political or ideological attempts to simplify and nullify complexity into certain dominant narratives – by mobilizing the autobiographical 'I', in this case, embodied in the duality of cultural studies student/producer. This chapter is therefore about contestations of interpretation, between the personal and the official. As Steedman puts it, 'Personal interpretations of past time [...] are often in deep and ambiguous conflict with the official interpretative devices of a culture' (Steedman 1986: 6). In that sense, this chapter is not meant to attempt a historical account of the power relations between Hong Kong and mainland China through the lens of pop music. It is more my own remembering of what I have done and what I have failed to do, with all the possibilities of resistance to and complicity with dominant narratives. This account favours 'the messy, subjective life of the historical agent rather than his/her more "objective" accomplishments or conditions', a shift from 'fact to the experience of fact' (Pollack 1998: 18). My purpose is to stake a singularizing claim of identity through critical personal self-reflexivity. 'Singularity' here suggests that this is not intended to be generalizable to other people's experience; this reflection is of this time, in the spaces I occupy, relevant primarily to the dual role I have and hopefully to our critical understanding of 'Chineseness'.[3] In Chapter 3, we will move beyond the autobiographical approach and discuss another contestation exercise of Hong Kong's pop music with hegemonic Chineseness, in the site of a particular music genre: China Wind. In Chapter 6, we continue to investigate Hong Kong's alleged co-production of hegemonic Chineseness in the case of Olympic songs.

Nationalistic songs

Songs like 'Descendants of the Dragon' are not rare in Hong Kong's pop music tradition: from the anthemic, heroic-sounding songs and sentimental, folkish ballads, generally known as *minzu gequ*, in 1970s and 1980s, to what I would call the neo-*minzu gequ* reinvented in trendier R&B or rap numbers during the turn of the century.[4] The difficulty in translating *minzu* to English is noteworthy. *Minzu* generally denotes 'the people', with an emphasis on lineage, more than race, which, however, tends to conflate with 'the nation'. In the standard English-Chinese dictionary used in mainland China, the entry 'nationalistic' is given two Chinese equivalents: nationalistic (*guojia zhuyi*), and people-listic (*minzu zhuyi*). While *minzu gequ* is often refined in the mainland Chinese musical context into the 'ethnic' and the 'nationalistic' – with the purpose of, respectively, preserving and promoting the 'ethnic minorities' and the 'nation', those *minzu gequ* that secure public airplay in Hong Kong are predominantly of the second type.

Although never really dominant in the local pop scene, these nationalistic songs appear frequently enough to carve out their own genre in a market otherwise monopolized by 'love songs'. This unusual cultural phenomenon, however, has attracted rather limited academic interest. In an edited volume on Hong Kong popular lyrics, Mei-kwun Cheung discusses the role these songs play in constructing a sense of home and nation prior to the handover in 1997 (Cheung 1997). Wai-chung Ho (2000) charted the tides of nationalistic and anti-nationalistic songs in the local pop scene to review the sociopolitical relations between Hong Kong and Beijing. For me, the power of *minzu gequ* lies in its tendency to privilege a particular performance of Chineseness by the tactic of excluding the marginal, be they foreign (mostly imperialistic) enemies or domestic dissidents, as well as the possibility of cultural resistance it offers.

The term *minzu gequ*, a common genre marker in music sites and shops in mainland China, has become a discussion item during the official CCTV Youth Singing Contest 2006. One of the adjudicators, the classical vocalist Jiang Dawei, noted the decreasing ethnic (*minzu*) element and suggested changing the term *minzu gequ* to Chinese songs (*zhongguo ge*).[5] In a related report posted on the CCTV site, the writer Zhang Liqiang (2006) comments: 'How we are going to deal with the term *minzu gequ* may be controversial [...] but *minzu gequ*] possesses the core element of our nation's musical culture development – Chineseness'. This is, in short, the predicament I am situated in when I, as a professional lyricist, am commissioned to work on projects that would force me to walk into the dangerous stadium of *minzu gequ* and do a performance of Chineseness. Informed by my understanding of power and resistance, should I take a bow and go? Or, is it possible to masquerade in a line or two and intervene in my own manner? I tried. In 1980 I sang a *minzu gequ*; by 2004 I penned one.

Another approach

I was (and still am) intrigued, and troubled, by the role such nationalistic songs might play in the construction of Chineseness, especially in connection with the so-called re-nationalization process of Hong Kong (Erni 2001). More specifically, the concern here is how certain Chinese texts (song lyrics) might be deployed to frame Chinese history and identity in the narrow terms of nationalism, thereby confining the possibility of defining Chineseness in other terms such as gender, class or regional spaces (Callahan 2006). While thinking how to theorize on the relation between Hong Kong's popular culture and issues of Chineseness, I was reminded of the danger of theoreticism (Hall 1996; Wright 2003) not so much in cultural studies but in myself. What possible contribution could my theorization make when many of my scholarly colleagues have been delivering valuable works in a similar vein (Abbas 1997; Chow 2000; Lee, G. 2002)? And, ultimately, what possible contribution? To what?

I thought I had one answer to offer: me and my lyric writing. For almost two decades, I have been writing lyrics for Cantopop (or Cantonese pop songs) in Hong Kong, and more recently, also in Mandarin or Putonghua, for the Greater China market. Instead of launching a third-person study on *minzu gequ*, I think it should be more my take to investigate: how 'I' have been dealing with issues of Chineseness through the pop lyrics I have created? More specifically, how this 'I' – someone growing up in colonial Hong Kong, now living 'overseas', in short, someone who can never take Chineseness for granted and whose Chineseness is never taken for granted – seeks to reclaim my speaking position on what is Chinese, and resist dominant, exclusive versions of Chineseness through acts of lyric writing?

Before embarking on such an inquiry, I want to elaborate on two points, which make my preference for an autobiographical approach more than a preference. First: as Wright argues, 'an autobiographical approach is employed precisely to be specific and in the attempt to avoid the pitfalls of overgeneralization and the authority of authenticity' (Wright 2003: 805). Such pitfalls seem to be particularly pertinent in discussions on Chineseness, where collective experiences are often overgeneralized and authenticated into collective identity. Scholars in area or sinological studies, in particular, are prone to speak in such collective terms of Chinese identity and culture.[6] In mainland China, as Callahan observes, academics have also been making their case for 'Chineseness', by essentializing and collectivizing values, traditions and culture (Callahan 2005).[7] It should be more appropriate, I believe, to speak as me, insisting on my individual experience, whose singularity is meant to wrestle with the collective. The singularity is to relieve Chineseness of 'pretensions to a "master narrative"' to become a 'somewhat humbler quilt of many voices and local hopes' (Pollock 1998: 18).

Second: I want to take up Meaghan Morris' (1997) question 'What do cultural studies do?' If academic writing is meant to intervene in reality and to express any discontent to that reality, so is creative writing. As both a cultural studies student and a cultural producer, I often wonder how I am supposed to make a difference in the 'real world'. Far more often, however, I would wonder if it is possible at all. If strategies of engendering cultural studies as praxis would include empirical research and performative acts (Wright 2003: 816), this very inquiry should serve as an interface between the two. This chapter is a chronicle of how I, a lyrics writer, try to write what I have read from cultural studies into a cultural product. It is also an occasion to interpellate me, a cultural studies student, to read the product back into cultural studies. As Chua Beng Huat reminds us, 'The life of a consumer product is very short' (Chua 2003: vii). My wish is to show how cultural studies may matter to such a short life, first of all, by giving birth to at least certain cultural products, and, in the final analysis, in resurrecting such cultural products from their consumerist existence into more endurable knowledge. This is the cultural studies student and cultural producer collaborating to try to understand what cultural studies do.

Re-nationalization I: Descendants of the dragon

> If there is something from my childhood and adolescent years that remains a chief concern in my writing, it is the tactics of dealing with and dealing in dominant cultures that are so characteristic of living in Hong Kong. These are the tactics of those who do not have claims to territorial propriety or cultural centrality.
>
> (Chow 1993: 25)

When I grew up in the 1960s and 1970s, English and Mandarin songs dominated my life. For a long time, I was served a daily diet of school anthems and Christian hymns, all in English. Sometimes we would also practise Chinese songs, in Mandarin, probably from a pre-war, pre-communist China. Again, very occasionally, we would also learn songs that must have been translated because the tones of Cantonese lyrics did not correspond to the notes of the melody, as required by the Cantonese listening habit. It was, in short, silly to sing in Cantonese. And I was growing into the hierarchy of languages and cultures, of the 'in-between' status of Hong Kong Chinese under British administration. But then, slowly, I opened my eyes to local television dramas and my ears to their theme songs, ushering in a localization process that finally ensured the cultural and market space for Hong Kong pop and a whole new genre defined by its locality and its local tongue: Cantopop.

The localization of pop in Hong Kong was intrinsically political, given its linguistic, cultural and political relationship to Britain and mainland China (Cheung 1997; Ho 2000).

It was, however, never really politicized – until the wave of *minzu gequ* swept over the city by the end of 1970s and early 1980s, precisely the period defined by Deng Xiaoping's concept of 'one country two systems' (introduced in 1978), the Sino-British negotiations and the signing of the Sino-British Joint Declaration (1984). For the second time in my life, I was wondering how I was supposed to fill in the nationality blank: the word 'Chinese' sounded as unlikely as 'British'. It was during such first moments of transition, of a sudden loss of a voice to articulate ourselves amidst the sovereignty negotiations between two nations, that I heard the city's young men and women start to sing songs such as 'Descendants of the Dragon'.[8] And I was thrust into the dilemma: do I consider myself a Hong Konger or Chinese? Back in 1980, the freshmen of that university year, in a movingly collective voice, articulated and thereby defined ourselves the following way:

> Black eyes, black hair, yellow skin
> Forever, descendants of the dragon.
>
> ('Descendants of the Dragon/龍的傳人' 1978)

Were we singing in a grand European-style hall or somewhere in the lawn with campfires? I am not sure. I do not even recall if I joined in the singing. I am always surprised by how some people seem to be so sure about so much, even their memories and histories, even their descent, destiny and enemies. What I remember was that among our group members, only two of us raised our hands to declare that we were Hong Kongers. It was a choice fabricated by the necessity of a choice. I felt betrayed, belligerent, eager to make a point, ending up making a person. To use Anthony Fung's words, I reckon my tactic at that particular historical juncture of mine, and perhaps not only mine, was to appropriate a local identity label 'to resist encroachment of the national' (Fung 2001: 591).

Re-nationalization II: Home and nation

As the negotiations between Beijing and London over the future of Hong Kong seeped into the consciousness of the city, *minzu gequ* occupied more and more airtime and public space. While the cultural backgrounds of these nationalistic songs will be identified in the following account, my primary concern is confined to how they were conceived and received in Hong Kong, constructing, I remember, at least two imaginaries: a home and a nation.[9] Such construction might be a personal response to the times Hong Kong was experiencing, like it was for Ivy Ku, a local singer-songwriter, who released a number of *minzu gequ* during the 1980s. Although she had never been to China at that point of her music writing, Ivy Ku told me she created those songs with 'true feelings for China' (personal communication, 8 November 2006). Less personally, local record companies were formulating new strategies to correspond to the changing political and economic relationship between mainland China and Hong Kong. As Jolland Chan, a veteran producer and lyric writer, recalled, record companies with local capital (such as Crown and Wing Hang Records) – unlike major international labels (such as Polygram and EMI) – were consciously promoting certain artists to the Chinese market by including tracks that expressed a 'positive attitude towards the motherland'. Citing the Hong Kong singer Cheung Ming-min as an example, Chan hinted at a central directive from Beijing, saying 'Cheung was given lots of opportunities by CCTV' (personal communication, 8 November 2006).

On the 'home' front, songs hit the charts where a rustic, idealized, vaguely Chinese or sinified space was carved out, luring audiences in Hong Kong to a home at last. These sentimental ballads, with their vivid invocation of a landscape quite alien to local urban dwellers, were singing nostalgia for something we were supposed to cherish, somewhere we were supposed to belong. But I did not. My landscape, crowded with skyscrapers and shopping streets, was more chaotic, noisy and contaminated. These ballads, pregnant with folkish melancholy and hints of homecoming, were celebrations of a more 'pure' brand of Chineseness:

> Walking on a country trail
> The old cow returning at dusk is my companion
> Blue sky and the setting sun on my chest
> Its colours are the clothes of the evening clouds
> Carrying a plough on their shoulders
> Farmer boys are singing
> And they are blowing a *dizi*[10]
> Remotely, cheerfully
> Sing a country song
> Let your thoughts free in the evening breeze
> Let your loneliness go with the evening breeze
> Let's forget everything on a country trail.
>
> ('A Country Trail/鄉間的小路' 1978)

While Ye Jieshou, a Taiwanese folk song veteran, was known for invoking idyllic landscape as a commentary on the increasing industrialization of his native Taiwan, 'A Country Trail' was perceived by me and many of my contemporaries as what a Chinese home promised to offer – freedom, community, an opportunity to start afresh.[11] The conflation between 'A Country Trail' and mainland China was also facilitated because a major performer of this and another of Ye's songs in Hong Kong was Cheung Ming-min, who, as noted earlier, was generally seen to be Beijing's favourite. Always dressed in costumes associated with the traditional and the revolutionary China, Cheung was responsible for popularizing many more explicitly nationalistic songs, including 'I Am Chinese', which will be discussed later.

And then, sometimes, the homecoming story would be enshrined in a personal narrative where home and nation became one. Such songs were making a certain past desirable, a 'Cultural China' imaginable (Eperjesi 2004). To paraphrase Chris Berry, it is not so much

China that makes these songs, but these songs help make China (Berry 2000: 160). 'Father's Straw Shoes', another of Ye's songs popularized by Cheung in Hong Kong, is a good example:

> Straw shoes are the boat, father is the sail
> Carrying grandmother's blessings
> And a seventeen-year-old dream
> With high hopes it embarks its journey
> Sailing to the shores of Yellow River
> Loading tons of yellow earth
> When night falls, it anchors at Qingshazhang
> When dawn breaks, it heads off to Shanhaiguan
> […]
> Straw shoes are the boat, father is the sail
> Listening to a faraway home calling
> Carrying half a century's drifting, the weary boat is about to come to the harbour.
> ('Father's Straw Shoes/爸爸的草鞋' 1981)

If home building is about nostalgia for an imaginary past, another major stream of *minzu gequ* during this period of Hong Kong's re-nationalization, is about nation building, about fighting for a better future. While the national signifier 'China' was generally absent in the home building songs, making way for a more cultural logic of inclusion (country trail, old cow, *dizi*, boat, sail, Yellow River), China and Chinese were the key terms in, for instance, 'I Am Chinese/我是中國人', which was written by the Taiwanese composer and director Liu Jiachang. While this song was intended as a celebration of Chinese nationalism in the political frame of Republic of China, the nation was conflated with mainland China, again through the mediation of Cheung Ming-min, who performed this song extensively not only in Hong Kong but also in mainland China:[12]

> Silence is not cowardice, tolerance is not indifference
> The traditional Confucian thoughts will guide our footsteps
> Eight years of bitter resistance against the invaders testified to our tough race
> Not until the very last moment, we would never declare war
> When I could bear no more, I would step forward
> I will always remember, to unify China, to restore our territories
> Wherever I was born, I am Chinese
> Wherever I am, I swear I will die a Chinese ghost.[13]
> ('I Am Chinese/我是中國人' 1982)

I could not help looking over my shoulders to see if all the Chinese ghosts surviving all the years of Chinese history would be right there, behind me, watching. I think they are. And the scariest moment is when they conflate into a monolithic ghost powerful enough to dictate who is Chinese and who is not. It is no longer the Chinese becoming ghosts, but rather the ghosts becoming the Chinese. The Confucian tradition, the resistance against foreign enemy, the unification, the steadfastness – what a bizarre act of exorcism it is, to expel all the non-conformist, the non-national, the non-committed to create a willing Chinese ghost called 'Nation'. The nation narrative is nothing more than a ghost story, I think. No wonder you need to be brave. 'Brave Chinese/勇敢的中國人', the first *minzu gequ* hit in Cantonese, was created for a television drama series broadcast in Hong Kong at the end of 1982. While the Sino-British negotiation became the prime concern of the city, this drama series, set against a backdrop of Japanese encroachment in Republican China with a patriotic student as its heroine, gained widespread popularity. So did its theme song, which was performed by its main actress Liza Wang, who, six years later, was appointed by Beijing to represent Hong Kong and Macau in the National People's Congress:

> My beautiful hometown was tarnished, my picturesque lake was saddened
> Take a look at the Chinese land, a spirit of righteousness is rising
> I vow to turn my suffering into anger
> Be a brave Chinese, use your hot blood to resist the enemy
> March forward, march forward
> Tens of thousands of us become one, fearless of difficulties, dissipating darkness
> Be a brave Chinese, use your hot blood to wake up the 'Chinese ghost'
> Tens of thousands of us become one, fearless of difficulties, dissipating darkness.
> ('Brave Chinese/勇敢的中國人' 1982)

Become one, such a tempting formula. For the mainland audience, as Dai Jinhua observes, these '"returned patriots" confirmed the integration and interpolation of the motherland by singing these pop songs' (Dai 2001: 172). And for the Hong Kongers at the time of imminent changes, we willed ourselves to be brave, to be Chinese, to become one with tens of thousands of those who at least looked like us. But it is not easy. It necessitates a logic of empowerment by conjuring up an enemy, the other, be it the Japanese during the Second World War or the colonizers since the imperialistic encroachments. It also necessitates a submission of the part of us alien to the whole, the part of the city alien to the nation, the part of the future alien to the past. Perhaps the bravery is to chop this alienation off to fit in, and the hot blood one can use probably sheds from such an act of self-mutilation. For many people in Hong Kong, there was no other choice but to emigrate, feeding into a variety of diasporic imagination that negotiates with the 'export of Chinese nationalism' (Sun 2005: 69), from challenging China as the centre of Chineseness (Tu 1994), foregrounding notions of transnationalism (Ong and Nonini 1997; Ma and Cartier 2002), to categorically questioning the necessity of Chineseness itself (Ang 2001). I left Hong Kong after the first wave of emigration, to witness how the rest of the city drove on with that powerful 'Formula One' to swerve through twists and turns of the decade. Until 4 June 1989.

Re-nationalization III: Performing acts (i) – writing against the grain

Minzu gequ reached its height in the year 1982, when both 'I Am Chinese' and 'Brave Chinese' were listed on Radio Television Hong Kong's (RTHK) Top 10 Chinese Pop Songs of the Year.[14] With the signing of the Sino-British Joint Declaration in 1984 and the future of Hong Kong decided, the local pop scene saw the emergence of a number of musical groups creating hit songs exploring, among others, issues of 'post-colonial identifications' (Chu 2000). I started collaborating with Tatming Pair,[15] an electronic duo, in 1988. The next year, pro-democracy demonstrations at Tiananmen Square were suppressed with violence, shattering a dream into thousands of questions. What does it mean to be a brave Chinese? What is Chinese? What have the Chinese done to fellow Chinese? Who are the enemies? I was staying in London during the entire crisis. Like many others in the city, I joined in rallies to cheer, to support and eventually to mourn. When the turmoil started settling down into a thickness of post-Tiananmen critiques and re-critiques, I learned from my demonstration days that I actually found it difficult to scream and shout the way demonstrators were supposed to. I learned at least two things about my position in activism and resistance: I should continue my activism in words rather than in the street; and I am scared of any unison of voices that silences other possible voices. In 1990, Tatming Pair released a new album; we had to make a response:

> The heaven is threatening with flames.
> The land is suffocated with words.
> The wind is flaring up clouds of violet.
> The people are embracing the dread.
> Who will arch his bow
> And shoot the tongues of fire?
> Who will steal the elixir
> And fly to the moon to escape her desire?
> Want to complain to the heaven?
> But the heaven is not to be questioned.
> Want to curse destiny?
> But destiny is not to be questioned.
>
> ('Don't Question the Heaven/天問' 1990)

In this song, I invoked a cursed landscape with Chinese mythical figures and classical idiom to allude to post-massacre China and to question the ideology of silence, of acceptance, conveniently assigned to be Chinese values and traditions, popularly known as 'the heaven' (*tian*/天) or destiny. I wanted to question not only the political system, but also the 'culture' that sustains it. The title and major theme of the song was borrowed from a poem written by Qu Yuan (circa 340 BC–circa 278 BC), whose honest but bitter advice to the regime of his time earned him a life of frustrations, pain and finally suicide. Legend has it that his poem was originally titled '*wen tian*', literally 'ask heaven', but the authorities worshipped, or feared *tian* to such an extent that it would be total disrespect to place *tian* at the end of the title – it had to come first. The title became '*tian wen*' ('heaven ask'). I knew I could avenge the censored scholar and revert to the title he intended. But that would be lying to the time we were experiencing; I decided to keep the twisted, yet more revealing title, to secretly ask: what has changed in these centuries of Chinese history? What kind of 'centuries-old curse' is this Chineseness? What sort of 'traditions' make the Chinese of our time accept what is thrust onto them? What I wanted to do was not to retrieve the meaning of Chineseness in Qu Yuan's or any other dynastic time, but to question contemporary, dominant versions of Chineseness, which are often said to be grounded in history. If indeed the Chinese have 5000 years of history, what historical baggage have we inherited? That would be my question to heaven.

After the song was released, it caused 'considerable discussion in the society' (Wong 1989) and most critics took up those issues on history and Chineseness. Chi Ching (1990), for instance, asks: 'Where is the Chinese courage? Does it only lie in the mythic world?' Elvin Wong (1989) writes: 'Although the question has remained the same for 5,000 years, we have to keep on asking, because we haven't got the answer'. 'Don't Question the Heaven' became the Best Chinese Pop Song of 1990, according to RTHK. But Tatming never got the chance to stage concerts in mainland China in the coming years. In 2005, Anthony Wong, the lead vocalist of Tatming, opened their reunion concert in the Hong Kong Coliseum with 'Don't Question the Heaven' (Figure 1.1).

One year later, Tatming finally had their first mainland concert, in Shanghai. This opening song was taken out from the final rundown, shortly before the concert was to take place. The rundown, I was told, had passed the official screening but was revised by the organizer at the last minute 'just to play safe'.[16]

My collaboration with Tatming and, after their suspension, with Anthony Wong has offered me opportunities to try to trouble dominant narratives on Chineseness. If, to borrow Duara's (1999) observation, a certain narrative (for instance, of descent) succeeds in privileging certain cultural practices as the constitutive principles of a community, I think my job is to (at least attempt to) deliver some potential 'counter-narratives' from Hong Kong (on the margins of Cultural China) popular culture (on the margins of Chinese Culture). My tactic of resistance, in short, is to write against the grain. Thanks to Tatming and Anthony's subversive desire, the local society's pre-handover anxiety and the music industry's relative openness (or, some would argue, shrewdness to market such anxiety), I was given the space to produce a number of lyrical texts on this tactical line.

Three years after the student demonstrations, I wrote some lyrics for Anthony's solo project in which I attempted to critique the crackdown and Beijing's refusal to 'apologize' from the perspective of patriarchy. If Confucian or Chinese tradition was supposed to cherish proper piety from sons to fathers, from subjects to leaders, my question would be: don't you remember when you were a son, a subject? The notion of a rebellious son was also meant to disrupt the dominant framing of the handover as a 'return', particularly

Figure 1.1: Tatming Pair performing 'Don't Question the Heaven' (courtesy of People Mountain People Sea).

as a depoliticized metaphor of a prodigal son returning to the family to which he should belong.[17] More personally, it was my own rebellion against the pious sentiments of 'Father's Straw Shoes' released precisely a decade earlier. 'How Great Thou Art/你真偉大' was my writing against patriarchy and power:

> Oh father, father, have you never committed a mistake?
> Oh father, father, have you never refused to budge?
> Yesterday you were proud when you fought the crazy prejudices
> And now you say I am too rebellious
> I am too naive.
>
> ('How Great Thou Art/你真偉大' 1992)

'Let's Play Again When the New Century Comes/下世紀再嬉戲', released in 1995, two years before the Hong Kongers became nationally Chinese, was written amidst fears of forgetting and the absurdity of remembering. It was the time when the local administration was busy preparing for the handover ceremony and the city was nervously struggling with the inclusion to and marginalization from the Chinese 'national imaginary' (Abbas 1997). I wanted to articulate one more time my indulgence with the past, reluctance to accept the present, confidence in the future, all of which was, after all, as naive and sincere as a child's game; the big guys were up there, deciding everything. Fragrance was my allusion to the Fragrant Harbour, what 'Hong Kong' was supposed to mean:

> Still trying to distinguish the fading fragrance,
> I remember how the flowers flied with grace.
> We were so indulgent in the games we played
> That we didn't even notice the weather changed
> On a particular day.
>
> I remember how we played among the flowers.
> Our laughter was so happy.
> I remember how we took a deep breath
> And dashed though one wonderful century.
>
> Now, I am afraid everything will be forgotten soon.
> Our remembrance becomes absurd, yet beautiful.
> Now, I am no longer playing with you,
> Shall we make a date?
> Let's play again when the new century comes.
> ('Let's Play Again When the New Century Comes/下世紀再嬉戲' 1995)

And then, in 1996, Tatming reunited briefly to release an album commemorating their meeting ten years earlier, which includes this song, 'A Black Moon in Gusty Wind'. We wrote two versions: the Sodom (Cantonese) version speaks with the voice of those who stay behind in the sin city:

> I go to hell, you to heaven
> This very night, our city may be even more glamorous
> But the moment you leave, don't ever look back.

In the Gomorrah (Mandarin) version, those who leave sing:

> I don't have time to take away everything
> This very night, would the city be more beautiful?
> You are behind my back, may I turn around?
> ('A Black Moon in Gusty Wind/月黑風高' 1996)

'A Black Moon in Gusty Wind', a crystallization of the many conversations between me, who left, and Anthony, who stayed, did not cast any serious shadows on the ongoing festive preparations leading to the handover ceremony. This song about migration, about the anxiety of leaving and staying, of the city that was about to become Chinese, did not stir up much discussion even though many Hong Kong people would have migrated by then. It was also one of my last, increasingly scarce, attempts to deliver counter-narratives to the celebrations of Chineseness from the margins of Hong Kong. The post-1997 economic difficulties, generally known as the Asian Crisis, succeeded in replacing, or at least displacing, the city's political angst with a more fundamental onslaught of vulnerability: how do I keep my job? When we live for the moment, it is embarrassing, if not downright cruel, to think of history. It was not the time to ponder issues of Chineseness, when the people of Hong Kong were entering a postcolonial reality that required them not only to accept Chineseness as their political, official identity, but also to embrace it as their economic, pragmatic alliance to secure a better livelihood. As John Erni puts it, 'Hong Kong is measuring its supposed "inferiority" against a modernizing and capitalizing China' (Erni 2001: 396).

Sharing what Wang describes as the Taiwanese 'anxiety over the "China Global" as an encompassing transnational structure that either swallows Taiwan in its stomach or elbows Taiwan out of the international society' (2004: 269), I turn my gaze away from the centre, to the south. In the last few years, the Hong Kong Special Administrative Region Government has been promoting a more specific alliance with its immediate mainland neighbours to form an economic entity, geographically south. While the Pearl River Delta project is carving itself into the public mind, I am thinking of my private act of carving. If it does not make much sense to launch a frontal critique of the powerful totality called Chineseness, should I try to carve out some cleavages from within? Could I interrupt the widening Chinese boundaries by inserting a 'Southern' identification? In 2005, Tatming Pair included this song in their twentieth anniversary album:

Forgotten your snowstorms
Forgotten your hidden tongues
Forgotten

You are perhaps a mythical bird in the North
That never flies away
I would rather stay in the south
And dance till I can't

You have your bright expectations
I have my secret passions
If we fall in love, we will only waste it
You will always remember
I will always forget

There is nothing but a ballroom
And the currency is a kiss.

('Ballroom of the South/南方舞廳' 2005)

Opening with a series of forgetting acts, this song was meant to acknowledge the beginning of a new period, a new future where southern Hong Kong must live on under the Beijing regime up in the north. For the rest of the song, however, I employed a binary structure in which a 'you/North' line would always be punctuated by an 'I/South' line articulating longings not necessarily oppositional but categorically different. I knew I could not ignore – but I could write against – the fait accompli of one nation, one people, by suggesting different destinies. The North, or the centre of power, may be as inscrutable, immutable, even indestructible as a mythical bird that never flies away. The South, nonetheless, would rather be a ballroom, a locality of pleasure, transaction and above all transience. Given the increasing economic integration of the South, I was hoping to invoke a commercial, almost frivolous Southern identification,[18] as a possible source of alliance against a politicized version of Chineseness, which predicates on a certain past, monolithic and serious.

Re-nationalization IV: Performative acts (ii) – writing with a twist

'Ballroom of the South' was the second plug of Tatming's new album. Enjoying a reasonable amount of airplay and becoming a minor hit, it never unnerved the way 'Don't Question the Heaven' did.[19] Once again I realized it was not only the city that was summoned to deal with the new postcolonial reality, but me too, as a lyricist. 'The relationship to China can no longer be oppositional in the old way' (Abbas 2001: 624), I agree with Abbas. I could not only write against the grain when my fellow Hong Kongers, for instance, warmed themselves to moments of Chinese glory (such as Beijing's successful bid for the 2008 Olympics and the completion of the first Chinese space mission) just as eagerly as they denounced incidences of Chinese shame (such as the initial cover-up of SARS and the exportation of contaminated products to Hong Kong). I have the feeling that the Hong Kong people have learned the trick to claim and celebrate Chineseness quite selectively. And it is not always harmless. As recently as 2005, tens of thousands of Chinese took to the streets to demonstrate against the Japanese, who allegedly were twisting history to their advantages. Similar demonstrations were organized in Hong Kong. When a democracy activist took the occasion to urge Beijing to respect its own history, he was jeered.[20]

Could I also claim Chineseness and twist it to my advantage? Like the city at large, the pop music industry in Hong Kong functions increasingly in a new economic landscape where the mainland market dominates. Local pop idols cannot rely on the older position of Hong Kong as the nodal point of global Chinese youth culture. They need to establish local popularity and extend it to the mainland to be real stars. Some of the Hong Kong-based stars have become so successful that they are regularly invited to become 'spokespersons' for official events or campaigns in mainland China, such as Leon Lai and Nicholas Tse. In Chapter 5, we will discuss in greater details the increasing marginalization, and some would argue disappearance, of Hong Kong pop music during this re-nationalization process.

In 2002, the first time China qualified for the final rounds of the World Cup, Leon Lai was invited by the Beijing authorities to create a theme song. He asked me to contribute the lyrical content. I was reminded of that summer night, more than two decades ago, when I was forced to raise my hand to the identity question: Chinese or Hong Konger. There and then, many of us wanted to be part of a grand narrative called China. And, for me, the fundamentally intriguing question remains: how else? I knew it did not feel right to be in the minority, to be stripped of the power to define by myself what is a Chinese. And now, when I was confronted with the chance to speak to the centre, I knew I had to speak like the centre – after all, it would be a song to celebrate Chineseness written in 'official' Chinese.[21] How else? Could I speak against the centre at the same time?

I could not resist the temptation, or challenge, to try the 'how else'. Locked in this triangular tension between speaking to, like and against the centre, I tried to write with a twist. If my collaboration with Tatming and Anthony Wong is (whenever possible) intent on interrogating Chineseness, my other tactic, looking back, would be more like claiming Chineseness in order to disclaim. If the typical disclaimer – for instance 'I am not a racist but …' – is first to negate, then assert, my kind of disclaimer is first to assert, then negate. I am a Chinese, but …. My identity as a Hong Kong Chinese living in the Netherlands also complicated my speaking position, invoking hopefully a sense of hesitancy among the audience in anything I claimed as Chinese. For the World Cup theme song, I tried this:

> Chasing after each other, full of possibilities
> The world is like a ball, full of competition
> Run and seek,
> Real are those who join the game
> If the gate is made of iron, I am a man of steel
> *I want your love your love your love*
> *Lay your lay your love on me lay your love*
> With your love I will be brave
> *Lay your lay your love on me lay your love*
> With your love I am always charged up.
> ('Charged up!/衝鋒陷陣' 2002; italicized lines sung in English)

Confined by the clear intent of such a theme song, I had to create something positive, upbeat, to boost up the national spirit. The verse quoted here, for instance, could very well be understood as a nationalistic summon to the Chinese people to be 'a man of steel', to 'run and seek' national glory in the international arena. In all probability, the preferred reading of that song must be that if it did secure the endorsement by the Chinese commissioning authorities. In that sense, I was complicit in this official campaign of Chinese nationalism. In an attempt, however, to open up some space for negotiated reading, I inserted certain twists. First, by avoiding words associated with victory, I tried to twist the aim of the game from winning to joining. If nationalistic sentiments were meant to boost a more militant spirit of fighting and winning, I tried to contain them by invoking a less predictable world of participation and possibilities. Second, by injecting the words 'your love' in a way that would also suggest personal, romantic, rather than national, love, I tried to twist a song of national pride into a mundane love number – I am Chinese, but I am also a mundane lover. When Leon Lai sings 'I want your love', does he want the love of the motherland or the love of a girl? Ambivalence, I thought, would be a good antidote to straightforward nationalistic longing. That some of the chorus lines were sung in English, not Chinese, were also meant to make it more problematic to take the Chinese nation or people as the object of love in this presumably nationalistic song.

My attempt to add twists to the dominant narrative remains, quite often, an attempt. For the World Cup song, it was 'untwisted' at least by the accompanying video, which opened with a collective waving of the red Chinese flags. Sequences of ping pong – communist China's ticket not only to the world of sports, but also to the community of nations – were montaged in to deliver a visual prophecy of China's achievement in the arena of football and perhaps not football alone. Then, a Chinese player, in his yellow team shirt, kicks a ball right in front of an aeroplane in the process of taking off. The ball swerves literally around the globe and flies through different European and American national and cultural icons. Somewhere during its journey to the West, the ball, amidst a crowd of cheering Chinese children wearing red T-shirts bearing 'China' (in English) on their front, waving red Chinese flags, manages to set loose the hour and minute hands of Big Ben in London, and finally knock off a gargoyle apparently belonging to the Chrysler Building. The music video of 'Charged up!' concludes with Leon Lai, in a space suit, floating out there, flashing a winning smile to the world below him – slightly more than a year before Yang Liwei became China's first astronaut and 'Space Hero'. The officially sanctioned visuals of 'Charged up!', in short, were to fix the celebration of Chineseness without the 'but'.

Nicholas Tse, representing the newer generation of Hong Kong stars, thrives on the re-nationalization process and operates in China even more intensively than his predecessors. As Beijing continued promoting its brand of Chineseness-cum-nationalism, not surprisingly in the site of sports, Nicholas Tse became the younger spokesman for a number of national events. We will discuss the recruitment of diasporic members to the state–capital nexus in transnational Chinese pop music industries in Chapter 7. Suffice it here to note that Nicholas Tse was raised in Canada, and holds Canadian nationality.

Two years after the World Cup song, I was commissioned to write the lyrics for a song to be performed by Nicholas as the theme song of the 'Chinese Champion League'. Again, I participated in an official campaign to promote nationalistic feelings. 'Hurry up!/快' could and would be read by many as an urge to hurry up and demonstrate that the Chinese are strong, heroic and proud. But for what? If I confessed to having injected a substantial dosage of urgency in this song to make it work as a national spirit booster, I also hoped to twist the direction of urgency to one's own chance and destiny. 'This is my time, this is my game', not ours. If I was reproducing hegemonic narratives of nationalism that tend to embody national chance and destiny in its people – epitomized, among others, in sportsmen of national stature – I was at the same time trying to disentangle them. It remained my modest hope that some, just some, listeners and singers of the theme song would feel the possibility of their own chance and destiny. To me, that would be a shift, however momentary, from the ideology of acceptance that I was writing back in 1989.

> Right now, a hero is appearing
> Right now, people are cheering
> Right now, everything is changing
> Hurry up! My chance is a step away
> Win or lose depends on who runs fast
> Hurry up! Destiny is a second away
> The strongest leaves the last.
>
> ('Hurry up!/快' 2004)

The same year, Nicholas Tse was invited to sing the theme song of the Seventh National University Games. Urged, again, by my memories of 1989, and by my probably stereotypical impression of a new generation of Chinese youth, who were more concerned with economics (not politics), with the future (not the past), with success (not fun), I tried to rebel against the Chinese with my notion of the youth. To ears attuned to more explicit lyrics on youthful rebellion, 'The Best of Youth/青春之最' must have delivered quite a harmless ode to the young students joining the Games. In many ways, it was. However, in a China where university students, the target consumers of this song, once rebelled, challenged and became violently silenced by the authorities, this song, I gathered, would at least serve to twist the dominant construction of Chineseness – predicated on, among others, discipline, sacrifice and punishment – with an (admittedly romanticized) idiom of freedom, indulgence and fearlessness, hopefully opening up spaces for cultural resistance, if not downright political rebellion. In fact, I wrote my lines with probably wishful thinking that they could very well be describing the demonstrations of 15 years ago. The official censors might have sensed something more disturbing than that; I had to change two references to 'going to the street' and 'staying all night long'.[22]

> Youth is a pair of arms
> Wave them and I can fly
> Shout to the city how young I am
> Youth is a party
> Miss it and you will regret […]
> When you are young, get the best of youth
> Indulge yourself today

Remember our meeting today
During the brightest moments, we are carefree.

('The Best of Youth/青春之最' 2004)

The most serious struggle I had with claiming Chineseness took place in the same year: Nicholas' producer asked me to write lyrics for a new song about being Chinese. 'You see', he said, 'during concert tours in the mainland, Nicholas would always perform this song "Chinese". It always works, the mainland audience just loves it, but it's not Nicholas's own song.' He explained, Nicholas would like to have his own song that would warm up his concerts as much as the other *minzu gequ*. Finally, I had the opportunity to write a 'pure' *minzu gequ* myself. I knew I could not possibly avoid the obligatory trope (the Great Wall, the Tang Dynasty), the obligatory narrative of common descent, common destiny, common enemy. Nor could I ignore China's newfound place and pride in the world. The lyrics, I reckoned, had to address such sentiments to be affective and effective. How else?

What I tried in the first draft was threefold. First, I decided to problematize the category of 'Chinese', constructed and guarded fiercely with hegemonic discourses, with the category of 'yellow', which, for all its mythical and therefore more fluid qualities, should be more open to interpretations and contestations. What is yellow? This question would be easier and safer to pose, given the necessity of censorship, than 'what is Chinese?' Risking grand narratives of Chineseness presumably inherited by the Chinese, I tried to put the historical burden back to the individuals of today, to give the 'yellowness' your own name, your own shape. Second, recalling the xenophobic tendency in some older *minzu gequ* and in the construction of Chinese nationalism through a performance of victimhood by 'foreign' enemies (Callahan 2006), I tried to trouble the narrative with indirect references to past tyrants in Chinese history. For instance, one of the original chorus lines read: 'Yellow people, who buried you with the dead?' It was an allusion to the imperial practice of burying people alive to keep a deceased emperor company during his final journey to the underworld. Another chorus line read: 'Yellow people, who caused you harm?', which was my reference to the 1989 crackdown. If Chinese people suffered, I was trying to suggest, the suffering was inflicted not only by foreign enemies, but also by the fellow Chinese. Finally, fearing this song would be an instrument for a collective performance of Chineseness, not unlike my experience in 1980, I tried to inject more – more histories, more possibilities and, ultimately, more me, instead of us. I tried to twist a narrative of cultural, national unity to individual plurality. And Chineseness, I learn from Butler (1990), is more a performance than an inheritance; it is everybody's turn to step onto the stage and perform their own version of Chineseness, which, according to me, should be heroic enough.

Some days later, I got a fax from the producer, containing the response from the censors. All the lines alluding to encroachment from within were marked. On the right upper corner of the fax was handwritten, in Chinese: 'Overall, inappropriate wording. The main thing should be to embody the pride of the Chinese people as well as their unyielding spirit.' And above this remark: 'Not approved.' Following a discussion with the producer, we decided – how else? – to give and take; I replaced the two chorus lines mentioned earlier with a prouder 'Yellow people, walk on earth'. I added in the magic number '5,000' to invoke the dominant narrative of China's long history. I did not, however, change the basic questioning tone. Nor did I add in the words 'Chinese' (*'Zhongguoren'*). This time, the lyrics were approved:

> Is it from the tidal waves that swept through 5,000 miles
> Or the wall that awaits reconstruction?
> History fades into all the yellow
> Condensing into the setting sun, on my back
> Is it from the sweat that dripped through 5,000 years
> Or the legendary Tang Dynasty?
> Jianghu stirs up all the yellow
> Waiting for me to give it a name, and a shape
> Yellow people, walk on earth
> Stick out a new chest
> Yellow people, walk on earth
> The world knows that I am not the same
> More chaos, more courage
> The more the world changes, the more adventurous I become
> With nothing, I go everywhere
> After 5,000 years it's finally my turn to step onto the stage.
>
> ('Yellow People/黃種人'[23] 2004)

It is finally my turn to step onto the stage, to perform in my own way what Chinese is, I thought. The music video opened with a vast expanse of desert – yellow earth – with Nicholas, wearing a modern sports suit, walking alone (Figure 1.2). When some gusty wind lays bare a terra cotta Qin(-looking) warrior in the desert, he comes alive in the body of Nicholas, who starts beating an ancient battle drum to rally thousands of subterranean warriors. After erecting a huge phallic monument and shooting fire arrows into its mouth, the Qin army joins a contingent of athletes all wearing the same modern sports suit as Nicholas's in the opening scene, all bearing a torch. The video – whose concept was developed by Nicholas himself with the director and the production heavily sponsored by the Chinese sports shoes brand using the song as its advertising campaign jingle (personal communication with executive producer Leo Chan, 6 February 2007) – is a visual journey from a solitary wanderer to collective success; a visual connection, if not conflation, between ancient glory and contemporary strength, between the great unifying era of Qin and modern China. In other words, while the lyrical content, I thought, was seasoned with a stronger dosage of pride, unyielding spirit, in order to preserve and serve the question – how do I perform my Chineseness at this moment of history? – this video was making the question rhetorical and the answer, or directive, was already spelt out in the censors' remark.

Me and the Dragon

Figure 1.2: Nicholas Tse in MV of 'Yellow People' (courtesy of Emperor Entertainment Group).

The CD, packaged in an oriental(istic) box, dealt me another blow. If one of my attempts in this *minzu gequ* was to twist a dominant narrative of collective identity into possibilities of individual performance, Nicholas gave his own twist to my writing. Undermining my attempt to avoid referring to a grand collective 'we', he inserted the 'us', the 'Chinese', back to the song, delineated by bloodline and an attitude of fury, obviously against 'them', the perceived Other, the non-Chinese 'everywhere in the world'. He delivered the following rap before the last chorus:

> Everywhere in the world you will see a yellow face
> Red blood flows in 1.3 billion people
> You say it's my fury
> I say it's my attitude
> Fearless, marching forward
> Are only us, the Chinese.

('Yellow People/黃種人' 2004)

Shoot the dragon

Let me conclude with some clarifying remarks. First, I do not want to leave an impression that I am always conscious about what or how I am writing in my lyrical works. The account I just gave should be taken primarily as a work of analysis and memory, and for that matter selective and artificial. Second, I do not want to leave an impression that my lyrics are always engaging with issues of Chineseness directly or explicitly. More often, I want to entertain, experiment and, in the meantime, earn some money. Third, whatever tactic I may have employed in writing otherwise, I always feel that I am playing tug-of-war with so much unpredictability: from censorship (both self and official), capitalistic logic, institutional structure, art and video directors, whims of the stars, to endless (ab)uses on the receiving end. Talking about a disclaimer, this, I think, will be mine.

What I do want to claim is that this inquiry is first and foremost autobiographical, writing of my experience in the duality of a cultural student and cultural producer. It is about me and my lyrics. Nonetheless, this singular experience of mine can be linked to more general issues of resistance and popular music. Following certain traditions that tend to position popular music as part of social movements (Hebdige 1979), assuming resistance to be explicit, conscientious and intentional, a number of studies on Hong Kong popular music have focused on identity and politics, framing local pop in a more macro scenario of political struggles (Erni 2007; Ho 2000; McIntyre et al. 2002; Witzleben 1999). The current inquiry seeks to add to their insights by laying bare what I would call the micro politics of resistance; it is an account of the personal-artistic-political matrix wrapping around an ideal of resistance. Resistance, for me, is an everyday negotiation of my work, my creativity, my identity and the dominant discourses on Chineseness, a testing out of personal and official limits. It is usually more mundane, probably less influential than I would ideally hope for. Sometimes, it may be complicity. But to paraphrase de Certeau (1984), it will be my 'making do'.

In discussing the ambiguity, or the possibility of ambiguity, of the Chinese identity, Allen Chun (1996) says provocatively: 'fuck Chineseness!' Allow me to indulge myself in this metaphor: is not my act of writing an act of ejaculation? I mean, for once in a trillion it may be consequential, for the rest I do it for pleasure. In that sense, the pleasure of a cultural student and producer may not be so different from the pleasure of a cultural consumer. In his conception of 'popular pleasures', John Fiske argues that consumers of popular culture derive both 'producerly pleasure' – of making their own meanings from the texts – and 'offensive pleasure' – of resistance to structures of domination (Fiske 1989: 55).

Such pleasure is also mine.

Notes

1 All song titles, lyrics and quotations from Chinese-language sources were translated by the author. Personal names are listed in pinyin, except those from Hong Kong.

2   For an account of 'the Chinese race' in modern China, see Dikötter (2003).
3   For that matter, I could also locate my inquiry into issues of 'Britishness', given the colonial past of my city and my own past. For the time being, I feel I could only afford to deal with issues of 'Chineseness', which, despite – or because of – my colonial past, remain closer to me.
4   Some may use another term 'China Wind', which we discuss in Chapter 3, to categorize such music.
5   It should be noted, for all the ambiguity surrounding the term *minzu gequ*, that my inquiry – and my memory – of *minzu gequ* does not cover the more 'ethnic' stream of the genre, for example the release of Sister Drum (in 1995/6 by Elektral/WEA). For a discussion on the politics of Sister Drum, read Upton (2002). For a more comprehensive and historical account of 'music with national/ethnic character', see Yang (2000).
6   See for instance Tu Weiming's (1994) notion of 'Cultural China'.
7   For a further discussion of academic nationalism, see Chow (2000) and Dai (2001).
8   'Descendants of the Dragon' gained popularity in Taiwan before catching on in Hong Kong. Hou Dejian wrote the song as a protest against Washington's decision to sever diplomatic ties with Taipei in favour of Beijing. That it was appropriated as a song with pro-Chinese feelings surprised Hou: 'You have totally misread my intention!' (Hou 1983). The vicissitude of 'Descendants of the Dragon' illustrates, as mentioned earlier, how a cultural product, regardless of its producer's intention, could and would be appropriated to serve the dominant ideology. My lyrical works are no exception. While intended to open up spaces for resistance, they might at the same time be complicit in constructing grand narratives on Chineseness. The relations between resistance and complicity will be elaborated during the analysis of my own lyrical works.
9   For a general discussion on the construction of home and nation in Hong Kong popular music, read Cheung (1997).
10 *Dizi* is a transverse flute, widely used in Chinese folk music.
11 For an account of the 'modern folk song movement' in Taiwan, see Zhang (2003).
12 It would be interesting, but beyond the autobiographical scope of the current inquiry, to chart the career of Cheung Ming-min and its political and cultural significance in terms of Chineseness as he mediated between Taiwan, Hong Kong and mainland China.
13 The Chinese character for 'ghost' here is '*hun*', which also carries the meaning of 'soul'.
14 According to Chow, these songs were popularized primarily due to anti-Japanese sentiments (Chow 1990). In August 1982, a Japanese history textbook allegedly distorted facts surrounding the Sino-Japanese War (1937–1945), causing widespread uproar among Chinese communities around the world.
15 Generally considered a rare example of balancing between mainstream and alternative pop, Tatming Pair enjoyed critical acclaim and intellectual attention in Hong Kong. See for instance Lok (1995) and Cheung (1997).
16 The identity of the informant is not disclosed as the conversation was conducted confidentially.
17 For an analysis of the dominant family metaphor surrounding the handover, see de Kloet and Chow's (2000) study on the Handover CD 'Born on the First of July'.
18 In terms of pop music, there are signs of an emerging Southern identification. Radio stations in the Pearl River Delta region, for instance, are partnering with their

counterparts in Hong Kong and Macau to form their own pop chart '9+2' and their annual music awards.

19 I have only come across one commentary that places the song in the context of Hong Kong's political destiny. The title of the *Asia Times* article, cited on the *Epoch Times* site, reads: 'Listen to Tatming's song and feel the Handover pain' (Ling 2005).

20 For an account of the event written by the activist, see Szeto (2005).

21 In fact, I have been writing lyrics increasingly in Mandarin. Although Cantonese lyrics remain the bulk of my creative writing, I share the 'intellectual concern about the danger of an annihilation of "the local" in the re-nationalization process' (Erni 2001: 409).

22 It is common practice in mainland China for record labels to submit materials related to a musical product to ensure that the songs and the CDs that contain them would have no difficulty in getting released. Official theme songs would first be screened by the commissioning authorities.

23 'Yellow People' also became the theme song of a martial arts television drama series broadcast nationwide in 2005.

Chapter 2

THE PRODUCTION OF LOCALITY IN GLOBAL POP - A COMPARATIVE STUDY OF POP FANS IN THE NETHERLANDS AND HONG KONG

Introduction

Marco Borsato's hit single, titled 'Rood/Red', topped the Dutch charts for 11 consecutive weeks in 2006, attesting to the abiding popularity of this local pop star. Shot in black and white with occasional streaks of red, the video clip of 'Rood' features Marco, in his typical casual wear including a T-shirt, a blazer and a pair of jeans, singing in a small club venue as if he were doing a live intimate gig. In the same year, his Hong Kong counterpart Leon Lai continued his spectacular shows in Shanghai, Beijing and a major casino in the United States after a series of concerts in his hometown the year before. The year 2006 also saw Leon directing and starring a feature film, and releasing two albums. Born in the same month in the same year (December 1966), the two pop stars share quite a few things in common: both entered show business through a local singing contest; both released their debut album in 1990; both have a repertoire of eclectic, updated and easy-listening pop; both reached the apex of their star status in the 1990s but still command a massive fan crowd. At the same time, while Marco is a married man with three children, Leon remains his city's desirable bachelor, and his love life has been a major source of entertainment news. Again, in 2006, paparazzi in Hong Kong, after spying on his residence for more than a month, or so they claimed, managed to 'catch' Leon with a female model, resulting in the publication of highly speculative but nonetheless explicit reports on their presumable sexual indulgence.[1]

Underneath a surface of similarity – in gender, age, sexuality, career path, musical choice and popularity, Marco Borsato and Leon Lai seem to be embodying rather different resources for local imagination, and making rather different stars for their local fans. In other words, even though they may follow the kind of career trajectory and perform the kind of pop music like many other pop stars in other parts of the world, they point to something more complex than global uniformity. Part and parcel of this complexity, as we will argue in this chapter, lies in fandom and its production of the local. In our current globalized time, a time when the global is often perceived as a threat to the local, fan cultures emerge around local stars, providing fans with a sense of place. However, studies of fan cultures by and large fail to reflect upon the locality of fandom, running the danger of producing a homogenizing discourse in which 'fan' is turned into a universal label. Furthermore, studies of fan cultures that have appeared over the past decades present a strong Anglo-Saxon bias (Fiske 1992; Jenkins 1992; Lewis 1992; Baym 2000; Lancaster and Jenkins 2001; Hills 2002;

Hodkinson 2002). Such studies are not particularly helpful in understanding the intricate ways in which not only global but also local stars are appropriated by fans outside the Anglo-Saxon world to produce a sense of locality.

As we will show in this chapter, fandom can be an important means for what Arjun Appadurai has called the production of locality (Appadurai 1996). In particular in the context of intense globalization, the importance of being rooted, to create a sense of home, has, according to David Morley (2001), increased. As Saskia Sassen puts it: 'the epochal transformation we call globalization is taking place inside the national to a far larger extent than is usually recognised' (2006: 1). Popular music, in conjunction with new technologies, provides ample opportunities for the construction of a mediated sense of home and belonging. Local stars, we will argue, play a pivotal role in the production of locality. This study focuses on two local stars in the Netherlands and Hong Kong: Marco Borsato and Leon Lai. Both sing in their own language. Marco's popularity is confined to the Netherlands (and, to a lesser extent, the Dutch-speaking part of Belgium) while Leon has fans not only in Hong Kong, his base city, but also in Taiwan, mainland China as well as the Chinese diaspora around the world. That we situate them as 'local' stars is not only in opposition to 'global' stars (such as Madonna, Justin Timberlake and other predominantly American and British stars), but also a reference to the more elusively cultural, rather than strictly geopolitical, context in which their popularity operates. This chapter is based on an analysis of fan websites and face-to-face interviews with fans. Online and offline practices of fandom conflate, as we will show, both revealing a strong embeddedness in their respective cultural context. In other words, the differences between fandom in the Netherlands and Hong Kong resonate with – that is, display and construct – cultural characteristics of both localities.

While this chapter serves in the first place as an empirical probing into the production of locality that fandom entails – production that has hitherto received scanty academic attention – it also builds on previous fan studies. While a large body of academic work on fans comes from the discipline of social psychology (for a lucid example, see Giles 2002; for more pathologizing examples, see Scheel and Westeveld 1999; Stack 2000; Lacourse et al. 2001), our study takes a cultural studies perspective (Fiske 1992; Jenkins 1992; Lewis 1992). We particularly share their appeal to take the everyday lives of fans seriously, and resist the pathologizing notions of fandom that continue to prevail in popular discourse (Jenson 1992). At the same time, we do not wish to fall into the trap of univocally celebrating fandom, and read it as a unique form of popular resistance (e.g. Fiske 1992; Jenkins 1992). In our focus on everyday life, we aim to move beyond a resistance versus compliance rationale, into 'what fandom does culturally' (Hills 2002: xii). Theoretically, this study aims to connect globalization theory with fan studies, two domains of inquiry that have so far largely ignored each other. Empirically, we aim to show specifically how local stars can be used for the production of locality. The locality issue will be taken up again in Chapter 5 when we discuss not the stars but where the stars are produced and stardom is performed: pop venues.

Globalization: A sense of locality

The debate on globalization is characterized by two opposite poles: one argues that globalization is a process of homogenization or McDonaldization (Ritzer 2000), while the other reads globalization as a process of heterogenization. The apocalyptic undertone of the first argument often includes a harsh critique of the United States. Contenders for this line of argument draw support from a multitude of popular cultural phenomena: Hollywood is the global movie factory, Madonna is the global icon, McDonald's is the global eatery, and so forth. Singling out pop music as 'the anthem of globalization', Rene Boomkens' account also refers to the Americanization process in world culture:

> Pop music presented itself initially as a foreign cultural item, a product of the cultural domination and colonising urge of world power number one, the United States. Pop music fits in many aspects with the idea of the McDonaldization of world culture. Just like the Big Mac, American pop music has always been the worldwide yardstick [...] There is much to say for the thought that pop music serves as part of the ongoing unilateral Americanization of the world: pop music as $ign of the times, expressed in dollars.
> (Boomkens 2000: 27–28, translation ours)

Boomkens is right in suggesting that the chances of a pop singer from Los Angeles breaking into the Brazilian market are higher than those of a colleague from San Paulo scoring a hit in the United States. But then, why should he or she want to? Secondly, the popularity of 'Latin face and sound' (Ricky Martin, Jennifer Lopez, Christina Aguilera) in American (and global) pop provides another set of problematics destabilizing the hegemonic narrative (see also Stokes 2004).

As earlier research shows, the notion of cultural homogenization – and the world being colonized into one singular Americanized space, as the outcome of ongoing globalization – remains more apocalyptic than appropriate in describing what is taking place in various cultural fields (Hannerz 1987; Appadurai 1996; Sassen 2006). Consequently, the other end of the debate interprets globalization as a process of increased heterogenization, with new cultural elements being cut and pasted with already existing cultural patterns, producing creolized cultures (Hannerz 1987), or propelling the indigenization of 'foreign' cultural forms (Appadurai 1996). Global cultural icons can therefore have different readings, and produce different fan cultures, in different cultural contexts. Or local stars can appropriate a global cultural form. Drawing on a historical overview of Hong Kong pop stars, Ho (2003) has shown how these stars from the 1970s onwards help produce a sense of locality while employing the globalized cultural form of popular music. Along the same lines, it can be expected that these local stars are appropriated by local fan cultures to produce a sense of locality (Appadurai 1996), or to construct a *heimat*, a feeling of home (Morley 2001). This raises the question of how local stars, who make use of this profoundly globalized form of popular culture, pop music, are used by their fans to produce a sense of locality.

Fandom: On fans of local stars

Following Richard Dyers' seminal volume on stars, questions on audienceship and its most visible form, fandom, are inevitable. As mentioned earlier, most fan studies that appeared since the early 1990s show a strong Anglo-Saxon bias. For example, Henry Jenkins' book discusses *Star Trek* fans in the United States, whereas, a decade later, Matt Hills' impressive overview of fan studies (2002) still uses predominantly British examples. Apart from the Anglo-Saxon bias, the parameters of most fan studies do not depart from class, gender and age. Dyer, for instance, while pointing out that 'virtually all sociological theories of stars ignore the specificities of another aspect of the phenomenon – the audience', continues to cite adolescents, women and gay men as displaying particularly intense star–audience relationships (Dyer 1982: 36–37). In her provocative juxtaposition of the obsessive fans with the dedicated professors, Joli Jenson (1992) foregrounds issues of status and class (for other class-related fan studies, see Bryson 1996; Brown 1997; Brown 1998; Nash 2001; Jancovich 2002; Stenger 2006). In the same collection, at least three contributions are devoted specifically to gender-related themes: Cheryl Cline on female rock fans; Barbara Ehrenreich, Elizabeth Hess and Gloria Jacobs on girls' hysterical adoration of the Beatles; and Stephen Hinerman on female fantasies over Elvis (for other gender-related fan studies, see Baym 2000; Fung and Curtin 2002; Kim 2004; Williamson 2005). As John Fiske notes, '[m]ost of the studies so far undertaken highlight class, gender and age as the key axes of discrimination' (Fiske 1992: 32). Apart from race (for a study in which fandom is linked to ethnicity, age and gender, see Ali 2002), which is quoted by Fiske as a needed additional axis in stars/fans studies, we would also draw attention to the under-examined global/local dynamics, of which race is sometimes a component.

We do not, of course, suggest that studies along demographic axes (gender, age, class and sexuality) are neither legitimate nor interesting, but they do not contribute much to the globalization debate mentioned earlier. If an enquiry on stardom is about 'how do stars fit into the ideological discourse' (Butler 1991: 11) and fandom is taken as a 'response to specific historical conditions' (Jenkins 1992: 3), the studies undertaken so far are not situated, at least, in these specific historical conditions of increasing globalization and its related ideological discourse. An investigation in the global and local in non-American pop stars and fans, we believe, will provide an important addition to currently available studies of fan cultures.

Methodology

We have therefore chosen to focus on two distinct, relatively small, non-Anglo-Saxon locales: Hong Kong and the Netherlands. Marco Borsato (Figure 2.1) and Leon Lai (Figure 2.2) are comparable, as noted earlier, in terms of personal background, popularity and music style. In addition to their entertainment career, both stars are also known for their participation in high-profile charity acts as well as in advertising campaigns. Given our primary concern with fans and their production of locality through Marco and Leon, we refrain from drawing

The Production of Locality in Global Pop

Figure 2.1: Marco Borsato (courtesy of Loe Beerens).

Figure 2.2: Leon Lai (courtesy of Paciwood Music & Entertainment Ltd).

too much from the textual content of their images. Suffice it to say: whether seen in 'real life', video clips or concerts, Marco mostly appears as an ordinary guy wearing casual outfits, while Leon is polished, trendy, showing a preference for what is generally considered sex appeal, glamour and spectacle. Our choice of Marco and Leon is also supported by their relative typicality in terms of Dutch and Hong Kong stardom. In the Dutch pop world, other bestselling colleagues, such as Frans Bauer and Jan Smit, project a similar guy-next-door look as Marco's. In Hong Kong, one of Leon's 'rivals', Aaron Kwok, donned in sexy and glamorous costumes, dared a singing-dancing-acrobatic act with a hanging, revolving pool in his 2007 concerts. Such extraordinary spectacles are not uncommon in Leon's or other Hong Kong pop stars' stage performance (de Kloet 2005b). We will return to this theme of (extra)ordinariness when we present our findings.

Our data was drawn from two sources: website postings and face-to-face interviews. From message boards, 100 postings were taken from the official Marco Borsato site (*www.marcoborsato.nl*) from 26 May to 3 June 2000, while 241 postings from the popular Leon Lai Happy 2000 Discussion Forum hosted by *www.hongkongcentre.com*, from 29 July to 5 August 2000. If we can trust the names used by the Borsato fans, it is clear that the site is predominantly populated by woman: 80 per cent.² Hong Kong fans make use of fake handles, making it impossible to trace the gender balance.³

We have subsequently interviewed five fans of each star, in both cases four women and one man. Their age ranges from 17 to 42, most of them (eight) are single. Fans were selected through snowballing, with the help of the respective fan clubs. Following a thematic analysis, using a data matrix (van Zoonen 1994), we have identified recurring themes in the discourses employed by the respondents, both in the online postings as well as in the interviews.

Production of locality: The linguistic and the heroic

Linguistic boundaries are employed to produce a sense of locality in cyberspace. The Dutch case is rather straightforward: their postings are only accessible to a Dutch-speaking community. The language use on the Leon Lai site is more spectacular as a linguistic boundary and identification with Hong Kong, rather than China:

(陰謀論)我想講0左好耐,唔知各位有無相同感覺,反黎報' 生果' 在報導有關 Leon 新聞時,經常刻意用一d Leon 影得差既相片刊登⁴ -- J

This excerpt, which criticizes a particular 'anti-Leon' tabloid, may read like Chinese. This apparently Chinese text, however, is not written in standard Chinese but in the Cantonese 'dialect' widely spoken in Hong Kong. Besides diction, typical Hong Kong Cantonese sentence structures and expressions are generally used in the guest book, drawing, at the same time, a boundary against all non-Hong Kong-Cantonese users, including Chinese from mainland China and Taiwan. As part of its 'Speak Mandarin Campaign', the Singaporean government tries to discourage Cantopop since it is considered a dialect that does not fit the ideal state-sanctioned Chinese-Singaporean identity (Khiun 2003). But the linguistic hybridization goes even further in these postings from Leon Lai fans. While standard Chinese is abandoned in all these messages, English is often used, mostly in a mixture with Cantonese. The use of English or Chinglish, the name Hong Kong has given to the mix of Chinese and English, on the site is a reference to the history of Hong Kong, which, after one-and-a-half centuries of British colonial rule, was handed over to China in 1997. Given Hong Kong's political and cultural marginality in the greater Chinese context, it is not surprising that the fans of a Hong Kong pop star would reject the standard national Chinese language and use its own mixture of Cantonese, English and Chinglish to mark out its own virtual territory. As Sandig and Selting argue, 'regional dialect can be used as a kind of "regional" style symbolizing the regional identity and allegiance of its speakers' (Sandig and Selting 1997: 141).

Looking at the content of the messages, we find that one of their most striking features is that they are *not* about music. The stars are more like local heroes. In the case of Marco Borsato, his affiliation with War Child is a topic that frequently recurs, like in the following quotes:

The Production of Locality in Global Pop

Wonderful that you make yourself available like that for War Child and that you went to Kosovo. I understand that you are so deeply moved by everything and that you must work it through. Wish you strength and success with all you do for War Child in the future.

Sabine

Hoi, Marco, good that you are back again! The photos of Kosovo are nice, but sometimes also very impressive. Sometimes it appears indeed just like Enschede ... Success on 14 June. I am proud to be a fan of someone who makes himself so available for others.[5]

Rebecca

Putting all these 'good work' messages together, one may invoke an image of Marco Borsato leaving home, flying around to save the world. For all his perceived altruistic merits – he is making himself available for such humanitarian cause – their local star is a hero precisely because he is human, with genuine feelings and concerns. To the relief of his fans, wherever Marco has been, he will return to his home (country), he is local. As apparent in the above-quoted and other messages, the idea of homecoming is strong among the fans. The important idea of home in these messages brings to mind Morley's argument that under current processes of globalization and de-territorialization, people are more, rather than less, inclined to articulate a sense of home or *heimat*, a sense that often involves a process of re-territorialization, a redrawing of imaginary boundaries (Morley 2001). Marco Borsato, however, is not only congratulated for the 'safe' return to his home country the Netherlands, but also literally to his own home – his family. Marco's wife Leontine (also a show business personality) and their children are often the recipients of 'best wishes' or kisses at the end of the fan messages (15 of them). Their marriage anniversary is also remembered by a number of fans.

Indeed, the messages on Marco Borsato's charitable acts, in their accents on his genuine involvement and return to his family, articulate and construct a local star not only as a good person of noble acts, but also a normal person of true feelings. Besides the messages on Kosovo and Enschede, many fans write as if they are simply relating to a person very close to them. For instance, 14 messages mention either a friendly request (asking Marco for coffee at a birthday party in a farm, to cook together), their daily lives (telling how they are eating chips and having a good time), or a simple greeting (asking Marco how he is doing). The ordinariness of the content underlines the perception of the star as an ordinary fellow being, who is supposed and is able to share in their mundane life. Following this notion of an ordinary, accessible star, it is hardly surprising that even more fans write in to link the more private, emotional happenings in their lives to Marco Borsato and sometimes to other fans. A one-minute silence is organized on the chat room for a boy who died. The picture that emerges here is of a very intimate virtual imagined community.

The fans of Leon Lai care less about his charitable acts. In contrast to the high proportion of charity messages on the Marco Borsato site, only 20 messages are sent in by the fans of Leon in relation to his one single charitable act: Leon would drive a local billionaire around in order to raise funds for charity. All these messages, however, only refer other fans to read related reports in the local press.

Among the rest of the 241 messages, two major themes stand out: a concern with Leon's prizes and the attention to his whereabouts. First, the prizes: in 2000, Leon Lai made an unexpected announcement that from then on he would not accept any (local) music awards any more. It became a point of discussion during this period because of the rumour that Leon agreed to stand for a regional reward, leading to some press comments on his integrity. Among the 108 messages sent to express their views, most posted in Leon's defence, like this:

> Leon has made it clear that he only 'refuses Hong Kong awards'. He didn't break his promise. There are simply too many annual music awards in Hong Kong, they are not representative at all. Leon is wise not to accept them. But this 'Global Chinese Hit-list' is adjudicated by many Asian radio stations. Very representative. It's worth joining in.
>
> a supporter

Quite apart from discussing whether Leon has broken his promise, messages similar to this supporter's also manage to construct discursively another set of moral standards to be applied in this case, namely, local awards can be dismissed, but a 'global' event organized by 'Asian' media is 'worth' their local star's participation. When it comes to winning an international battle against international opponents, the local hero must go and fight for the local honour.

A related but less spectacular display of concern (14 messages) is related to a cyber-voting for the best Hong Kong actor hosted by a Japanese website during this period. Leon's fans make an appeal, after noticing that Leon lags behind Takeshi Kaneshiro, an actor of Japanese-Chinese descent, who is also active in the Hong Kong film industry:

> Please go vote to this Japanese Homepage. Leon is second now. First is Takeshi Kaneshiro.
>
> Jojo

Such collaborative effort is indicative of the urgency to join forces and help their local hero to fight for the local honour – in this case, in Japan, against a half-Japanese opponent. Indeed, if saving the world is what Marco's fans expect of a Dutch hero, fighting for local honour seems to be the mission in Hong Kong. In this honourable mission, one does not find the other constructions related to the local star Marco Borsato, such as his feelings, ordinariness and closeness.

The second major group of messages (53) posted on the site is, instead, organized around informing one another – either by providing information directly or referring to other media reports – where Leon is. Unlike the Dutch fans who underline the home-coming of their star, the Leon fans seem to be equally eager in telling everyone that Leon is or is not in town. In the meantime, they invariably mention what Leon is actually doing – or working, to be exact. If fans of Marco Borsato would simply welcome him home, their

Hong Kong counterparts often add a working dimension to his homecoming. Mermaids' message is typical:

> Leon came out from airport like he was walking on the catwalk modelling not for clothes but … for Snoopy.

What Mermaids refers to is the well-known commercial involvement of Leon in the promotion of Snoopy suitcases during that particular period– among the various advertising activities he does for other sponsors. When he is not in Hong Kong, Leon's absence is also discursively linked to the notion of work. For instance:

> When is Leon coming back? – Angela
> Leon should be back soon, he is in Malaysia to start a movie. – Vicky

Distinct from the humanitarian, ordinary person Marco is – as displayed in the messages left by his fans – the Leon invoked by this group of messages is someone who is busy flying around and working. After all, what is at stake, according to the messages, is honour, not feelings; while feelings may come naturally, honour must be earned. No wonder none of the messages, in sharp contrast to the Marco site, is devoted to the kind of emotional expression by the Dutch fans.

Production of locality: The social, the charitable and the personal

Three aspects stand out when analysing the face-to-face interview materials: (1) a strong sense of community among the fans, (2) the charitable activities of the star and (3) the star's character.

Community

Previous studies on fan culture have convincingly presented the importance of affective bonds between fans, and the related emergence of fan communities that meet both online and offline (Jenkins 1992; Jenson 1992; Hills 2002). In our study, two sets of discourse on such community feeling are most obvious: first, among anonymous crowds and second, with fan-cum friends. Among the former, concerts are invariably mentioned as occasions invoking such collective sensation. Nok-ming,[6] from Hong Kong, recalls:

> Like going to a concert. So we would be swaying our fluorescent sticks all together. Wow! I don't know these people sitting next to me, but it feels like we are friends. [So you would be very happy?] Yes, yes, I would be very very happy.

Accounts similar to Nok-ming's abound in interviews with other fans. Marco Borsato fan Erik says:

> It was simply a fantastic show. Together with Mattijs we distributed lighters for Veronica. We covered the main area, at least 5,000 lighters, a very beautiful experience. When the first number 'Speeltuin' ('Playground') started, all the lighters were lit up. And you saw Marco look at them and wow. We were standing by the side, where Marco played acoustically. It's so beautiful … It's really an unforgettable experience.

Besides concerts, the community feeling is also constructed on a more personal and smaller scale. Fung-yi, when asked about her relationship with other Leon fans, says:

> We are quite close. We started off because we all liked Leon, and then we became good friends. Some of them feel like aunties to me. We go to his concerts together, and we become closer and closer. Sometimes we would go on vacation together.

Debbie's experience on the other side of the (pop) world sounds almost identical:

> Yes, you wait for his performance. And then at a certain moment you start feeling close to a particular type of people who are also waiting. You have contact with one another and start talking for hours … Now it's no longer only about Marco, like we spent a weekend together at Vlaardingen and Marco had nothing to do with it.

In the case of Tin-yan, the only person with whom she shares her admiration for Leon is her brother, who is three years older than her:

> He would buy magazines, while both of us would buy our own CDs.

Tin-yan's collective experience as a fan together with her brother points to another facet of the fan community: its conflation with the family, particularly in the context of Hong Kong. Besides Tin-yan, three other Leon fans also have (extended) family members sharing the same admiration. Nok-ming, for instance, finds a ready partner in her older female cousin when she needs to discuss matters concerning Leon, like his clothes. Tze-ying's daughter was as enthusiastic as her mother before she started her full-time job.

Sometimes the respondents reiterate the stereotypical images of 'obsessed individual' and 'hysterical crowd' as described by Jenson (1992), while distancing themselves from such fans; Nok-ming decides against joining the fan club because she does not have 'that kind of mentality' while Nathalie, on the other hand, observes that by taking up the fan club 'job', her affiliation with Marco becomes socially 'acceptable'. It is of interest, however, to note that the other dominant image of fan – a loner – is not at all invoked in their discourse. Marco's and Leon's fans we interviewed may claim to be less or equally frenzied as other 'super fans'; they never admit to be lonely themselves, neither do they hint at other fans as solitary outsiders.

Charity

As is seen in the messages left in the guest books of the Marco and Leon sites, the charitable acts performed by the two local stars receive enthusiastic approval from both groups of fans. Yet far from foregrounding the emotional and human dimension of charity as the Dutch fans do, the Hong Kong fans prefer to talk about, indeed, the more-than-human greatness of Leon and the honour and pride he brings from out there to his fans and fellow people here. Stressing the difficulties Leon has to survive, Fung-yi says:

> I think he's great. Going to such remote places like Rwanda and Ganxu [in China] must be very tough. You have to get lots of injections beforehand. I think as an artist, he really serves as an example not only for us fans, but for everyone … I think he's great. I can only use this adjective 'great' to describe him.

The greatness of her local star is further connected with the idea of honour and pride:

> I am his fan, I also share the honour. Not every artist in Hong Kong is willing to spend so much time on charity. And so enthusiastic. I feel very proud.

Both Nok-ming and Chun-fai respond emphatically that they, like Fung-yi, feel honoured by what Leon has been doing for charity. While Nok-ming cannot name the kind of honour she feels ('an unspeakable feeling'), Chun-fai says: 'It's an honour for the Chinese!'

If difficulty, greatness, honour and pride are the key words in the discourse of these Hong Kong fans on their local hero, their Dutch counterparts construct Marco's charity using a different set of terms, where involvement, emotion and humanity dominate. Unlike Leon's fans who speak more about the physical difficulty Leon may encounter abroad, especially as a star, Marco's fans prefer to comment on the emotional burden Marco has to carry, as a human being. Nathalie, for instance, explains why his fans are touched by his work in Kosovo:

> Because it was so clear that he was concerned … He was there and that touched me quite a lot. I don't know if you have seen the documentary. It was a small village, on one side was a playground and next to it was a mass grave. And almost every child lost a father or mother, and he looked so unbelievably around, like he's thinking: how is it possible. And the fans sat there crying, watching how concerned he was.

Compared to Leon's fans who articulate their sense of honour in Leon's difficult missions outside Hong Kong, Marco's fans are more eager to point out the domestic acts of their local hero in the Netherlands. Nathalie, for instance, when asked if she wants Marco to do more overseas charity work, replies:

> He also does a lot for the Netherlands. Jantje Beton, Ronald McDonald House. Overseas work doesn't have more value than in the Netherlands.

From the discourse of Marco's fans, greatness and honour that the local star may reap from his global acts seem much less important than the humanitarianism he shows. Given the person of feeling that he is, Marco would simply carry out his good deeds wherever it is, as articulated by his fans. In any case, while both groups of fans attach significance and support to the charitable acts their local stars have been doing, how their notions of charity are constructed diverge – Leon's fans 'glorify' his good deeds in terms of what he brings to himself (greatness) and his fellow people including the fans (honour), while Marco's fans 'personalize' his charitable work into who he is. To put it differently, Leon becomes more a star because of what he does for charity, while Marco, on the other hand, becomes more a human being for the same reason.

Character

For the Dutch fans, the ordinariness of Marco Borsato as a real person, as a real human being is another important marker of their admiration. Despite his obvious public, celebrity status, all Marco fans refer fondly to his being *gewoon*, a common Dutch word that can be translated as 'normal', 'ordinary', perceived therefore as unpretentious and authentic. Nathalie says:

> He is very honest. Some people think that it's only an image, but he simply shows the way he is. If he is cheerful, he shows it; if he is sad, then he cries. On stage, on TV.

Marco is thus perceived as normal as a friend or a neighbour, and sometimes is approached by the fans likewise, for instance, when they drop by to visit him. Erik says:

> Once I had this unique experience at his place, he came out unexpectedly with his little son. There were four of us. Marielle and I kept an eye on his little son, who was smart and nosy. I wondered whether it's okay to take a picture. Then the boy walked away, and there were a lot of canals there, so I wondered whether it's okay to pick him up, and it was OK with Marco.

If the name Marco Borsato is taken away from this narrative, one may indeed wonder if Erik had simply gone to the residence of a new neighbour, who happened to come out with his little boy. No wonder he says:

The Production of Locality in Global Pop

It may sound very strange, but I see him simply as a person. He is obviously the biggest star in the Netherlands, but the star status is very relative and Marco has changed very little. He hasn't changed at all through the years. Marco is simply a person and that's the way I approach him.

In Erik's discourse, the ordinariness of Marco as a person is all the stronger because of and, at the same time, in spite of his star status. Such double mechanism is also at work in the following account by Tessa who, before Marco moved out in summer 2000, lived in the same city as him:

Marco knows that he actually can't. He can't walk in the street anonymously, but how often I have seen him do that. If you didn't know he's a star, you wouldn't tell. He simply walks in his old ragged trousers.

As underlined by Tessa's discourse, Marco's anonymous walk in the street becomes significant because he is supposed to be well-known and, he is still doing it. His insistence on being ordinary is thus cherished. The intricate relationship between the star and the person is perhaps best illustrated in the following sentence of Tessa:

Sometimes a person becomes a star, and sometimes a star remains a person. That is Marco.

According to Tessa, celebrity claims its origin in the ordinary, while, at the same time, ordinariness is being celebrated. One may, in turn, trace this celebrated ordinariness in the Dutch culture, which is often said to be tilting towards the ordinary. Some fans draw the link themselves. For instance, Debbie states:

I think there is no other country where the people and the artist are so sober.

When asked if there could ever be a Dutch Madonna, Nathalie says:

No, the Netherlands won't take it. If you do it so big and are so big in the Netherlands, they would find you arrogant and tell you to behave normally. You go and buy French fries by the Febo and do not behave bigger than you are.

Here, the popular local fast-food chain Febo (not the McDonald's) is used to underline the typical Dutch ordinariness while the pet phrase, often considered to capture the spirit of the Dutch people *doe maar gewoon* ('behave normally'), is also quoted by Nathalie to talk off the possibility of such extraordinary global stars in the Netherlands.

The Dutch fans are also eager to articulate the emotional importance of Marco's music. Tessa, for example, who labels herself as 'a person of feelings', gives a detailed account of how her endeared grandmother ('My grandma and I were one') wanted to fulfil her last wish, namely to have an official wedding ceremony. For both significant occasions, the wedding and, shortly after, the funeral, Marco's songs were used. Tessa recalls:

> I find it so special that my grandma chose my Marco. If someone dies, I play Marco; if I am happy, I play Marco.

Miriam says:

> After my father died, this song – I was lying on the lawn and staring at the moon – I don't even remember the title, I don't know – the song touched me in a way just like I was with my father.

In stark contrast, their Hong Kong counterparts attach no emotional significance at all to the music of their own star. When asked when she would listen to Leon, Tze-ying simply replies: 'Doesn't really matter.'

Tze-ying's reaction is typical of other Leon fans who, likewise, do not articulate any connection between their emotional life with Leon's music, or with music in general. What is remarkably different from Marco's fans is their discursive nonchalance in severing their music-listening act from any other emotional justifications, such as, like Marco's fans, mood management or crisis support. In general, such resistance to reflect or explain (away) their acts in 'deeper' terms leads frequently to curt, fragmentary answers from Leon's fans – as if to correspond to the fragmentary, chaotic life of their city, which allows limited space and time for display of feelings. On the other hand, as indicated by the quotes cited above, Marco's fans are more ready to volunteer lengthy replies, which, apart from echoing the general tenor of laying bare their feelings (like their star), may also be anchored in the dominant discourse emphasizing emotional expression and honesty in contemporary Dutch society.

The categorical difference of Leon's fans from their Dutch counterparts is not only confined to the articulated use of music: Leon Lai's star appeal is also constructed differently. While Marco Borsato is fondly compared to one's friend or neighbour – being ordinary – with almost no attention paid to his physical attraction, Leon is anything but ordinary. Not being cast as the boy next-door, he is referred to as 'the prince on the white horse' by Fung-yi. In less dramatic terms, Nok-ming and Tin-yan also mention the good looks of Leon. Regarding the physical appeal of Marco Borsato, only Nathalie says she finds Marco 'sexy' since one year ago, because of 'his little belly and thinner hair'. Interestingly enough, Nathalie immediately contains such sexual appeal in a more normal, domestic setting by adding that she also finds her husband sexy for the same reasons.

Leon's fans do not foreground him as a person of feelings. Instead, he is a persevering worker. Tze-ying, when asked of her views of what a star is, says:

> Actually I haven't really thought about it. But, well, I think Leon is very hardworking. And he tries his best in everything he does. He is very demanding to himself.

Tin-yan says:

> I think he works very hard in everything he does. But he won't shout to everyone. He bites his lips and keeps on working, quietly.

Indeed, Leon's frequent flying to other places of the world is, in its turn, also perceived from the perspective of work. In the extreme case where Leon emigrates to another country, none of his fans seem to object, provided, like what Tin-yan says, he continues what he is doing. Fung-yi even says:

> Well, if he suddenly leaves, I wouldn't be happy. But on the other hand, I would also be happy – a bit contradictory – because Leon has a new place to develop his career, I would be happy for him.

Compared to their Dutch counterparts, who value the closeness of their local star far above the inaccessibility of global ones, Leon's fans seem to be more able to negotiate distance and separation with work and career – and, again like in their articulation of Leon's charity acts, honour. Chun-fai, like Fung-yi, would not mind Leon basing himself in another place if that would add to his popularity. Cherishing the possibility of Leon becoming a global star like Madonna or Michael Jackson, Chun-fai says:

> Of course I want that. I would be very happy … I would feel proud.

Tin-yan states:

> That would be Hong Kong's honour and his fans' honour.

Indeed, the idea of leaving behind one's place of origin, working hard for a better future, and bringing honour (and money) to one's family is not an alien thought in the context of Hong Kong. The often quoted post-war metamorphosis of Hong Kong into a prosperous city puts the stress on the enterprising spirit of mainland Chinese refugees. Later, in the uncertain years before British Hong Kong was reverted to Chinese rule, in 1997, the necessity of working hard for a better future, in the sense of earning enough money and emigrating abroad, is reiterated. Leon's fans' welcoming reaction to Leon's hard-working ways – even at the expense of leaving them behind to become global – is in stark contrast to Marco fans, who would rather keep their ordinary, local star close to themselves, both geographically and emotionally. Some of Leon's fans go further than envisaging Leon as global star – they actually see Leon already as one. Fung-yi says:

> He has fans all over the world. To some extent, he is famous everywhere. His fans are distributed all over the world. In whichever corner there are fans of his.

It comes, therefore, as no surprise when they are asked to speak on their favourite music video clips of Leon, all of them choose those filmed on locations outside Hong Kong, such as Miami and Korea – signs of his outward expansion. In the case of Marco's fans, all of them point precisely to the localities within the Netherlands in the Marco video clips, like Bloemendaal, Leiden and Rotterdam.

Conclusion

It is clear that both groups of fans have managed to create their own community around their local stars, whether in cyber or 'real' space – with similar and divergent characteristics. As far as online community is concerned, both show linguistic features reminiscent of their respective societies at large. While friendliness and rapport is generally displayed, the Leon community leans on sharing information and opinions, but not in, conventionally speaking, private or emotional matters, in contrast to the various emotional exchanges in the Marco community. Such contrast may reflect different cultural accents perceived in the two localities.

At the centre of the fan communities are, of course, the local stars Marco and Leon. In both online communities, they are constructed as local heroes, who either go to save the world (charity) or fight for local honour (prize-winning). Fans' beliefs in the local participation in global setting as well as in the local as home are communicated at the same time. During the process, however, the local stars are invested with different characters. While the perception of Marco Borsato as an ordinary person of feeling and humanitarianism is foregrounded, Leon Lai is largely constructed as an important someone, who is busy flying around, both working and striving for honour. Also opinions on charity diverge: as far as the Dutch fans are concerned, their notion of charity is, again, anchored in Marco's feelings and humanity. On the other hand, their Hong Kong counterparts emphasize the greatness and honour their local star may bring.

In general, while the Dutch fans see Marco as an ordinary person, the Hong Kong fans characterize Leon as an extraordinary worker. Marco's fans' notion of ordinariness, with its associated constructions of having feelings, being authentic and accessible, also leads to articulations of strong emotional ties to his music – entirely absent in the discourse of Leon's fans. Besides his good looks, Leon's most remarkable character trait is work: his hard-working perseverance and constant attempt to seek improvement and honour. The different characterizations, we argue, are in turn informed by the dominant discourse on being ordinary, emotionally honest and humanitarian in the Dutch society at large, as well as that on being more than ordinary, hard-working and proud in the Hong Kong context.

Fans use the stars, thus, to produce a sense of locality (Appadurai 1996) or home (Morley 2001). Debates on cultural globalization (or Americanization, for that matter) should not be only about cultural products (e.g. the musical form or content), about cultural icons (e.g. pop stars), about cultural flows (e.g. the United States to the rest of the world); they must also be about the cultural practices of audiences. 'Consumers' of cultural products, cultural icons and cultural flows must not be taken as passive recipients, fanatics or even victims, but active participants in the production of meaning in their daily lives (Fiske 1992). Even when the music of Marco and Leon sounds not unlike that of their global counterparts, even when they look not unlike their global counterparts, their local fans 'use' them differently.

We do not wish to celebrate the local, and are aware of the danger of cultural essentialism that may be read from our analysis. It is important to acknowledge that these stars are part of a profoundly globalized political economy. They are contracted by global record companies (Universal and Sony respectively), and provide for these companies a way to conquer local markets (Negus 1999; Hesmondhalgh 2002). In other words, the production of locality is often implicated in the logics of global capitalism. Fandom is thus complicit with the global political economy, which, however, does not necessarily disempower fans – they can and still do appropriate the texts in their own intricate ways. What this comparative study has shown is how fans use local stars to gain a sense of home, to become part of a community that is neither fluid nor transnational, but one that is instead profoundly rooted and quite fixed.

Notes

1   The incident has in turn sparked off a discussion on the (mal)practices and ethics of local paparazzi.
2   It is of course possible that Marco Borsato's fans are also using fake names. Nevertheless, it is interesting to note that their preference for 'real' names seems to underwrite the penchant for the 'personal' in their postings, which is absent in the postings of Leon Lai's Hong Kong fans. See further analysis in main text.
3   To provide an additional checking-mechanism on our data, a brief follow-up study was conducted in 2006, involving a comparative analysis of the fan websites of both stars, yielding similar results.
4   All the Dutch and Cantonese-Chinese messages are translated by the authors.
5   On 13 May 2000, an explosion in Enschede, a city in the Netherlands, took away the lives of 21 local residents and turned an entire neighbourhood into scorching debris. This officially declared 'national disaster' led to, among other fund-raising events, a charity concert in which Marco Borsato pledged to join.
6   All the interviewees agreed to the use of their names for this publication.

Chapter 3

BLOWING IN THE CHINA WIND: ENGAGEMENTS WITH CHINESENESS IN HONG KONG'S *ZHONGGUOFENG* MUSIC VIDEOS

> China Wind is an unprecedented current. [Chinese-language] popular music is no longer monopolized by romantic love songs, but is now moved by an irreducibly dense current of Chinese culture.[1]
>
> (Lan[2] 2007)

So opens a cover story article featured in the 22 July issue of the Chinese-language *Yazhou Zhoukan/Asiaweek* in 2007. Indeed, when you tune in to any pop station in any Chinese community, it is quite likely that you would come across a song that the local presenter will tell you is another *zhongguofeng* single. The best-selling Chinese pop[3] idol at this moment, Jay Chou, whose song 'Lady/娘子' featured in his debut album in 2000 arguably earned him the reputation of 'father of China Wind', pledged that he would have at least one China Wind song in his releases (Cao 2006). As in other musical styles or genres, it is difficult if at all possible to pin down what exactly China Wind popular music is. It can be defined musically, by its juxtaposition of classical Chinese melody and/or instruments with trendy global pop styles, particularly R&B and hip-hop. It can also be defined lyrically, by its mobilization of 'traditional' Chinese cultural elements, such as legends, classics and language, implicitly or explicitly in contemporary contexts. While songs with distinct Chinese characteristics, whether musically or lyrically, have always been part of local pop history, 'China Wind' is a novel phenomenon.[4] Above all, China Wind owes its production and circulation as a discursive formation to its endorsement by mainstream artists, notably from Taiwan, as much as to its popularity among audiences in Greater China. In fact, the term has become so en vogue that it is no longer exclusively or even predominantly applied to popular music, but also to popular culture at large; key the Chinese words of *zhongguofeng* in any search engine, one will be confronted with top hits covering a wide range of items from fashion accessories, design, animation, packaged tours, to anything that is modern and yet traditional.

While China Wind pop is yet to be systematically documented, researched and analysed, popular and media attention has generally focused on: (1) Taiwan-based artists: in addition to Jay Chou, critics also regularly refer to music by Leehom Wang (who has coined a term 'Chinked-out' in 2004 for his brand of China Wind), David Tao, Ken Wu, TANK and girl group S.H.E. in their reports on China Wind (see for instance Cao 2006; Chen 2007; Fung 2006; Lan 2007); (2) lyrics: although China Wind is also defined musically, critics tend to zoom in onto the lyrical dimension of the songs, citing substantial portions of the lyrics to illustrate China Wind's evocation of the Three Kingdoms, Lao Zi, Confucius and so forth. This resonates with a general tendency in popular music studies to privilege lyrics in the analysis, assuming, as Frith points out, that 'words determine or form listeners' beliefs and values' (Frith 1998: 164). As if to underwrite the lyrical importance of China Wind, Fang Wenshan, generally considered the most important lyricist of China Wind pop, published a book in 2008, connecting 34 pieces of his China Wind lyrics to Chinese rhetorics, culture and tradition, or what he calls *guoxue*, the study of Chinese classics (Fang 2008).

Given the focus on Taiwan-based artists and the lyrical dimension, discussion on China Wind has been framed by the specific political entanglement across the Straits. The *Yazhou Zhoukan* cover story, for instance, situates China Wind in the 'de-Sinification' (*qu zhongguohua*) policy implemented by the Taiwanese authorities, inferring from their temporal coincidence China Wind's (potential) power to unite culturally what is severed politically. In the words of the Taiwanese scholar Xu Wenwei, 'The [China Wind] phenomenon stitches up wounds inflicted by tearing apart. When politics tears apart, popular culture brings stability' (quoted in Lan 2007). In a more general sense, China Wind has been accredited with the attempt if not achievement of reinserting and reasserting sanctioned, 'sinocentric' versions of culture and history to a younger generation. The 'Chineseness' that China Wind has been articulating and constructing is largely assumed to be part and parcel what the Chinese are supposed to learn, about themselves and about their culture. As Eric Wolf notes, 'the cultural assertion that the world is shaped in this way and not in some other has to be repeated and enacted, lest it be questioned and denied' (1990: 593). Jay Chou's rap number 'Compendium of Materia Medica/本草綱目' – the title draws from a Chinese medical classic allegedly dated from the Ming Dynasty – is an extreme but nonetheless indicative example. Hailed by *China Newsweek*, a mainland publication, as a 'progressive song in celebration of Chinese culture' (Cao 2006), the song proceeds, amidst the names of 16 ancient medicinal herbs: 'If Master Hua Tuo were reborn, he would cure your favour-currying attitude towards foreigners/let foreign nations learn the Chinese language/stir up our nationalistic consciousness.' As Anthony Fung observes in his research on Jay Chou, 'his most popular songs trigger the audience's emotions in a celebration of Chinese tradition and values' (2008: 73). Similarly, Wang Peiwen, commenting on Fang Wenshan, Jay's lyricist, notes 'his works show a consistent creative ideal of restoring and returning to traditional Chinese culture' (2007: 51).

In this chapter, rather than focusing on what is considered the main 'source' of China Wind songs, namely Taiwan, we have chosen China Wind songs originated from Hong Kong and their music videos as the primary site of enquiry. Although our analysis primarily draws on the visual aspects of the music videos, we follow Sarah Pink's observation that no experience is ever purely visual (Pink 2008). We will hence examine not only the visual but also the lyrical text of such videos. Our central concern is: how do Hong Kong's China Wind music videos engage with hegemonic versions of Chineseness? In that sense, it can be read as an extension of the autobiographical inquiry in Chapter 1, where one particular Hong Kong lyricist's attempt to contest hegemonic versions of

Chineseness is discussed. The choice of Hong Kong is informed by our empirical interest in the complex entanglement of cultural and political power which the postcolonial city is presumably going through. On the one hand, many scholars on Hong Kong popular culture have observed a 'process of re-nationalization' following or even prior to the political handover to Beijing rule in 1997 (e.g. Erni 2001; Ho 2000). On the other hand, as a hybrid city, which has no claims to 'territorial propriety or cultural centrality', and which is embedded in its 'in-betweenness' (Chow 1993), Hong Kong continues to show resilience in troubling dominant narratives of Chineseness by reinventing local culture and identity (Abbas 1997; Chow and De Kloet 2008). We are interested in finding out empirically how popular culture, in this case, China Wind pop, is shaping and being shaped by this tension between nationalistic longing and the city's hybridic 'capacity to think otherwise' (Chan 2005). It can also be taken as a supplement to a number of studies on Chinese musical nationalism (e.g. Kagan 1963; Kouwenhoven 1997; Tuohy 2001; Wong 1984), which seek 'to examine the mutually transformative process of making music national and of realizing the nation musically' (Tuohy 2001: 108). At the same time, our choice of Hong Kong is more than empirically driven; it is, in theory and in praxis, a correspondence with the ongoing debates on Chineseness – debates on not only what but also who defines it (Ang 2001; Chow 1998; Lim 2006). By privileging Hong Kong, we are in line with scholars who choose to interrogate dominant versions of Chineseness by invoking Hong Kong as a case study that troubles any essential claim on Chineseness (Abbas 1997; Chow 1998; Leung 2008). If China Wind, as a whole, shows signs of becoming what Tu Wei-ming may call a Cultural China project, Hong Kong's variant is resisting and this study can be seen as a tactic to contest China Wind's culturalist strategies. In short, this chapter is also meant to reclaim a speaking position for Hong Kong, which can never take Chineseness for granted and whose Chineseness is never taken for granted, on questions of Chineseness (Chow 2009a), to let the hybridized hybridize.

For the purpose of this inquiry, we have scanned the pop chart of Commercial Radio Hong Kong from 2006 till the moment we finished collecting data for this study, which was the first week of October 2008.[5] We have identified 18 songs that would be generally recognized as China Wind, among which eight originated in Hong Kong: two in 2006, four in 2007, and two so far in 2008. The rest were performed almost exclusively by artists from Taiwan, who are known for their China Wind pop, including Jay Chou (six), Leehom Wang (two) and Ken Wu (one), and the remaining one by Ah-Niu, a Malaysian-born artist who reached pop stardom in Taiwan. Of the eight Hong Kong China Wind songs, six were released with accompanying music videos. While this group of songs and music videos forms the primary body of data, we also make occasional comparison with the rest to enrich our visual and textual analyses. We will first show how the Hong Kong videos destabilize Chineseness by rendering it as distant, ambiguous and something to struggle with. We will then concentrate on a conspicuous dimension of Hong Kong China Wind, that it is mostly embodied by female artists. We will conclude with some thoughts on further research.

Table 3.1: China Wind entries to Commercial Radio pop chart January 2006–October 2008

Song title	Highest chart position	Performer (based in)	Composer	Lyricist
2006				
Error in a Flower Field	01	Leehom Wang (Taiwan)	Leehom Wang	Chen Zhenchuan
Huo Yuanjia	03	Jay Chou (Taiwan)	Jay Chou	Fang Wenshan
Peach Blossoms Everywhere	19	Ah-Niu (Taiwan)	Ah-Niu	Ah-Niu/ Youdi
Hair, Like Snow	05	Jay Chou (Taiwan)	Jay Chou	Fang Wenshan
Sweet Dumplings	01	Fiona Sit (Hong Kong)	Khalil Fong	Zhou Yaohui*
Goddess of Mercy	01	Andy Lau (Hong Kong)	Khalil Fong	Lin Xi
Beyond a Thousand Miles	07	Jay Chou ft. Fei Yu Ching (Taiwan)	Jay Chou	Fang Wenshan
General's Decree	07	Ken Wu (Taiwan)	Ken Wu	Ken Wu
Golden Armor	08	Jay Chou (Taiwan)	Jay Chou	Fang Wenshan
2007				
Chrysanthemum Terrace	15	Jay Chou (Taiwan)	Jay Chou	Fang Wenshan
Daiyu Smiles	01	Vincy (Hong Kong)	Weng Weiying	Zhou Yaohui
Flowers	02	12 Flowers ft. Shirley Kwan (Hong Kong)	Chen Huiyang	Lin Xi
Small**	18	Joey Yung (Hong Kong)	Jay Chou	Fang Wenshan
Falling Leaves Returning to Their Roots	10	Leehom Wang (Taiwan)	Kuang Yumin	Kuang Yumin
Big Red Robe	2	Denise Ho (Hong Kong)	Benson Fan	Chen Haofeng
Jan – 2 Oct, 2008				
Sword and Snow	4	Denise Ho and Sammi Cheng (Hong Kong)	Benson Fan/ Denise Ho	Wyman

Blowing in the China Wind

Mountain and Water	6	Shirley Kwan (Hong Kong)	Plet Blank/Rene Runge/Andreas Kaufhold/Chist	Xiazhi
Fragrance of Rice	17 (as at 2 Oct)	Jay Chou (Taiwan)	Jay Chou	Jay Chou

*Zhou Yaohui is the pinyin of Chow Yiu Fai, one of the authors of this chapter.
**Although 'Small' is written by the Taiwanese Chou and Fang, it is included in our analysis as a Hong Kong song as its performer Joey Yung is based in Hong Kong and generally perceived as a Hong Kong star.

Destabilizing Chineseness

As expected of visual embodiments of China Wind songs, the accompanying music videos evoke a diversity of imaginaries conventionally coded as Chinese, or, more precisely, traditionally Chinese. From sinified objects such as silk-screen and orientalistic costumes, to sinified genres such as Cantonese opera and swordsman play, these imaginaries of Chineseness, in a general and collective sense, do create 'an occasion for constructing Chineseness as a territorially dispersed, yet ethnically integrated imagined community', as John Eperjesi (2004: 28) argues in his analysis of the film *Crouching Tiger, Hidden Dragon*. However, making Cultural China imaginable is never a fait accompli; rather, it is a dynamic, power-ridden and therefore unstable project. The six Hong Kong China Wind videos under our scrutiny demonstrate a paradoxical

Figure 3.1: 'Goddess of Mercy' (Andy Lau) (courtesy of East Asia Music (Holdings) Ltd).

Sonic Multiplicities

Figure 3.2: 'Goddess of Mercy' (Andy Lau) (courtesy of East Asia Music (Holdings) Ltd).

act of evoking and undermining Chineseness at least in three ways; they have constructed Chineseness as distant gaze, as ambiguous space and as ongoing struggles.

Of the six videos, 'Small/小小' and 'Goddess of Mercy/觀世音' are visually the least sinified. In 'Goddess of Mercy', despite its title and the Buddhist sentiments of the lyrics, the only sinified object, a Chinese Buddha statue, occupies one single shot in a video that is largely built on news footages of starvation, poverty and disasters in the world. Evoked as a source of spiritual wisdom ('When there is a crisis, we need advice from the higher power'), the Buddha, however, stays high up (established by a shot tilting from low to high), overlooking, but never intervening, whether visually or narratively, in the suffering of the world. In the end, it is Andy Lau (performer of the song) who guides a spoiled boy to stand up, venture to the sun, to the sea, and drop a message in a bottle to nature: peace. In a similar but extended fashion, Chineseness is mobilized as distant gaze in the video of 'Small'. Here, a large silk screen with sinified red flower motif functions as a recurring backdrop to a story of childhood romance and lost love. While fragments of a boy and a girl, playing hopscotch, rope-jumping and wedding, intertwine with fragments of a solitary woman, Joey Yung (performer of the song), the silk screen stands there, unmoving and unmoved, bearing silent witness to the past and of the present yearning for the past. If memory, according to the lyrics, wears the face of 'a folk story-teller, speaking with the accent of hometown', visually the silk screen is transforming that nostalgic Chinese face into a more impassive facade, watching but never intervening, like the Buddha.

Figure 3.3: 'Small' (Joey Yung) (courtesy of Emperor Entertainment Group).

The Chineseness constructed in another two videos is marked less by distance than by ambiguity. In 'Daiyu Smiles/黛玉笑了', lyrically a feminist re-reading of the main female character Lin Daiyu in the Chinese literary classic *Dream of the Red Chamber*, 'hand-drawn' Chinese ink paintings open up a two-dimensional fantastical space in which the physical person Vincy (the song performer) exists. Similar to and yet radically different from the silk screen in 'Small', the ink drawings in this video do not only function as a backdrop, but also as a real world that Vincy interacts with. For instance, at the beginning of the video, Vincy would only stand on an ink painted bridge pondering at a pair of ink-painted fish swimming; she steps down later on to the pond and plays with the ink-painted fish. As if to trouble her role as the melancholic, vulnerable Daiyu, Vincy in the video is sometimes dressed in black, sometimes in white with a style that defies easy periodization. This ambiguity between tradition and modernity, fantasy and reality, absence and presence, characterizes the Chinese world conjured up by the ink paintings in 'Daiyu Smiles'. It is interesting to note that ink also features in the video of a Taiwanese China Wind song 'General's Decree/將軍令'. The video begins with Ken Wu (the song performer) dipping a brush into a bowl of ink and ends with him completing the three words – 將-軍-令 – in traditional calligraphic style. This piece of ink writing, after Ken Wu defeats a group of black guys in basketball, singing 'In your world you speak a b c d, but on my soils, sorry, you have to speak Chinese', functions as a symbolic act of completion, commendation and confirmation, very different from the ambiguous symbolic order in the other ink-painted world.

The video of Fiona Sit's 'Sweet Dumplings/糖不甩' takes the element of ambiguity further. Like 'Daiyu Smiles', 'Sweet Dumplings', rather at odds with its lyrical exploration of a traditional sweetmeat and romantic sweetness, features one single female person throughout the entire video. However, unlike Vincy, who traverses her ink-painted world, sometimes in white, sometimes in black, but always wearing a pensive expression, Fiona is not only torn between, but visually torn into, two fantastical spaces sinified by bamboos, red lanterns, paper fan and waxed paper umbrella. When Fiona inhabits the dark world, she is dressed in a dark robe revealing her belly and her legs, with dark mascara smeared over the edges of her eyes; she becomes a temptress. When she inhabits the white world, she dons a long white gown, with long hair hanging down, exuding breaths in wonderful colours; she becomes a fairy. In other words, if the ambiguous space of Chinessnness confuses Vincy, hence her pensiveness, it infuses Fiona, splitting her up in two selves poised in tension. Strengthened by unsteady camera movement and focusing, the tension is finally resolved in the last scene where the white Fiona is sitting in front of a laptop seeing herself in the monitor; the ambiguous space is therefore contained in an act of modernity, presence and reality.[6]

This ambiguous space, however, becomes the site of explicit, ongoing struggles in the videos of 'Big Red Robe/大紅袍' and 'Sword and Snow/劍雪'. Mobilizing Cantonese opera as well as a well-known opera singer/actress as its sinification tactic, the video of 'Big Red Robe' features Denise Ho (the song performer) as a rebellious apprentice struggling between the wishes of her teacher (to play, like her, female roles on stage) and her own (to

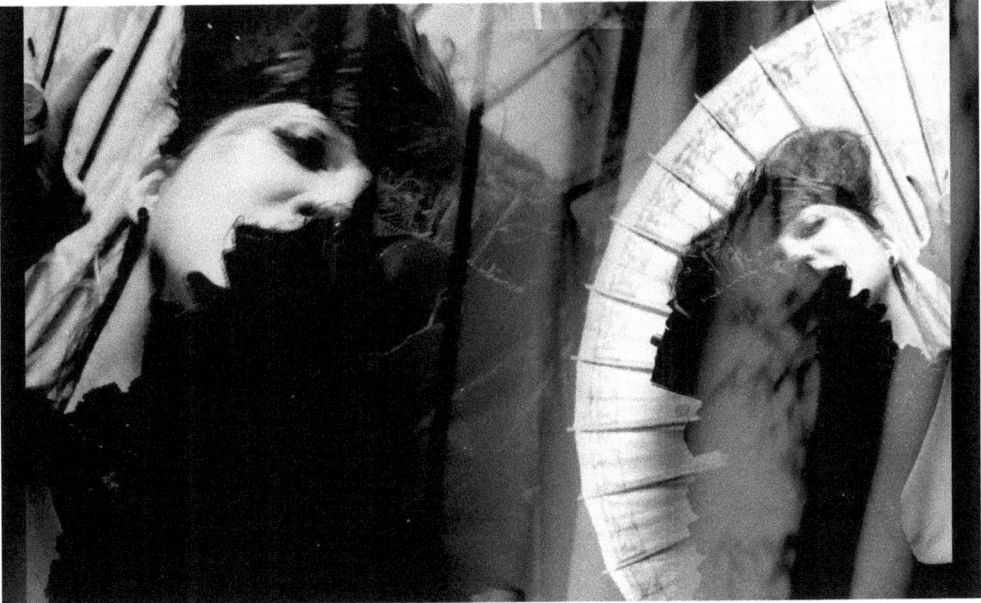

Figure 3.4: 'Sweet Dumplings' (Fiona Sit) (courtesy of Warner Music Hong Kong).

Figure 3.5: 'Sweet Dumplings' (Fiona Sit) (courtesy of Warner Music Hong Kong).

play, instead, the male roles – it is a common practice in Cantonese opera to have woman play the role of man). Her internal struggles are dramatized throughout the video: in Denise' facial expressions, in her being alone despite her opera troupe, in secretly practising male roles, in her wearing a black and a white T-shirt intermittently. Performing Chinese tradition, be it opera or obedience, is represented here as a series of struggles. (We will leave a fuller discussion on another performance, gender, to the next section.) While 'Big Red Robe' is filmed largely in a realistic style, the video of 'Sword and Snow' adopts the Chinese swordsmanship genre, in which Sammi Cheng and Denise Ho (performers of the song), in quasi-orientalistic costumes, return in time, separately, from some futuristic apparatus to a large piece of primordial grassland and engage in constant sword fighting.[7] The sinified space opened up by this video is a space of danger, of uncertainty, of struggles. That the two swordswomen return to a piece of grassland and fight, forms a telling contrast to the video of Taiwanese China Wind song 'Fragrance of Rice/稻香'. There, a middle-aged office man, after being fired, falls into a depression, seeing his wife and daughter leave; he returns to his hometown, to his elderly mother and to a piece of rice field where finally his family is happily reunited. Instead of fighting, Jay Chou (the song performer) and a guitar-playing companion are singing in this rural landscape: 'Do you remember, home is the only fortress?' Rice, rice field and the concomitant Chineseness are evoked as an idyllic home/town, a space for reunion and happiness.

Feminizing Chineseness

As alluded in the last section, gender is an important dimension that the Hong Kong group of China Wind songs has foregrounded and reasserted into dominant, often masculinist constructions of Chinese tradition, value and culture. Of the six Hong Kong China Wind songs, only one is performed by a male artist,[8] a stark contrast to the Taiwanese situation, where China Wind was presumably initiated by Jay Chou and has been almost monopolized by him and fellow male artists. It is of interest to note that the only China Wind song that has stirred up any significant controversy is delivered by S.H.E., a Taiwanese girl group. Their single 'Zhongguohua/Chinese Language' has been criticized for being too pro-Beijing, claiming that the girls should not sing 'the whole world is learning Chinese language (*zhongguohua*)' but 'Taiwanese language (*taiwanhua*)' (Lan 2007). This controversy has laid bare not only the political nature of the China Wind phenomenon, but also the masculinist attempt, to borrow Rey Chow's analysis on Chen Kaige's *King of the Children*, 'to rewrite culture without woman and all the limitations she embodies' (1995: 141).[9] Following this line of thought, it would not be unreasonable to suggest that the sharp gender division of China Wind in terms of Hong Kong (female-dominated) and Taiwan (male-dominated) has less to do with coincidence than with the city's hybridity and its inherent discomfort with dominant narratives, with certain claims to Chineseness.

If Hong Kong China Wind pop is to feminize, to intervene by rewriting Chinese culture with a female voice and to use gender as a means to trouble dominant narratives (Hershatter 2007: 108), what does it say? We believe we hear echoes of her uncertainty, of her history and of her womanhood. First, uncertainty. While Ken Wu, in 'General's Decree', knows exactly how a Chinese man should act (including the nationalistic-racist act of beating a group of black guys and the sexist act of dancing with some thinly clad ladies), Vincy, in 'Daiye Smiles', keeps on wondering about the fate of a Chinese woman, in this particular case, Lin Daiyu. She takes a long walk through a sinified space of ink paintings, doing exactly the opposite of Ken, that is, not acting. Again, it is hardly a coincidence that in four of the Hong Kong China Wind videos, three of them feature a single female persona in both black and white outfits, while the other one shows a world with two female characters in fighting. In other words, the Female in these videos is always represented in somatic duality, in psychic schism, a visual device to underline their bewilderment, uncertainty and inner turmoil in the space called Chineseness. Consequently, onto all the ambiguities and struggles in the Hong Kong China Wind videos, a gender dimension must be added.

The notable exception is 'Small', where the female protagonist Joey Yung is visibly enjoying some fond memories of a long lost past. 'Small' is intriguing, however, not only because of its representation of a solitary woman confronted and yet content with her personal history, but also because of its intertextuality with another Taiwanese China Wind song 'Chrysanthemum Terrace/菊花台', that also has history as its main theme. The two

Figure 3.6: 'Daiyu Smiles' (Vincy) (courtesy of Emperor Entertainment Group).

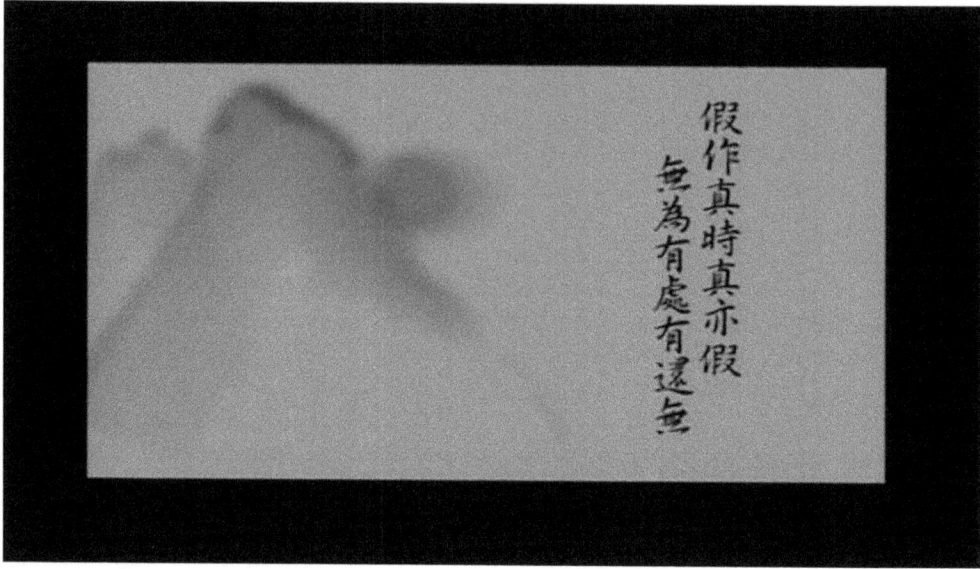

Figure 3.7: 'Daiyu Smiles' (Vincy) (courtesy of Emperor Entertainment Group).

songs share both the composer Jay Chou and the lyricist Fang Wenshan, but the Taiwanese one is performed by Jay himself and the Hong Kong one by Joey. In addition to the production team, the two songs share remarkably similar structure in their accompanying videos – sequences of the past (with other people) intersecting sequences of the present (with merely the performer). As the theme song of Zhang Yimou's *Curse of the Golden Flower*, the video of 'Chrysanthemum Terrace' collects a large selection of footage from the film, a court thriller set in dynastic time, in which Jay Chou also stars. We are therefore presented with Jay in imperial costumes juxtaposed with Jay in contemporary clothes. This visual duality, however, is different from the female duality with its embodiment of uncertain or conflicting longings. While the imperial Jay is caught in dazzling glimpses of drama, power and glory, the contemporary Jay is seen sitting, immobile, in a confined interior stylized in traditional Chinese fashion, playing a *guqin* during the extended music break. His occasionally extended arm, at once a hip-hop gesture and an invitation, is luring the audience into a masculinist version of history. This history is grandiose, public and violent. That history is at once escapist and inescapable. No wonder that in 'Small', Joey would rather indulge in her smaller, more personal and intimate history. The more 'antagonistic' video of 'Sword and Snow' can be read as an alternative reimagining of history. Two women, not men, appear at the dawn of time, in nobody's (grass)land and fight; they end up, literally and figuratively, standing close to each other, dropping onto the grass, shedding their swords, surrendering their bodies to the falling snow. Their history has possibilities of intimacy.

Figure 3.8: 'Sword and Snow' (Sammi Cheng and Denise Ho) (courtesy of East Asia Music (Holdings) Ltd).

Figure 3.9: 'Sword and Snow' (Sammi Cheng and Denise Ho) (courtesy of East Asia Music (Holdings) Ltd).

Figure 3.10: 'Big Red Robe' (Denise Ho) (courtesy of East Asia Music (Holdings) Ltd).

The two Chinese words *jian* (sword) and *xue* (snow) make a revealing intertextual reference to the middle (stage) names of two legendary Cantonese opera performers, Ren Jianhui and Bai Xuexian. Both performers are biologically female. Ren, however, always performed male roles onstage and Bai was typically his female partner. Besides performing as a heterosexual couple onstage, the two also led their entire offstage lives as two women cohabitating, close to each other.[10] Their middle names were the ones their apprentices would inherit – *jian* for the male-role performers, and *xue* for the female-role performers. The allusive mobilization of these two words is not only instrumental to the reconstitution of history as 'her-story', or swords giving way to snow; it also hints at another historical product, the performance of gender. This is the major theme in the video of Denise Ho's China Wind song 'Big Red Robe'. If the question for Vincy is 'What should I act', for Joey 'What should I remember', that for Denise is 'What should I perform'.[11]

As mentioned earlier, the video narrative of 'Big Red Robe' is set in a Cantonese opera troupe, which also functions as a school; in other words, it is a space where Chinese tradition and culture are supposed to pass on from one generation to another. The video opens with a sequence of short fragments showing a Cantonese opera actress doing her make-up, practising as well as performing. When the narrative develops, we are increasingly aware of the reluctance of Denise to perform the gendered roles being imposed on her. Interestingly, the actress-teacher in this video, Xie Xuexin, is a professional opera performer in real life, an apprentice of Bai Xuexian, hence the middle name Xue.

Figure 3.11: 'Big Red Robe' (Denise Ho) (courtesy of East Asia Music (Holdings) Ltd).

Figure 3.12: 'Big Red Robe' (Denise Ho) (courtesy of East Asia Music (Holdings) Ltd).

At one point, Denise Ho rewrites her teacher's name from Xuexin ('snow-heart') into Jianxin ('sword-heart'). As noted earlier, Denise intermittently wears white and black T-shirts to underwrite the apprentice's internal struggles. Most conspicuously, she wears almost no make-up throughout the video – until the last moment when she puts on her make-up and costumes, and, unlike her teacher, performs manhood onstage.

While this final metamorphosis can be interpreted as a (misogynist) preference for manhood, it articulates an oblique rejection of the traditionally tragic roles female actresses are traditionally wont to perform: they suffer to become heroines, to win the applause of the audience. The cutting, at this point, from close-up to medium and long shots, finally revealing an empty theatre, shifts the fundamental question 'what gender do you perform?' to 'for whom and for what?' In the context of the video, if Denise chooses to perform her gender accordingly, she would have secured the blessing of her teacher, acceptance by the theatre troupe and promise of a good career. By betraying operatic and Confucian traditions, she risks losing her parent (teacher), family (troupe) and future (career). In one sequence, we see Denise, in a black T-shirt, eating a bowl of rice with her fellow troupe members, inside; in the next sequence, Denise, in white T-shirt, stands on her own, outside.

Interestingly, questioning gender performance and its oppression never constitutes an important theme in the video of the Taiwanese China Wind song 'Error in a Flower Field/ 花田錯', despite a strikingly similar mobilization of Chinese opera. This song, performed by Leehom Wang, owes its title to the Peking opera *Huatiancuo*, and a substantial part of the video, like 'Big Red Robe', features sequences of an operatic performance. Comparable to the generic comedy of errors, this Peking opera is built up on the dramatic tension of cross-dressing, mistaken gender and misplaced eroticism and love, finally resolved by two heterosexual marriages. None of this playfulness, if not critique, of gender performance is translated to the video text. Instead, we see Leehom undisputedly and happily as a man, engaging in various romantic dates with a woman wearing, typically, long straight hair. This is perhaps what the female voices of the Hong Kong China Wind have to offer: the courage to think otherwise, to feminize and thereby problematize Chineseness, to suggest that the Chinese tradition, value and culture evoked so positively in the male-dominated China Wind pop may not necessarily be something to celebrate if you are not one of them. Born to a first-generation Taiwanese migrant family, Leehom grew up in the United States and, at the age of 19, secured a recording contract while he was visiting his grandparents in Taiwan. For a detailed discussion of the intricate connection between Chinese diasporic youth and transnational Chinese pop music, see Chapter 7.

Whither China Wind?

At the end of the aforementioned *Yazhou Zhoukan* article, Zhou Fengwu, a Taiwanese Chinese Studies scholar, suggests that only time will tell whether China Wind will have long-lasting cultural impact or disappear as a commercial fad (Lan 2007). While not disagreeing with Zhou's remark, we hasten to add: which China Wind? In this chapter, we take Hong Kong's China Wind songs and their music videos to examine how they engage with hegemonic versions of Chineseness. This is both an empirical and theoretical act. Drawing on Hong Kong's historical in-betweenness and its current location in the re-nationalization process, we seek to turn Hong Kong's hybridity from a noun to a verb: to hybridize. Our textual analyses show that while Hong Kong's China Wind pop evokes Chineseness, it also undermines it in two major ways: first, it renders Chineseness as distant gaze, as ambiguous space and as ongoing struggles; and second, it feminizes Chineseness, opening up a space for questions on history and gender performance. In other words, the Hong Kong China Wind that we have analysed articulates something quite different from a triumphalist celebration of Chinese tradition, value and culture. If China Wind, as a whole, is a culturalist project to rewrite Chineseness in an authentic, monolithic and indisputable way, Hong Kong's variant is resisting.

Obviously, more research is necessary to understand the China Wind phenomenon. Given the scope and purpose of this chapter, we have chosen primarily the music videos of Hong Kong China Wind for our textual analyses. We have compared them to a number of Taiwanese China Wind videos. How is the situation in other Chinese pop production locations such as Malaysia, Singapore as well as the perceived centre of Chineseness, mainland China? How would the audio dimensions of China Wind construct and contest versions of Chineseness, such as musical instruments, singing style and, more importantly, the (regional) language used? And we have not covered issues of audiences and political economy in connection with the production and reception of China Wind (see notes 6 and 7). With all the limitations of this study, the insertion of Hong Kong in any debates on Chineseness, we contend, is a contestation of who has the authority to speak as Chinese, to define Chinese. The issue is not to define who has the authority, but precisely to un-define. If China Wind lends itself to a monotonous anthem of sinification that drowns the rich polyphony of dissident voices, the underlying tunes of Hong Kong's China Wind are to hybridize, to think otherwise. To pursue the China Wind metaphor further, we argue that what Hong Kong pop can offer, and is offering, is precisely to stir up a little whirl of alternative Chinesenesses, a little confusion, a little unsettling, a little uncertainty of where it will take the Chinese, or where the Chinese should go. After all, the history of Chinese pop music, and perhaps of Chinese culture itself, is yet to be written.

Notes

1. All the translation from Chinese texts to English is by the authors.
2. Chinese names quoted in this chapter will be noted in pinyin, except for singers who will be presented with their names known to the public.
3. For easier reading, the term 'Chinese pop' used in this chapter denotes 'Chinese language pop'.
4. It is of interest to note that back in 1992 when a group of mainland Chinese artists were invited to perform in Hong Kong, the concert was also titled 'China Wind'.
5. All the three pop radio stations in Hong Kong host their own charts. The one of Commercial Radio 2, also known as 903 Top 20, is arguably the most respected and prestigious. The station claims to base chart performance entirely on air plays.
6. 'Sweet Dumplings' was also used as the jingle of a computer brand commercial, which might have accounted for the non-diegetic insertion of a laptop in the video. Advertising sponsors, a common phenomenon in Chinese pop world, and therefore the influence of corporate economy on cultural production in general and China Wind pop in particular is an important issue, which, however, cannot be addressed properly within the scope of this chapter. See final section.
7. *Sword and Snow* was the theme song of Asian Games Fair and High Resolution AV Festival 2008. See also note 6.
8. The other two Hong Kong China Wind entries that are not included in our analysis are also performed by female artists.
9. It is worth noting that in mainland China, Li Yuchun, the androgynous Supergirl winner-turned-idol, has released an EP shortly before the Beijing Olympic Games 2008, titled *Youth China*/少年中國.
10. For a book-length account of cross-dressing in Chinese opera, see Li (2003). It is interesting to note that while cross-dressing, both from male to female and female to male, existed in

Chinese operatic traditions, the former has become the more dominant practice. According to Li, 'While women in European theatre were emerging on stage from the early modern period, female performers in late imperial China lost ground to male players from the 17th to the 19th century. Female cross-dressing in Chinese society experienced the same reverse development compared to Europe' (55).

11 Denise Ho is well known for taking up issues of (home)sexuality in her music and other creative activities. In 2005, she initiated and starred in a musical that zoomed in on the homoerotic subtext of the Chinese classic *Butterfly Lovers*, in which a young woman cross-dressed as a young man in order to attend school falls in love with her/his classmate.

Chapter 4

SEX, MORALITY AND CANTOPOP

> The spectacle is not a collection of images, rather, it is a social relation between people that is mediated by images.
>
> (*Proposition 4, The Society of the Spectacle*, Guy Debord 1995 [1967]: 12)

Picture Gate

In early 2008, the singer-actor celebrity Edison Chen's private pictures with a range of female stars became public after he had taken his computer to a repair shop. Within hours, millions of Chinese across the globe watched Edison Chen in various sexual positions with several female Chinese celebrities such as Gillian Chung, Bobo Chan and Cecilia Cheung. This privacy infringement case soon turned into a high-profile process of public lynching, forcing all those involved into hiding from a proliferation of moral judgement and condemnation. Media reports of the incident are characterized by a discourse on what we like to label *the extreme moral*, focusing on fidelity, privacy, family life and moderate ways of living. At the same time, we also detect an intriguing conflation of the extreme moral with what can be termed *the extreme material*, as exemplified by detailed reporting on the gadgets the stars are seen using and the manner in which Edison Chen staged his comeback. Thirdly, alongside the moral and the material, a *juridical* discourse was mobilized by both the alleged victims as well as the authorities aiming to delineate the good from the bad and to define the true culprits. In particular the moral as well as the material discourses emerged on the Internet and in magazines, constituting, as we would like to argue, a mediatized space in which the stars and their bodies are turned into spectacular sites onto which capitalist dreams in conjunction with a less-than-liberal or liberating morality are mapped.

Taking the Edison Chen scandal as our case study, we aim to do the following. After a brief revisit of the theories on moral panic and a literature review concerning studies on the Edison Chen scandal, our inquiry will take this scandal, this moral panic to its particular intersection of time and place, namely the time of the spectacle and the fluid transnational Chinese/media sphere. Our analysis of Chen's public statements, the concomitant media reports, and his recent comeback will unravel the shift from the spectacular, and its visual representation of possible carnal pleasure and disruption of the capitalistic order, to the moral, material and juridical discourses as they proliferated in the mediatized space of Hong Kong. We will show how high capitalism conflates – despite its so often articulated ideology of freedom and liberty – with moral fundamentalism. This point may well be summarized by paraphrasing Max Weber: 'The Confucian cum Victorian Ethic and the Spirit of Global Capitalism.' We argue that the media space is a contradictory space through which moral, material and juridical desires are articulated – a space also where ideological fault lines are drawn and performed. Following on from this, the chapter will end with a reflexive note on possible implications for our thinking on China at large.

Indeed, the sex photo scandal brings to mind old cultural studies work on moral panics by, among others, Stanley Cohen and Stuart Hall. Cohen (1972) argues that society needs what he calls folk devils, those who are outside the central core values of consensual society and who pose a threat to both the values of society and society itself. As he writes, 'more moral panics will be generated and other, as yet nameless, folk devils will be created. This is not because such developments have an inexorable inner logic, but because our society as presently structured will continue to generate problems for some of its members ... and then condemn whatever solution these groups find' (Cohen 1972: 204). As Erich Goode and Nachman Ben-Yehuda explain, the 'folk devil' is a 'deviant': someone engaged in wrongdoing and whose actions are considered harmful to society. They are deemed selfish and evil and thus substantial steps must be taken to 'neutralize' their actions, in order to allow a return to 'normality' (Goode and Ben-Yehuda 1994: 29).

In the case of Edison Chen, however, it is the main actor himself who through public performances reclaims normality and the status quo, while those responsible for the distribution of the pictures are being portrayed as the 'real' folk devils. Hence the mobilization of a juridical discourse, which helps to divert the attention away from the 'dangerous' polygamous corporal pleasures the pictures contain, pleasures that hold the potential to disturb hegemonic discourses on sexuality, fidelity and family life. Hall zooms in on the role the media play in this context – and it may well be fair to add that the Internet helps facilitate the globalization of moral panics – and for him, mediatized moral panics are vehicles for the transmission of dominant ideologies. The press thus amplifies public anxiety, reading a scandal as signifying a deeper moral malaise in society and as a sign of social disintegration. Subsequently, a parade of specialists, moral entrepreneurs, fans, citizens, victims, culprits and so on, appears in the media (Hall et al. 1978; Killingbeck 2001). Before probing further into the moral, material and juridical dimensions of the scandal, based on the materials collected from different media, let us first explain the scandal in more detail and summarize related studies conducted so far.

The Edison Chen scandal

When Edison Chen brought his crashed, pink, custom-made Apple laptop nicknamed 'cotton candy Mac' to the repair shop, he could never have imagined so much more was about to crash. On the 27 January 2008, pictures started to emerge on the Internet featuring Edison Chen with different female celebrities.

For readers who are not familiar with Chinese popular culture, imagine the leaking of pictures of Justin Timberlake enjoying sex – predominantly oral sex – with celebrities ranging from Cameron Diaz to Lady Gaga and Britney Spears, and one may start to grasp the magnitude of this scandal in the global Chinese/media sphere. Within three weeks, in spite of an extensive police crackdown and continuous legal threats towards those who might show or distribute the pictures, the global (rather than East Asian) media sphere was saturated with what came to be dubbed as the 'Sexy Photos gate' (Farmer 2009: 73). As Brett Farmer claims, 'the Chen scandal was unprecedented in scope and intensity, drawing ire and condemnation from various quarters across the entertainment, political and social spheres, effectively scuppering the careers of all involved, and occasioning a very public set of debates about everything from sex, gender, and public morality to celebrity cultures, privacy laws, censorship, globalization, and new technologies' (2009: 73).

Soon, on the Internet, subsequent to the viral spread of the sex pictures, different pictures emerged, aiming to show that the celebrities were not just photoshopped, but were really the true celebrities (see Figure 4.1). Even a timeline appeared, on which we can see in what

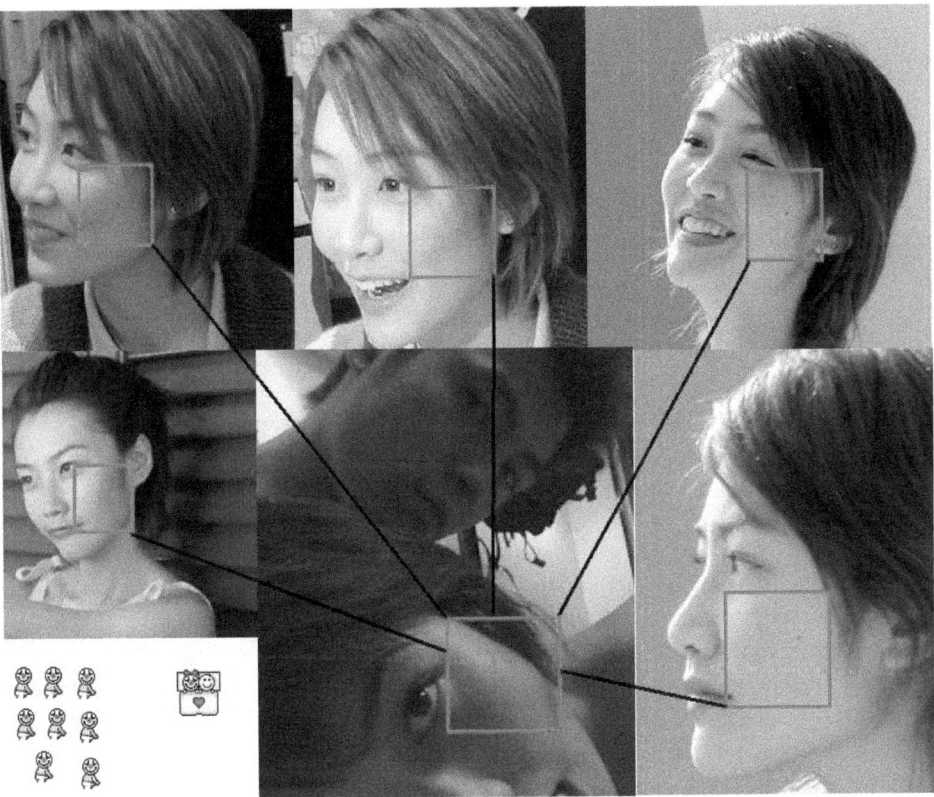

Figure 4.1: Internet circulation of the proof that these are the real celebrities being depicted.

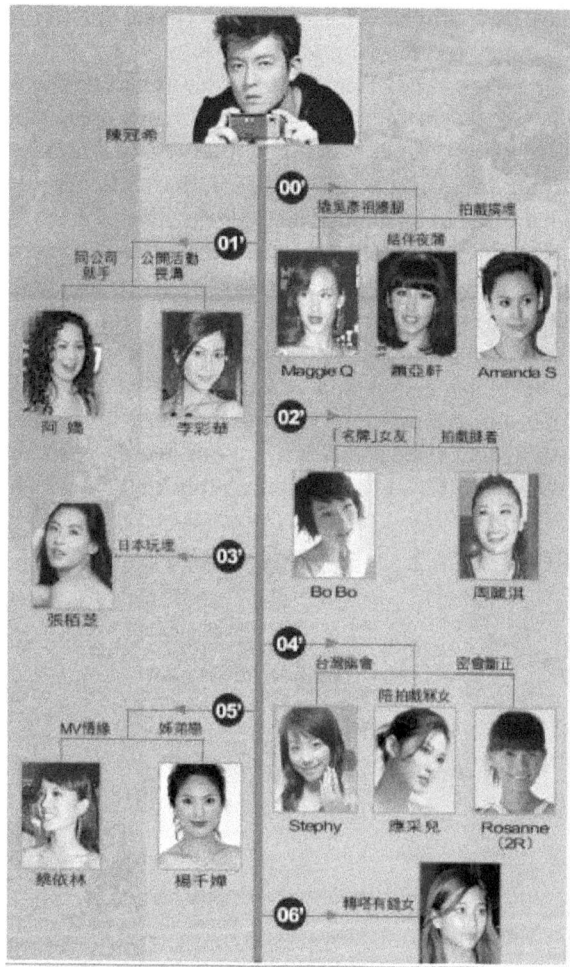

Figure 4.2: Taken from the Internet, a timeline of Edison's sexual life.

years Edison slept with which girls (see Figure 4.2). The scandal that unfolded was also geared towards the computer technician, 24-year-old Sze Ho-Chun, who leaked the pictures to the Internet, and who was sentenced to eight months in jail. But in public discourse he was not considered the (only) culprit, on the contrary, it was Edison Chen and his partners who were blamed for being reckless, obscene and immoral. As Katrien Jacobs observes, 'An anti-Edison movement organized by feminists and evangelical Christian organizations portrayed him as a male sex criminal and his lovers as female "victims". There were very few alternative readings of the gender dynamic. The female celebrities in the images were seen as "gullible and manipulated"' (Jacobs 2009: 607).

Farmer reads the case as a complex, multi-mediated moral panic. He points at how different factions within society used the scandal to strengthen their own moral position, thus, 'much of the critical and political significance of the scandal issued from the way it revealed divisive fractures in social consensus, with different factions coming out in protest over the morality of variously: the images; those depicted in them; those who illegally procured and circulated them; those who consumed them; and, even, the police and judiciary for their differential treatment of the above' (Farmer 2009: 74). Drawing on celebrity studies, he argues that in particular celebrities are contradictory, profoundly polysemic signs that allow for such semiotic battles. He further points to the transnational, in-between position of both Hong Kong as well as of Edison Chen (Canadian born, Chinese-Portuguese background), that only adds to the complexity and polysemy of the case. We will discuss the complex relationship between the Chinese diaspora and transnational Chinese popular music in the final chapter. Edison Chen's multi-ethnic background does indeed further complicate the scandal. In a study on the transnational transmedia celebrity phenomenon in China, Anne Ciecko observes that 'movie and transmedia stars Daniel Wu and Edison Chen represent globalized/westernized/cosmopolitanized images of youthful Chineseness as ethnicity, rather than nationality' (2011: 187). Edison's hybridity or polysemy feeds into his stardom, it sets him apart from 'Chinese' stars, his embraced otherness is turned into transmedia star capital (ibid.). Ciecko reads the unfolding scandal as a movie script, she writes 'Tales of triad threats, bounties and postal-mailed bullet; images of tearful implicated female participants depicted variously as victims, hypocrites, morally tainted, or chastened, permeated the media as if part of a film script' (ibid.: 192). The image of a star can in the end never be fully controlled or contained, the star text is 'fed or bled by ancillary media activities' (ibid.).

The Taiwan-based scholar Josephine Ho published a paper that came out of a seminar she organized around the scandal. In it, she argues how the response to the scandal betrays a general sexual conservatism of East Asian societies (2008). Like Ho, Katrien Jacobs focuses more strongly on the discourse on sexuality that proliferated following the case. She claims, rather sweepingly, if not in an orientalistic vein, that 'Hong Kong citizens feel pressured to dissociate from "modern decadent" experiences and want to engage in sexual relations that are part of a socially responsible, subdued and private lifestyle. Many believe in the power of an age-old principle that steers their actions and differentiates them from the West' (2009: 606). Jacobs critiques the moral conservatism of Hong Kong media culture, and shows how in her teaching the scandal opened up a discursive space for students to speak openly about sexuality and porn. Whereas Jacobs considers this univocally good, we are less sure; after Foucault it has become difficult to celebrate open sex talk or pornography, which may in turn become part and parcel of disciplinary regimes. Finally, Matthew Chew's paper (2008) connects the scandal to the steady decline of Hong Kong's culture industry, contending that the discourse surrounding the scandal was saturated with expressions of general discontent about the Hong Kong culture industry by fans; a music culture has transformed itself into a shallow celebrity culture.

The scandal is thus read as a complex, contradictory, transnational discursive spectacle, as betraying the sexual conservatism of East Asia, as showcasing a moment in which the polysemic and hybrid star text is being undermined by the media, as a moment that provoked a public sexual discourse, and as a sign of the decline of Hong Kong's entertainment industry. While these readings carry their thrust of academic and political concern, they also moralize, in the sense of moralizing the spectacular event into something loaded with norms and values, relegated to the realm of the moral. Here, we note the fundamental shift from the visual, where past enactments and thus future possibilities of carnal and exorbitant pleasure are represented, to the moral. And the momentary disruption of the capitalistic order launched by the free online circulation of photographs is ignored. While our inquiry resonates with the aforementioned studies, we would like to open up the focus on the moral in discussions of moral panic, and pose a slightly different question, namely, how do the extremely moralistic, the extremely materialistic and the juridical paradoxically function together in the spectacle society and celebrity culture of Hong Kong? Our inspiration for this question comes from a closer look at the gossip magazines of Hong Kong. During the scandal, one would come across ample pictures presenting Edison Chen, an alleged style icon, pointing at the clothes he was wearing, expressing their retail value. Ironically, when the visual returned to the spectacle as personified by Edison Chen himself, he was far from being a naked body seeking pleasure; he was fully clad with all the desirable items of our capitalist society. This rather bizarre focus on the material dimension is what we like to label the extreme material.

The Confucian cum Victorian ethics and the spirit of global capitalism

Among the numerous photographic representations of Edison Chen during the scandal, we take Figure 4.3, coming from *Oriental Sunday*, one of Hong Kong's most prolific gossip magazines, as an illustration (Figure 4.3). It was taken more than a year later, when Edison Chen for the first time commented on the scandal for CNN. The extreme material is articulated in all the references to the expensive clothes Edison wears: an 18K Cartier love bracelet, worth HK$33,000, a Levis Penom X Clot 505, worth HK$10,000, and Comme des Garçons Converse shoes, worth HK$980.[1]

What we see here is a blatant but typical visualization of global capitalism, one that cannibalizes and capitalizes on each possible moment to unfold itself, one that needs scandals as yet another spectacle, as Guy Debord claims in the thirty-fourth proposition of his manifesto: 'The spectacle is capital accumulated to the point where it becomes image' (1995 [1967]: 24). The image – Edison Chen – has turned into a commodity, a sign embedded in global capitalism, a sign that is required to act and behave properly, so as not to contaminate the spirit of global capitalism. We thus see a movement towards the articulation of the extreme material, a moment where capitalism hijacks the scandal, to be followed by an apology as if to sanitize that articulation. This conflation of the extreme material with the extreme moral comes to the fore in two public apologies made by Edison Chen. The

Figure 4.3: Edison Chen in *Oriental Sunday* (Issue 599, 2 June 2009).

first apology was delivered on 5 February in front of some 400 journalists and 200 police officers, 80 of whom formed a human chain around him as he left the building (Jacobs 2009: 606). Not only Edison Chen, but also some of the female stars delivered public statements as an attempt to regain their celebrity status. Edison Chen has a very basic, simple hairstyle during the apology, just as he wears a plain white T-shirt. This feeds into his attempted performance of being the boy next door, naughty and mischievous maybe, definitely not the real culprit; no, a folk devil cannot have good and expensive taste, can he? We will examine this materialistic dimension further when we discuss later his more recent performance not as the boy next door, but naughty and mischievous as few other professions would allow him to be – his comeback as an artist.

In his first statement, Edison Chen started with the following words:

I've decided to break my silence today and make this statement to the media and to all people involved in this strange ordeal. Recent documents being posted online have been intentionally hurtful and malicious not only to the victims but to our whole community.

The language being used here is indicative of a juridical discourse, with victims being harmed by malicious material. The juridical here is connected to the moral, the materials are claimed to be hurtful to 'our whole community'. With these words, Edison Chen thus implicates *all* citizens from Hong Kong in the scandal, assuming them to be hurt. Following the operating logic of a media scandal, he mobilizes juridical terms that are embedded in a hegemonic discourse, to amplify the meaning of the scandal to society as a whole. Consequently, he follows with words that present him as a responsible citizen, who obeys the rule of law, when he claims that:

> I have already handed matters over to the police and have been assisting them with this case from the first day onwards. Due to ongoing investigations, I am unable to comment any further upon this case.

To follow with, first, he issues a public apology – hereby reclaiming his moral self – and a subsequent appeal to everybody to 'help the victims', thus, again, implicating all citizenry into the scandal, for which he uses the euphemism 'ordeal'.

> The lives of many innocent people have been affected by this malicious and criminal conduct, and in this regard I am filled with pain, hurt and frustration. I hereby use this opportunity to apologize to anyone who has been affected by this strange, strange ordeal. I now call upon everyone to help and assist the victims of this case. If you have ever downloaded any of these images, please do not forward them to anyone. Please do not send them to anyone. If you are still in possession of these images, I urge you to please destroy them immediately. Let's help the wounded heal their wounds. I urge you to help the victims and not make anything worse.

His second statement further expands the moral horizon of the scandal by including the trope of the family and the innocent young. He states (http://blog.zdnet.com.cn/html/72/313972-1164424.html):

> During past weeks, I've been with my mother, my family and love ones to show support and care, and at the same time, have their support and care for me. [...] I would like to apologize to the ladies and their families for any harm and hurt on their feeling. I am sorry. I would also like to apologize to my mother and father for the pain and suffers that I caused. Most importantly, I would like to say sorry to all the people in Hong Kong. I give my apology sincerely to you all, unreservedly and with all my heart. I know young people in Hong Kong look up to many figures in our society. And in this regard, I failed as a role model.

He reclaims his moral self by articulating the importance he attaches to family life, just as he claims to be particularly concerned about his bad influence on innocent young people, who are so easily influenced. What we see here is a moral hegemonic discourse in which family life is valued above anything else, in which young people (and frequently also women) are those lacking agency and in dire need of role models and guidance, and in which the star himself claims to be a role model. To 'heal his soul' in his quest for salvation, he needs to retreat from society, thus performing another part of his role as arole model with high moral standards:

> However, I wish this matter will teach everyone a lesson. To all the young people in our community, let this be a lesson to you all. This is not an example set for you. During my time away, I made an important decision. I will wholeheartedly fulfill all commitments I have to take. But after that, I decide to step away from the Hong Kong entertainment industry. I decide to do this to give myself an opportunity to heal myself, and search my soul. I will dedicate my time to charity and community work in the next few months.

After these articulations of what we term extreme moralism, and the adjective extreme appears applicable given that the case involves the portrayal of assumed pleasurable acts of consensual sex, he retreats once again to a juridical discourse:

> I admit that most photos being circulated on the Internet were taken by me. But these photos were very private and never been shown to people, and never intended to be shown to any one. These photos were stolen from me illegally and distributed without my consent. […] I've been assisting the police since the first day the photos were published, and I will continue to assist them. After this press conference, I have the obligation to help them with their investigations and hope this case can end soon as everyone I think has the same wish. I would like to use this opportunity to thank the police for their hard work on this case. Thank you.

Once again he is not only trying to restore the moral hegemonic order, but also the juridical order with which it is so closely intertwined. His statements are drenched in a conservative moral discourse, one in which the family functions as the cornerstone of society, where children need to be protected from any sign of sexuality, where sex is referred to as sinful in any case, where pictures indeed threaten to undermine the community as a whole. The idea that he or they may have enjoyed the sex is ruled out, what we see here is a culture of shaming, of victimhood, devoid of any pleasure.

A similar conclusion can be drawn when we read the statements of the female stars, for example, from Twins' Gillian, at the time of the scandal the girlfriend of pop singer Juno:

> I was very naïve and very stupid. I was working very hard to establish our image. We are the idols of many young kids. This affair will affect our image. When we meet these young kids, I don't know how to face them. I have no one to blame but myself for doing that stupid thing.

The singer Cecilia Cheung claims:

> I was so scared [...] I went to my son's room – he was then seven or eight months old – and I hugged him. I was so frightened I do not know how to describe it. My legs turned to jelly. I nearly lost my balance. But then I thought to myself that if I, as an adult, could not get back on my feet, how could a helpless child stand on his own? I yelled, 'I have to stand up for the sake of my son.'

What we see here is, again, the proliferation of extreme moralism, in which families, children, heteronormativity, shame and victimhood overrule any other possible reading.

Following the aforementioned literature on moral panics, it is clear that the stars involved may not be so much the folk devils as the victims of a fraudulent computer technician. At least this was the metamorphosis they were trying to achieve in the spectacle society and the celebrity culture of Hong Kong and the transnational Chinese community at large. The latter features as the culprit who deserves detention. But to label him a folk devil would be to go too far. The juridical dimension of the case also changed from the issue of privacy infringement in our current digital times towards issues of free speech and censorship, as well as the differences between Hong Kong and mainland China. The scandal instigated heated debate on who is to blame, and whether possession or distribution of such photographs can be grounds for prosecution. The question of who is to blame started with the arrest of 29-year-old Chung Yik-tin, for uploading one image. Later, more people were detained by the police and charged for distributing the photos. When the police declared that those possessing the pictures could be in breach of the law, about 300 netizens in Hong Kong went to the streets to protest, urging the release of Chung Yik-tin. A commentary in Hong Kong's tabloid *Apple Daily* critiqued the intimidation of netizens by the police, and referred to 'the hypocrisy in law enforcement' for arresting people without bringing in the main source and victim – Edison Chen – for interrogation (www.zonaeuropa.com/200802a.brief.htm). An opinion poll revealed that 52 per cent of the Hong Kong citizenry perceived the case of Chung Yik-tin as one of wrongful prosecution, and 65 per cent believed that the incident damaged the reputation of the government, holding the Hong Kong police responsible for this (www.zonaeuropa.com/200802a.brief.htm). Later, Chung Yik-tin as well as the others were released. Instead, Sze Ho-chun, the computer technician, was convicted on 13 May 2009 for obtaining illegal access to a computer and received a sentence of eight-and-a-half months.

In China, the *Tianya* forum became the primary site for information on the photographs. The Chinese authorities removed posts several times, resulting in the following response from the forum master (www.zonaeuropa.com/200802a.brief.htm):

> I just received the news that the post had been deleted. [...] This was a tall building with more than 600 stories, and it was deleted without even a hello! The forum master refuses to accept the blame! I have raised hell within the organization. I have decided to

go against the operational rules and restore this post. I may lose my job as forum master, but I will seek justice for the entertainment gossip section.

The scandal thus triggered a debate on censorship in mainland China and Hong Kong. It was claimed that in Hong Kong, people could march on the streets to critique the police, but the pictures themselves were immediately deemed inappropriate. In China, on the other hand, such protests would be impossible, yet the pictures themselves seemed far less sensitive, and were only blocked after a few weeks. Interestingly, for several weeks, mainland Chinese sites were permitted to disseminate the images, making blogger Roland Soong, whose eastwest blog contains an elaborate archive of the full case, observe that 'in summary, in Hong Kong, YES for political dissidence but NO for pornography; in mainland China, NO for political dissidence and YES for pornography. How is this "one country, two systems" thing going to work? What will happen in 2047 when the two systems are supposed to have converged?' (www.zonaeuropa.com/200802a.brief.htm).

The unfolding juridical discourse shows that what appears to be a rather straightforward scandal can unfold in different and unexpected ways. But the juridical discourse is mostly limited to media savvy bloggers, the police force and politicians; in the larger public sphere the juridical discourse is overshadowed by the sexual spectacle that unfolds on millions of computer screens around the world. These are the images that are considered harmful for the weak and innocent; these are the images that destabilize the social order of Hong Kong, as they open up a heated debate in which, as Jacobs claims, sex talk was rendered possible. The scandal triggered a display of the extreme material; we get to see in detail which items the stars are wearing, from which brand labels, and their worth. The scandalous star is smoothly transformed into a commodity used by brand names to promote their products. This subsequently conflates with a performance of extreme morality in which also a juridical discourse is mobilized.

Spectacle and image

Debord's society of the spectacle rightly privileges the visual as the modus operandi of the spectacle of capitalism. The pictures of Edison Chen serve as a good reminder of the power and the danger of the visual, in particular in current Internet times in which its distribution depends on just a click of a mouse. In our ocularcentric times, it is images that hold the potential to disrupt and to challenge, but more often also to conform and to stabilize. The scandal disrupted the order of Hong Kong and the global Chinese public sphere, but the subsequent performances by its main actors, the media, the public and the authorities all seem to work towards a symbolic closure, despite the debates being stirred up over censorship and freedom of speech. The case rather quickly morphs into yet another show of commercial branding, as yet another show of global capitalism. As we have seen, the scandal that unfolds is more complex than just a moral panic; instead, it propels not only a moral, but also a material as well as a juridical discourse. Working together, these discourses succeed in containing the visual and the disturbing possibilities of carnal and exorbitant pleasure as discussed earlier, in stabilizing the spectacle and the celebrities, and eventually the spectacle society and the celebrity culture themselves.

The scandal reveals societies' unease with sexuality: even though the scandal may have opened up a space for a more public discourse on sexuality, the corporal pleasures of sex remain by-and-large undiscussed. When we read the scandal as a mirror, what is it that produces such a moral outrage? What is it that glues people to the screen of their computers and mobile phones? Is it possible that the pictures also show us sheer hedonistic pleasure? Is the outrage not underpinned by a collective jealousy, in which we secretly want to be Edison or Gillian? Are we offered a glimpse of an alternative and indeed eventually more utopian sexual economy? The Edison Chen scandal presents society a mirror, a mirror depicting what it is not – and the work done by the actors involved is to smash that mirror into pieces, to re-establish the status quo of society, to deny the corporal and reclaim the moral, the juridical as well as the material. Families, children, victims are all dressed properly in this parade of the decent moral self through which the nation-state, the entertainment industry and global capitalism aim to re-establish their hold on society. Foucault famously asserts, 'visibility is a trap' (1979: 200). The image, and the multiple processes through which people are turned into a mere image, is deeply implicated in global capitalism.

In a recent paper, Robin Visser (forthcoming) argues that:

> [s]pectacle is the discursive content of the appearance of capitalist society; it does not control its subjects by force but through manipulating the consensus of collective desire. Surface appearances effectively control people, in Debord's account, because they render the rational techniques that manufactured them invisible and what remains is the desire to possess the signifier of the sign. [...] Debord's 'situation', then, accepts a Gramscian paradigm of hegemony where mediation involves dynamic engagement with forces of capital. Capital in this sense is neither absolute nor antihuman because its hold must be continuously rearticulated by social actors.

It is this re-articulation that is at stake in the Edison Chen scandal: the glimpses of utopia that broke loose through the scandal had to be contained; the mirror ought to be broken so as to restore the moral ideological order. After all, the incredible speed at which the sex photos travelled, the vast expanse of Chinese homes and offices they entered, and most significantly, the intense appeal they seemed to exert on the transnational Chinese/media sphere was unsettling. It comes, to us, as no surprise that theorizations from the 1960s and 1970s – coming from Cohen, Debord and Hall – still prove adequate in our current globalized times. The power of the image has since then only amplified, and even though its viral, uncontrolled spread holds the power of political change (think of the tank man of 1989 in China, think of the photos of the Iranian girl Neda Agda Soltan, see Buck-Morss 2004), it more often than not tends to keep people, ideas, thoughts, desires etc. in their contained, regulated space. When confronted with the cock of a celebrity, the unified image of that celebrity is distorted; a utopian space unfolds, offering us a mirror, one that has to be refolded back, so as to undo and erase the image of the cock. The image lives on, lingers on, of course, but the public rituals, as we have observed, have served a purpose. They diverted the attention back to the discourse on the extreme moral, with its juridical underpinnings, a discourse that – given its intricate links with the extreme material – offers the prospects of another possible transformation. This transformation is not that of transgressive, hedonistic corporal pleasure, but that of decent yet conspicuous consumption, of us, aspiring the similar pink Apple computer, the same Levi's jeans – as they may bring the new self, if not salvation, we are hoping for.[2]

Eye see you as I see you

Edison Chen's reappearance in the East Asian entertainment industry was also made possible by expanding to other fields such as art. In 2010 he held his first solo exhibition titled 'I hate you for looking' under the name Etalier des Chene in Singapore. The local daily *Strait Times* claimed that 'Edison hits back with pop art', remarking: 'One work is an image of an eye pieced together with cigarettes, and fitted with a video camera that tracks anyone who looks at it. Another piece, Maona Lisa, combines the iconic images of Mao Zedong and the portrait by Leonardo da Vinci. But unlike Mona Lisa, Maona Lisa has eyes that are wired to a sensor and avoid a visitor's gaze. […] The works are for sale and the priciest of Chen's pieces are three Saiyan fibreglass statues at S$28,000 each, modelled on the manga Dragon Ball but recreated with the actor's face.'[3] Edison Chen's appropriation of the scandal and its ironic comment on the visual culture itself shows how malleable the moral and the material are; within two years, he capitalizes on the scandal by turning it into an art project, which in turn, as (Chinese) modern art at large, is enmeshed in global capitalism. This time, it is not his clothes and accessories that bear a price tag, but his artistic work.

Edison Chen's pop artwork revolves around the topic of visual culture – gazing and surveillance. In 2011 he joined the Beijing Art Fair in partnership with Madeln Company (founded in Shanghai by artist Xu Zhen). When we attended the opening of the fair, his booth was crowded with fans and journalists, obviously the most popular of all booths. We were all stopped from taking pictures, but this ban was either a feeble attempt or a downright ironic gesture, given the omnipresence of mobile phone photography of our time. T-shirts were dangling in the booth with prints like 'Poser' and 'Suck It', alluding unabashedly to the sex photo scandal triggered by Edison Chen himself just three years earlier (see Figure 4.4). A cartoon-like figure was drawn on the wall, with dollar signs as eyes, and the text 'Don't believe what your eyes see, believe only what you hear'. Elsewhere on the wall more explicit sexual references were written, like 'Do you want 2 fuck' and 'Like to suck'. As if to re-enact, and at the same time parody, his own photographic acts that caused so much controversy, Edison Chen took the occasion to take pictures of an older man in the booth (see Figure 4.5), and of

Figure 4.4: Edison Chen's Beijing 2011 art show.

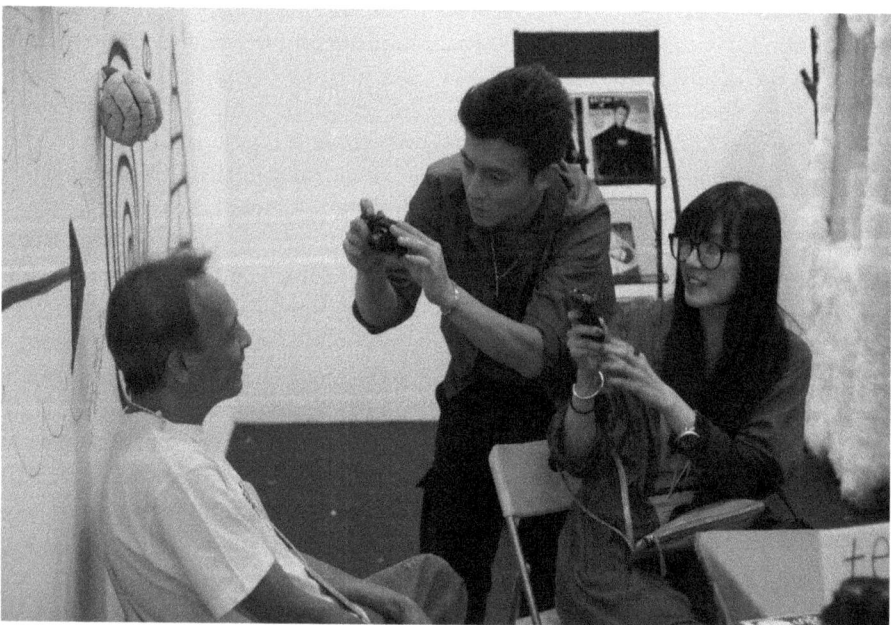

Figure 4.5: Edison taking pictures – again.

him spraying words on a piece of paper. In that sense, Edison literally cashed in on his scandal by morphing the visual actualized primarily as a result of pleasure, to the visual defined by aesthetics and, probably more importantly, capitalism. In this bizarre move, capitalism, now in the guise of the global art world, shows its flexibility and malleability once again.

By navigating towards another moral plateau – that of criticality – the scandal is once again capitalized, this time not in the shape of a Cartier watch, but in the form of an artwork. The words accompanying the piece are indicative of how the star image is in constant change, and how he tries to reclaim his agency through the domain of art:

> His art works include oil paintings, installations, sculptures, as well as other new media. Most of them are based on topics related to 'observation', composing a creation language out of personal experiences and surroundings' elements and presented in the form of interactive media works, that reflect today's social phenomena of watching and being watched. [...He] will pursue his creations using various media and art, to stimulate people's mind on these controversial topics.

The discourse on sexuality in this work does not denote pleasure, but rather provocation, or a performance of provocation. At one point his photographs were celebrations of his carnal pleasures, circulated for free (however illegal it might be), dislocated (however transiently) from the capitalistic order. Now the artist Edison Chen moulds the scandal into a direction that helps him regain credibility, reverts to a celebrity-as-commodity, whose photographs and other creations are to be bought at an art fair. It was a clever move. The art world is a relatively safe arena for Edison's self-referential playfulness, as it takes place by-and-large outside the scrutinizing eyes of the tabloid press. The aura of criticality that he aims to radiate is far removed from his public apology, demonstrating yet again the material and moral flexibility a star has to mobilize to regain his stardom and thus his market value. Probably the only casualty was the possibility of carnal pleasure and dislocation from capitalism that those first fleeting moments of the scandal once promised.

Coda

> The spectacular character of modern industrial society has nothing fortuitous or superficial about it; on the contrary, the society is based on the spectacle in the most fundamental way. For the spectacle, as the perfect image of the ruling economic order, ends are nothing and development is all – although the only thing into which the spectacle plans to develop is itself.
>
> (*Proposition 14, the Society of the Spectacle*, Guy Debord (1995 [1967]: 15–16)

Celebrities are images, signs upon which fans and the public project hopes, fears and desires. This requires a large amount of image control in order to present a unified entity.

As Andrew Mendelsohn (2007) argues, we need to think 'of celebrities less as individuals whose privacy is threatened and more as entities trying to present the most unified image possible in order to increase their cultural and economic power. Through this frame, the paparazzi fit squarely within a normative model of journalism, and can be thought of as investigative journalists attempting to uncover another "truth" of celebrities' (169). When artists are transformed to entity or image, they cannot rally to conventional discourses constructing the musical talent, and they cannot rally to discourses on authenticity, on rebellion, on soul, on musical talent to elevate them above judgements on moral calibre. In the absence of such discourse, celebrities have to resort to the most conventional discourse on moralism, to a reiteration of publicly accepted morals, which are drenched in hegemonic discourses.

The spectacle that unfolded on millions of computer screens worldwide is constitutive of a neo-liberal and highly moralistic society. To conclude this chapter, we would like to insert a reflexive note on the possible implications for our thinking on China at large. In popular discourse it is often believed and sometimes asserted that China's economic growth will slowly but steadily result in its political opening up. Capitalism, in such narratives, is equated with freedom, a liberating force that helps bring democracy. The Edison Chen case shows us a quite different picture: capitalism is deeply rooted in moral conservatism, it needs the visual spectacle to further promote consumption, and to celebrate conspicuous consumption, but it subsequently requires a moral closure, in which the stars ask for forgiveness, in which corporal pleasures are erased. Commercialization or commodification does not, as feared, lead to loss of morality; quite the contrary. How, then, do we disrupt this vicious cycle of the extremely materialistic and the extremely moralistic, both of which are mobilized together with a juridical discourse? How are we able to accommodate more? How do we enable the possibility of more carnal pleasures that cheerfully ignore or refuse to accept Victorian- and Confucian-inspired modes of living and behaving? How can we make it possible that both Edison Chen as well as Gillian Chung, Bobo Chan and Cecilia Cheung,[4] and the other women involved, would, alongside their discomfort with the leaking of images that are meant to be private, also articulate the pleasures they experienced, the fun of sex, and the additional fun of taking a picture of that? How do we enable a more heteroglossic discourse in which different possible sexual selves are being explored? If there is no outside to today's global capitalism, as Michael Hardt and Anthony Negri claim (2000), then how to make this possible from within, with the help of which media, which technologies and which actors? Blogs like the one from Roland Soong, in which the scandal is discussed and in which its juridical dimensions are teased out, do open up a space for debate, yet they are framed by notions related to an open public sphere and human rights, notions that conveniently ignore sexual rights. How to reclaim the sexual from the moral, the material and the juridical: this is the final question that we believe needs to be asked, following the Edison Chen case, and it is a question that has not been asked enough in public debates.

Notes

1. Such 'pricing' treatment is a common practice among celebrity magazines in Hong Kong.
2. This, obviously, warrants further studies among consumers of this scandal.
3. http://www.straitstimes.com/BreakingNews/Lifestyle/Story/STIStory_583958.html.
4. Arguably the hardest hit of all, Gillian Chung left the hugely popular duo Twins right after the scandal. After a retreat from the entertainment industry for slightly over a year, Gillian came back primarily as a solo artist, occasionally performing with her former partner. However, her singing, acting and product endorsement popularity has never reached the level of her heydays with Twins. By the time the sex photos were posted on the Internet, Bobo Chan was about to get married. Her wedding was suspended and after an extended stay in the United States, she returned to Hong Kong and started her jewellery business in 2009. Like Gillian, Cecilia Cheung's entertainment career was immediately put on hold. A popular and prolific actress, she signed her first film contract in October 2010, more than two years after the scandal broke out.

Chapter 5

BUILDING MEMORIES – A STUDY OF POP VENUES IN HONG KONG

> Changing cities produce many sights that are unfamiliar. But rapidly changing cities, cities without brakes like Hong Kong, produce something else as well: *the unfamiliar in the familiar*; that is, the unfamiliar that is half-seen or seen subliminally behind the seen/scene of the familiar.
>
> (Abbas 1997: 78)

Fluid sounds

Indeed, for someone living in a fast-changing city, the landscape may resemble a war zone, where space is structured by a tug of war between disappearance and appearance, between the unfamiliar and the familiar. Ackbar Abbas' interest is essentially visual; his inquiry into ways of seeing a fast-changing city like Hong Kong is located in visual cultures such as architecture and photography. Our concern is to include the audio with the visual. Informed by the global importance of the local sound – Cantopop – in the 1970s and 1980s and its perceived disappearance by the end of the new millennium, and intrigued by the series of the so-called comeback Cantopop concerts around the year 2000, we find our unfamiliar in the familiar at the site of a music venue: the Hong Kong Coliseum. In this chapter, we will begin with a discussion of the 'death of Cantopop' and some of its possible readings. Following a different approach to analyse and understand cultural consumption, we will zoom in on pop venues, which are prime sites for this emotive, audio-visual form of popular culture. We argue that one way of seeing, hearing and understanding the fast-changing city in the twenty-first century is to seek temporality in stability, or in the buildings that stay.

What happened to the sound of Cantopop, which 'in its heyday in the 1970s and 1980s [...] defined the look, feel and – with its lush, ultra-refined production values – even the sound of Chinese cool' (Burpee in Chu 2007: 2)? At a symposium on the development of Cantopop held in Hong Kong in March 2008, discussion was centred on the decline, if not the death, of Cantopop. In his doctoral thesis, the veteran Cantopop lyricist and composer James Wong pinpointed 1997, the year Hong Kong was handed over to the Beijing authorities, as the end of the Cantopop era (Wong 2003). Figures are quoted to quantify its disappearance: in 1995, Cantopop sales amounted to HK$1.853 billion, while three years later sales had dropped to HK$ 0.916 billion (Wong 2003: 169). Cantopop and its over-commercialization is referred to as a reason for its own sad fate. 'People are getting tired of mainstream Cantopop because it rehashes the formula of big ballads and cheesy dance tunes year in, year out' (Lee 2002). Economy and technology are also cited as accomplice. According to Stephen Chu, 'It is widely believed that the fall of Cantopop was caused by a combination of a bad economy, piracy and file sharing' (2007: 3). This gloomy narrative became even darker after the deaths of the Cantopop superstars Leslie Cheung and Anita Mui in April and December 2003.

A decade after the publication of Ackbar Abbas' acclaimed book *Hong Kong - Culture and the Politics of Disappearance* (1997), Cantopop, which played such a pivotal role in the construction of a Hong Kong identity, is according to the above accounts declining, dying, or at least, disappearing. It seems as if Hong Kong is haunted by the spirit of disappearance, as if the return to the 'motherland' could only result in its erasure as the unique city so aptly described by Rey Chow: 'What is unique to Hong Kong, however, is precisely an in-betweenness and an awareness of impure origins, or origins as impure' (Chow 1998: 157).

It is, however, precisely the disappearance of this in-betweenness, some would argue, that underwrites the perceived disappearance of Cantopop. Stephen Chu, for instance, asserts that '[t]he rise of a global Chinese music industry and media and the subsequent loss of the hybridity of Cantopop [...] is the major reason behind its recent decline' (2007: 13). In the globalization of Chinese music culture, Cantopop, performed in Cantonese, a regional language, is increasingly superseded, at least in terms of sales figures and the number of stars, by Mandopop, sung in official, nation-wide Chinese. Such cultural development resonates with the general 're-nationalization' process in Hong Kong after the city joined the nation (Erni 2001) – it is no longer about 'impure origins', but rather 'pure origins.' (For particular instances of co-option of Cantopop stars Leon Lai and Nicholas Tse into the mainland market, see Chapter 1.)

In addition to placing the perceived disappearance of Cantopop in a wider political, cultural context, it is our wish to challenge such a reading and pose questions regarding the very 'fact' of the disappearance itself. Anthony Fung and Michael Curtin, for instance, turn their gaze away from the traditional carriers of Cantopop, such as airplay and music release, to more recent forms of music consumption (Fung and Curtin 2002). Taking karaoke as their field of inquiry, Fung and Curtin argue for a different framing of the discussion. In addition to the disappearance narrative, which is largely framed by declining sales figures and dead stars, they urge to situate pop-music consumption in general, and Cantopop in particular, also in the realm of the uncountable, the personal and the emotive. We want to take this line of inquiry further. In proposing a counter-narrative to the story of disappearance, we will show how the uncountable, personal and emotive consumption of music is grounded in solid buildings – the music venues – that help sustain a Hong Kong identity and that defy disappearance in the post-1997 era.

Furthermore, to substantiate a story of disappearance by looking at sales figures and the number of stars misses, from our point of view, the changing landscape of popular music consumption. Even if the actual number of CDs being sold has declined rapidly, it does not necessarily mean that audiences are listening less to music. Apart from karaoke, there is a great deal of evidence to support the contention that there is continuing heavy emotive investment in popular music: ring tones as well as songs are frequently downloaded to individualize mobile phones; a quite astounding 34.8 per cent of the 530 million mobile subscribers in China use their phones to listen to music, compared to 5.7 per cent in the United States.[1] YouTube is used to upload clips of subscribers either singing or mimicking songs, activities that turn the consumer into a producer. MySpace has opened up a space for bands to promote and share their music. Digital production techniques such as GarageBand have become accessible to many people, enabling the easy production of music.

Meanwhile, it seems that pop-music consumption is becoming more and more personally oriented through the use of mobile audio devices, such as the mobile phone or the iPod, which enable users to fabricate their own soundtrack while traversing the city (Bull 2000). In short, there are signs that new modes of pop-music consumption are not only challenging conventional producer versus consumer distinctions, but also subsuming the collapse of such distinctions into the realm of the personal and the emotive. In the following, we will continue our inquiry into Cantopop on the sites of pop venues, particularly the Hong Kong Coliseum. We aim, through such an inquiry, to offer a different way of seeing, hearing and understanding music consumption in the city of Hong Kong. It is our contention that music venues, in particular, operate as emotive landmarks in the consumption of popular music. They allow citizens to feel that they belong to the city, as part of the city, of its citizenry and of a collective landscape of sight and sound. In short, they facilitate the construction of a collective emotive memory.

Monumental buildings

Ten years after the handover of Hong Kong, a theme song titled 'Hong Kong Always Has You/始終有你' was commissioned and produced by the official authorities to commemorate the special occasion. Part of the lyrics runs as follows:[2]

> Hong Kong always has you (Hong Kong always has you)
> Let people applaud for a century
> Hong Kong always has me (Hong Kong always has me)
> A hundred thousand more surprises in this century
> Thank you who have made a big world out of a small island
> you never give up, you are so persevering, despite all the difficulties
> that's why Hong Kong is so amazing, because Hong Kong always has you
> the Lion Rock is connected to the Great Wall, we share the same blood
> Hong Kong always has you (Hong Kong always has you)
> […]
> you never give up, you are so persevering, despite all the difficulties

that's why Hong Kong is so amazing, because Hong Kong always has you
(Mandarin: Because you're here)
Let people applaud for a century
Hong Kong always has me
(Mandarin: Because I'm here)

Lyrically, the song confirms the assumed link between Hong Kong and the mainland, while simultaneously stressing Hong Kong's alleged unique characteristics. The Han-centrism of such lines, as 'the Lion Rock Hill is connected to the Great Wall, we share the same blood', is strengthened by the insertion of the Mandarin line 'Because I am here'. While we may wonder who the 'I', 'you' and 'me' are referring to, or why certain lines have to be sung in Mandarin instead of Cantonese, the lyrics evoke a rosy image of post-handover Hong Kong. After applauding all the efforts and the perseverance of Hong Kong citizens, who have made the city into a prosperous place, the lyrics claim that reversion to Beijing rule serves as a guarantee for an equally prosperous future.

Moving beyond the lyrics, we are confronted with the accompanying video clip showing the familiar images of the skyscrapers of Hong Kong. The clip starts with a rather unimaginative, postcard-like parade of skyscrapers, all the modern monuments of economic power, the images of Hong Kong as a city skylined by global capital. One scene includes a window cleaner at work. According to the writer of the lyrics, Chan Siu Kei, the producers deliberately included this window cleaning shot to emphasize the human element in the city's success story. At the end of the clip, we can see a parade of another sort, this time a series of pop stars. This particular visual celebration of Hong Kong is primarily an act of collaboration between the government and pop music. (Apart from contributing to this project, Chan Siu Kei was also involved in the Beijing Olympics theme song production. See Chapter 6.)

Yet, the venues where music is performed in Hong Kong are conspicuously absent in the clip. They never operate as landmarks of the city. Most if not all of the landmarks of Hong Kong are either super-modern economic buildings pointing not only to the sky, but also to the future, or archaic, colonial architectures accommodating what would normally be called tradition or history. The latter draw our attention less frequently, but nonetheless sharply, when they are under threat, for instance, the case of the high profile campaign in 2007 to save the Queen's Pier in Hong Kong.[3] It seems that Hong Kong has to be imagined predominantly in terms of the future and occasionally in terms of the past; in other words, Hong Kong is largely imagined in terms of money and tradition, in terms of construction and destruction. And academics and activists privilege these two types of architectures, the economic ones and the heritage ones, as the prime site of their analytical concern or preservation efforts, of their understanding of contestation and resistance (Abbas 1997).

This chapter, however, is not about skyscrapers or colonial architectures, but about pop venues. It is about what Sophie Watson calls 'mundane and commonplace spaces of the city where people simply muddle through or rub along' (2006: 16). Our concern is the relation between public space, in this case pop venues, emotion and the possible production of identification and citizenry through the lens of collective memory. To paraphrase Saskia Sassen, this is an attempt to ground the soul of the city or a fragment of that soul in the materiality of the city, that is, pop venues (Sassen 2001). And among the venues, we are particularly interested in the Hong Kong Coliseum, which is generally considered the quintessential pop venue in Hong Kong. When the Hong Kong electronic duo Pixel Toy performed in Hong Kong at the Sheung Wan Civic Centre in July 2007, the band claimed on its leaflet: 'we may not be playing at the Coliseum, but we can still turn this into a big party.' The Coliseum is the local temple of a global popular culture. The massive concerts that it has been hosting are a major source of collective emotion and memories for the people of the city.

In contrast to the dominant gloomy narrative surrounding Cantopop in the post-1997 decade, Hong Kong culture, particularly pop culture, was characterized not so much by the politics of disappearance but by the politics of reappearance. This reappearance was not only facilitated by new modes of music consumption as discussed earlier, but also embodied in a series of comeback/reunion concerts. Older pop stars who had retired or simply been fired by the culture industry reappeared in all their former glory. Bands that had broken up or become inactive, such as The Wynners and Tatming Pair, staged high-profile reunion gigs. All these comeback or reunion concerts took place in the Hong Kong Coliseum.

The most talked about comeback concert series was probably the one by Sam Hui, the godfather of Cantopop. Sam Hui was the first to stage concerts at the Hong Kong Coliseum. That was in 1983. Twenty-one years later, he launched his series of comeback concerts. It became an instant hit, or as some would say, instant hype. In total, 38 concerts were staged, with almost half a million people witnessing Sam Hui's comeback. And the venue was of course the Hong Kong Coliseum. A local music critic attributed the success of his comeback to the local need for collective memory, which could be located in the context of fear. It was fear of disappearance, which hovered over the city before and after its handover to mainland China, a fear that could be relieved by the return of the legendary stars that helped to collectively remember the city called Hong Kong.

But then, if all these concerts had not been held in the Hong Kong Coliseum, would they still function in the same way? If all these comeback, reunion concerts symbolize certain articulations of a Hong Kong bygone but not quite, we may wonder whether these concerts might have become more a reminder of a Hong Kong bygone, totally and resolutely – had they not been held in the Hong Kong Coliseum. In a way, our questioning is not unlike Susan Fast's reflection on her experience with Live Aid in London, in 1985. For her, the best moments of that concert were during the performance by the band Queen, but none of the written accounts she came across afterwards carried any reference to Queen at all. She started to ask the most fundamental question: 'whose memory is it?' (Fast 2006: 138). And if this is a legitimate and relevant question, then our question would be: whose collective memory? And even: why is collective memory possible if our individual memories are so selective? We believe, as will show in our analysis, that the answer, or part of the answer, lies in the venue, literally and figuratively.

The nostalgia, the emotive expression of collective memories and the articulation of cultural identity requires not only the software of pop music, but also the hardware; after all, it requires a space, a public space, a venue where people can gather, to confirm and affirm they share the same memories, to confirm and affirm their emotions, to confirm and affirm their collectivity, to confirm and affirm their sense of belonging, identification and citizenry. Such space may perhaps be what Pierre Nora calls a *lieu de mémoire*, a material, functional, and symbolic site where memory crystallizes and secretes itself (Nora 1989). According to Abbas (1997: 65), 'architecture [...] has the dangerous potential of turning all of us, locals and visitors alike, into *tourists* gazing at a stable and monumental image.' But a massive and monumental venue like the Coliseum refuses, in its ordinariness, if not ugliness, to be turned into a tourist fetish. Instead, it turns Hong Kongers, indeed, into Hong Kongers. For the identity to be iterated and reiterated, the venue has to remain the same – far from disappearance, the venue may exude a strong sense of persistence, of defying disappearance. This is perhaps also why Hannah Arendt draws our attention to what she calls the 'permanence of public space' (1958: 55). The permanence of certain public spaces, like the Hong Kong Coliseum, serves to comfort city dwellers with the feeling that something has stayed and will stay essentially the same; in other words, that something will continue from some recent past into some near future. Pop venues are not only the embodiment of culture; they also help to construct and sustain a city and its culture.

Building memories

In the following, we will distinguish four stages in the development of pop venues in Hong Kong. In doing so, we will also try to connect the venues to the larger cultural formations of the city.

The first phase can be termed the pre-pop venue years, during which the British Hong Kong government, apart from pursuing predominantly economic and political interests, did make some effort to establish a cultural life in Hong Kong. The inauguration of the Hong Kong City Hall in 1962 was heralded as a major breakthrough in providing the city with cultural facilities. While opening the city hall, the governor at that time, Sir Robert Black, proclaimed: 'We in Hong Kong are the beneficiaries of two great estates of culture [...] This City Hall will bring light and pleasure to the people of Hong Kong, to the enrichment of their lives and the lives of their children!'[4] But how inclusive is the 'we' really? The venue mainly followed the colonial logic and played host to cultural events and genres for the privileged local elite and expatriate circles. During this phase, there seemed to be a dislocation of experience and identity. Dislocation, because the building itself, through colonial education, was branded for Hong Kongers as a marker or even an icon of the city, something the citizens identified, or should identify, Hong Kong with. Yet, most of the local population would have never stepped inside and experienced the space and its cultural activities. Figure 5.1 presents a typical old textbook image of the City Hall, isolated, dominant and proud. Now, four decades later, it is dwarfed by its more powerful neighbours (see Figure 5.2), a very visual account of the change in Hong Kong as a whole.

Figure 5.1: City Hall (courtesy of Hong Kong Public Records Office).

The second phase, in the late 1970s and early 1980s, saw the appearance of, first, the Academic Community Hall (1978, see Figure 5.3) and, then, the Queen Elizabeth Stadium (1980, see Figure 5.4). This was also the time when colonial elite culture was being contested, when local pop music, Cantopop, gradually established itself as a major musical genre and market in the colonial city. However, it was also a market characterized more strongly by a 'workshop' logic, in the sense that pop stars as we knew them later in the pop history of Hong Kong had not yet been produced. As both of these pop venues were able to host respectively audiences of 1300 and 3600 people, they were perfect locations for smaller concerts. Subsequently, this phase also saw the emergence of the 'collective' in terms of memory and emotion, when the local audience started to have a sense of gathering together to share some common experience. However, given the smaller venues and smaller gatherings, such experience remained fragmentary. Instead of privileging one dominant collective memory, there was a fragmented collection of collective memories. The venues and their concerts were not yet massive

Figure 5.2: City Hall dwarfed amidst the Hong Kong skyline.

Figure 5.3: Academic Community hall.

Figure 5.4: Queen Elizabeth Stadium.

and monolithic enough to elevate the collective into collective identity, at least not in the sense of a Hong Kong culture and identity. If they were remembered, those venues would be more likely spoken of fondly as reminiscent of the days of folk songs, of the student era, but not of the city.

In the third phase, from the 1980s until now, the definitive venue was constructed, the Hong Kong Coliseum. It was opened on 27 April 1983. With an audience capacity of 12,500, it was much larger than any other performance venue built so far; it ushered in the experience of cultural activity at a different level of intensity and collectivity. According to 2007–2008 figures, more than 1,862,000 people attended activities held at the Hong Kong Coliseum, compared to 334,000 at the Queen Elizabeth Stadium.[5] This was the phase when local pop music was maturing and canonizing into the genre of Cantopop, while the industry saw the full implementation of a more factory-like system when stars were largely seen to be manufactured, packaged and sold on a massive scale.

The Coliseum became the venue not only for performing stars, but also for producing stars. It was, and still is, the only venue. Even today, new stars must pass through this temple of pop to be fully baptized into stardom. Collective memory is gradually changing from being experiential, even existential, into the expected. Audiences who go to a Coliseum concert these days are not only aware that they will collect memories; they expect to feel stirred emotionally and they also want to own records of their emotions and memories. For instance, DVD recordings of

Sonic Multiplicities

Figure 5.5: Hong Kong Coliseum.

live concerts are one of the bestselling pop genres in Hong Kong. Guy Debord once described a spectacle as 'capital accumulated to the point where it becomes image' (Debord 1995: 24). In this case, the image has also become another form of capital, that circulates, to be owned by people who have seen the spectacle. The Hong Kong Coliseum's monopoly over audience expectations and therefore fulfillment of collective memory has turned this unique space into an important producer of Hong Kong culture and Hong Kong identity.

The fourth phase is more difficult to pin down. New venues have been built since the Coliseum, including the Hong Kong Exhibition and Convention Centre, which was conceived and completed in conjunction with the handover ceremony in 1997; Star Hall, at the Hong Kong International Trade and Exhibition Centre; and Asia World Arena, close to Hong Kong's international airport. However, up to now, none has offered a serious challenge to the function of the Hong Kong Coliseum in the production of collective memory and identity. At the end of 2008, the Coliseum was closed for large-scale renovation, and was reopened in 2009. At the same time, one new venue may arise as part of the West Kowloon Cultural District project, a government-initiated project that aims to promote Hong Kong as a creative city. The venue, in the plan referred to as a mega performance venue, will host up to 15,000 people, and thus a larger audience than the Coliseum. It remains to be seen whether the project will be actualized in this form, and whether such new venues will be able to replace the emotive power of the Coliseum.

Figure 5.6: Hong Kong Exhibition and Convention centre.

Figure 5.7: West Kowloon Project.

The Coliseum

Given the central role the Coliseum has played in Hong Kong pop culture, it comes as a surprise that so little has been written about it. On the contrary, however significant the Hong Kong Coliseum might remain for the local people, Hong Kong is generally described by the western media and local English media, most notably the *South China Morning Post*, as lacking venues for international stars. In particular, the lack of large outdoor venues presumably favoured by western mega stars or pop festivals is a recurring point of concern, although whether Hong Kong, given the heat and humidity, is a suitable location for outdoor events is another question altogether. This discourse sometimes conflates with the general shortfalls of Hong Kong, in terms of competitiveness, suggesting that it is in imminent danger of losing out to other Asian metropolises. Sometimes it conflates with the alleged lack in the ability of Hong Kong or the Chinese to party, to enjoy culture in an exuberant way. This criticism can partly be understood as Eurocentric, as an attempt to impose certain western experiences and values onto another locality, neglecting or ignoring local specificities.

It is clear that for the people of Hong Kong, the Coliseum is not only a public space; it is also a factory, literally, a production site, of collective memory, and a temple of experience and identity. Of all the venues, the Hong Kong Coliseum has not only the mechanics but also the magic to invest those collective memories with collective emotion and identity. To end our discussion on the Coliseum, we would like to pose a few questions for further deliberation in connection with the central inquiry of venues and memory. First of all, the Hong Kong Coliseum, being the canon of pop stardom, the temple of pop music, also hierarchizes, uniforms or even monopolizes the memories of Hong Kongers, while the Academic Community Hall and Queen Elisabeth Stadium, given their much smaller scale, would have more potential for multiplicity or collectivity in the plural. It remains to be seen how the dominant position of the Hong Kong Coliseum will impact on the writing of Hong Kong's cultural history.

Another question concerns the Coliseum's 'side effect' in facilitating a separation of space, emotion and identity. The Coliseum is an inside space, confined, forever connected to the city's entertainment, leisure and fun. By and large, Hong Kong only has inside, confined pop venues, and no outside, public venues. Outside venues are always linked with major pop concerts/festivals such as Woodstock, Band Aid, Live8 in the West and the rest of the world, where pop and politics and activism form allies, being visible, being part of the public space in the city. There is, however, a clear line of demarcation in Hong Kong: outside venues, such as Victoria Park, can be used for political rallies but not for pop events. Inside venues, such as the Coliseum, are 'only' for entertainment, rendered invisible, not directly part of the larger public space. This makes Saskia Sassen's question on who has claims to the city more complicated. Sassen observes outdoor festivals such as gay parades or Caribbean street walks not only in terms of a moment of showing off, but also in terms of certain groups of people laying claim to the city. However, if a city has developed a habit of celebrating its pop events indoors, how are we to understand its public politics? If live performances staged in the confined space of the

Coliseum help generate a collective memory, a Hong Kong identity, how are we to understand such essentially indoor, private moments, which seem to refuse to engage with Hong Kong's larger political landscape? Even more specifically, how are we to understand the identity politics embodied in the Coliseum during the political transition of the city from British to Beijing sovereignty? Would the Coliseum serve to erase a colonial capitalist history from the Hong Kong identity, producing nostalgia without melancholy, pain and a sense of struggle? Can we see the Hong Kong Coliseum, with its closed, massive and tomb-like monumental architecture, as a monument that seems to naturalize power – as monuments usually do?

Belonging and temporality

These are some of the questions that we believe require further exploration. For the purpose of this chapter, we have argued that instead of thinking of Hong Kong and its sound, Cantopop, in terms of disappearance, we consider that the changing modes of music consumption and the related emotive investments signal a continuous negotiation of what it means to live in Hong Kong. In our view, music venues, the material, stable embodiment of sight and sound, operate as emotive landmarks that help to invest memory with emotion and therefore identity. The Coliseum has served, as we have shown, an important function in producing stars, creating collective memories and reinventing the stars from decades ago, precisely in the significant time-span during which Hong Kong became part of China.

This was also the time when Hong Kong was shocked by the untimely deaths of two of its stars. The suicide of Leslie Cheung and the death of cancer-stricken Anita Mui robbed the city of its most celebrated legends, shocked it into an identity crisis, and ushered in the comeback phenomenon. The Hong Kong Coliseum has offered a space for the performance of a collective Hong Kong identity that refuses to disappear, helping to create a sense of belonging to a city that seems to be in constant flux.

Then what, to conclude, does this inquiry tell us about postmodernism and Hong Kong? At the beginning of the new millennium, the acclaimed volume on *Postmodernism and China*, edited by Arif Dirlik and Zhang Xudong (2000), was published. The idea of postmodernity is intricately linked to the issue of temporality. The constant state of in-between ness, of being always in flux, makes it tempting to claim Hong Kong as a postmodern city. However, the 'post' in postmodern produces an unjustified temporality, suggesting that the postmodern follows upon the modern. Based on our analysis, we believe it makes more sense to think of the postmodern in conjunction with the modern, in other words, to insist on the coevalness of the modern and the postmodern. If we translate these concepts into 'temporality' (the 'postmodern' idea of reality and identity being in constant flux) and 'stability' (the 'modern' idea of a stable, solid grounding of reality and identity), our study of popular music shows how the two can be considered mutually constitutive.

Pop can be considered a temporal sound, it produces hits that make us think back to a specific summer; pop is a transient sound, with stars that come and go. 'Pop is a performance of the artificial self; it is a spectacularization of the present. Pop's banality and artificiality render the music profoundly ambiguous, and it is this ambiguity that makes pop such a popular yet opaque musical form' (de Kloet 2005: 334). These reflections on the temporality of pop resonate with Chua Beng Huat's observation on the transience of consumer products: 'the brevity of life of a consumer object and of a consumer trend makes it unavoidable that all published materials on consumer products and trends are by definition "historical"' (Chua 2003: vii).

Pop serves as a marker of time. Today, with the possibilities of new technologies and the arguable collapse of production and consumption, audiences have become producers, sharing and personifying sounds and images. Pop is intricately connected with temporality, memory and nostalgia. Drawing on Rey Chow, Helen Hok-sze Leung argues that 'nostalgia is not simply a yearning for the past as though it were a definite, knowable object. Rather, nostalgia involves a "sensitivity to the movements of temporality." Understood in these terms, a nostalgic subject is someone who sits on the fence of time' (Leung 2001: 430).

However, pop is not only to be heard; it can also be seen. Sometimes, the sound needs material embodiment, a sight, to manifest itself. This is where the stable, gigantic and 'modern' structure of the pop venue comes in. The Hong Kong Coliseum illustrates how a pop venue serves as a massive, monumental fence of time, producing collective emotive memories that are being recorded on DVD's, mobile phones and cameras that are, in turn, being sold and shared with others on the Internet. Pop venues, as prime sites of this emotive, audio-visual form of popular culture, offer one way of seeing, hearing and understanding the fast-changing city in the twenty-first century: to seek temporality – the passing of time, the memory, the emotion, the sound, the fluid – in stability, or buildings that stay. Pop venues anchor pop, something that is temporal and in flux. Probably more than the skyscrapers that we see on all the postcards of Hong Kong, more than the monumental colonial buildings that ask for preservation, it is the Hong Kong Coliseum that helps the city to remember itself. It is a place, simply put, where you must have been, if you consider yourself a Hong Kong citizen.

Notes

1. From http://edpeto.com/the-next-generation/, accessed 10 June 2008.
2. Translated by Vincent Zhu.
3. See http://www.nowpublic.com/hong_kong_heritage_site_queens_pier_about_be_demolish_hk_government, accessed 10 June 2008.
4. See http://www.grs.gov.hk/PRO/srch/english/imgdisplay.jsp?RecordKey=799511&s=HKPRO_Archive_web&version=internet&page=2.
5. See http://www.lcsd.gov.hk/CE/Entertainment/Stadia/HKC/en/about.php and http://www.lcsd.gov.hk/CE/Entertainment/Stadia/QE/index.html, accessed 10 June 2008.

Chapter 6

OLYMPIC CELEBRATIONS AND PERFORMATIVE CONTESTATIONS

An aesthetic politics always defines itself by a certain recasting of the distribution of the sensible, a reconfiguration of the given perceptual forms. [...] The dream of a suitable political work of art is in fact the dream of disrupting the relationship between the visible, the sayable, and the thinkable without having to use the terms of a message as a vehicle. It is the dream of an art that would transmit meanings in the form of a rupture with the very logic of meaningful situations.

(Jacques Rancière 2004: 63)

'Beijing Welcomes You' may well have been the most played song on Chinese radio in 2008. In its accompanying clip, we see a parade of Chinese stars, who welcome the foreign visitors to Olympic Beijing. We would like to ask, whose Beijing are we then being welcomed to, given that these stars are from all over the 'Greater China' region? And since the lyrics of this song are written by probably the most prolific and popular lyric writer of Chinese language popular music, the Hong Kong lyricist Lin Xi, is it his version of Beijing maybe? Also, given that a major producer of this Olympic song is a veteran Hong Kong music professional, Chan Siu Kei, does it further suggest that the Hong Kong re-nationalization project is closer to its consummation? Is Hong Kong finally joining the celebration of the Chinese nation-state? In the clip, we see the Hong Kong-cum-Hollywood star Jacky Chan spreading his arms in front of the Great Wall, with the Olympic Slogan 'One World, One Dream' behind him in huge letters placed on the mountain. The first association these letters evoke is the Hollywood Sign, the famous landmark in the Hollywood Hills area of Mount Lee, in the Santa Monica Mountains, Los Angeles, California. The song is infectious, and easy to sing along with, at home, while driving or in karaoke bar, but are we all singing the same sentiments?

The authorities hope we are. The Beijing Olympics provided the Chinese authorities with a unique opportunity to promote the nation to both its citizenry as well as the world at large (Chong 2011; Landsberger 2009; Nyiri et al. 2010). For the grand spectacle of the opening ceremony, China mobilized its most prominent cultural producers, such as the filmmaker Zhang Yimou and the visual artist Cai Guoqiang. Popular music played a crucial role in both the opening ceremony and the Olympic project of 2008. The Olympic songs are seemingly univocal in their meaning; they celebrate China, its past, present and future, and do so in an explicitly nationalistic way. Following the thrust of this book, we must add: China is not one, and Hong Kong's perpetual in-between position always immediately complicates and contaminates any claim on pure Chineseness.

In this chapter, we aim to show that even in songs – the Olympic songs – that are produced so readily and earnestly to celebrate the nation, it is impossible to achieve a semiotic closure, impossible to contain alternative possibilities of meaning and affect. Different from, but corresponding to Chapters 1 and 3, where the focus is on how one Hong Kong music professional and Hong Kong's China Wind music videos negotiate and contest hegemonic articulations of Chineseness, this chapter seeks to engage with these polysemic possibilities by zooming in on the performative instabilities in the alleged Hong Kong co-production of Chinese nationalistic sentiments. We will show how these celebratory songs as a whole (Hong Kong and mainland) are part of a complex web of entanglements that involve different actors, none of whom can claim exclusive rights to contain the fluid process of signification.

The constative and the performative

How can we conceptualize the complex and transnational web of signification that propels the production and consumption of the Olympic songs, and how can we analyse the potential they hold for a slippage of meaning, away from the authoritative discourse of Chinese nationalism? To probe into these questions, we will draw on Alexei Yurchak's work on the late days of the Soviet Union titled *Everything Was Forever Until It Was No More* (2005). Yurchak's book starts with a peculiar paradox: how was it possible that up to the 1980s, citizens in the Soviet Union felt that the regime would live on forever, yet, when it all of a sudden collapsed, they were not that surprised either. Or, in the words of Yurchak, 'although the system's collapse had been unimaginable before it began, it appeared unsurprising when it happened' (2005: 1). While we do not wish to engage with speculative questions on the future of China, we do consider useful his theorizations with which he tries to unpack this paradox. Yurchak starts critiquing the binaries that have haunted analyses of Soviet life, binaries like official versus unofficial culture, the state and the people, totalitarian language and counterlanguage, truth and lies, morality and corruption, and so on (2005: 5). Not only academic, but also particular journalistic discourse on contemporary China remains stuck in a similar binary framework, one that can be traced back to a Cold War logic in which China is perceived as the ultimate totalitarian and authoritarian state. Such binary flattening of complex realities makes one label assumed 'official' cultural forms, too quickly, as univocally authoritative, and its 'underground' opposite as simply 'resistant'. These binaries generally reproduce the image of an omnipotent and powerful state with a docile citizenry.

How, then, can we move out of this binary? How can we avoid a Cold War logic, and how can we account for the continuous slippages of meaning in written, sung and visual language? Inspired by performance theory – referring to authors like Mikhail Bakhtin, John Langshaw Austin and Judith Butler – Yurchak develops a twin pair of concepts to analyse cultural products: the performative and the constative. The starting point for his analysis is the observation that we 'need to consider discourse and forms of knowledge that circulated in everyday Soviet life not as divided into spheres or codes that are fixed and bounded, but as processes that are never completely known in advance and that are actively produced and reinterpreted' (2005: 18). Speaking itself constitutes a voice that is never bounded or fixed, but always already dialogical, as Bakhtin has argued. Language is thus productive in itself, it does not need to be read as coming from a unified 'subject', but is inherently multi-vocal and already allows for constant changes and mutations in meaning.

The constative dimension of speech refers to what is stated, to the actual contents, to its literal meaning. Statements like 'my name is Joe', 'it is cold' or 'I am a man' are constative statements; they can be either true or false. But language also includes a whole class of utterances that *do* something. When someone declares 'I name this ship the Queen Elizabeth', this is a performative act. 'Constative utterances convey meaning and can be true or false; performative utterances deliver force and cannot be true or false – instead they can be felicitous or infelicitous' (2005: 19). When one votes during an election, the vote itself refers to one's preference for a certain candidate – the constative meaning, but the act of voting is simultaneously a performative act with which one performs a commitment to or belief in democracy. 'The unity of the constative and performative dimensions makes the vote what it is: a statement of opinion that is recognized as having consequences in legal, administrative, institutional and cultural terms' (2005: 23). The constative and the performative are thus dimensions that coexist; they are indivisible and mutually productive.

However, their importance may shift over time. According to Yurchak's analysis, in the late Soviet Union, it is the performative that gained importance, at the expense of the constative. He observes 'a rise of the performative dimension over authoritative discourse during late socialism. This also made the constative dimension of discourse increasingly unanchored, indeterminate, and often irrelevant' (2005: 25). As Yurchak writes, 'precisely because authoritative language was hegemonic, unavoidable, and hypernormalized, it was no longer read by its audiences literally, at the level of constative meanings' (76). The performative shift allowed for new and unexpected meanings to proliferate; it enabled 'the engagement in different new meanings that were not described by the constative dimension of these rituals and texts, [this] still did not preclude a person from feeling an affinity for many of the meanings, possibilities, values, and promises of socialism' (2005: 28). This point resembles James Scott's observation that 'the greater the disparity in power between dominant and subordinate and the more arbitrarily it is exercised, the more the public transcript of subordinates will take on a stereotyped, ritualistic cast. In other words, the more menacing the power, the thicker the mask' (1990: 3). Whereas for Scott, power is something that groups really possess, a pre-Foucauldian position, for Yurchak as well as for us, power is something more fluid, more relational and more productive. Hence, our preference to think and speak in terms of the constative and the performative, rather than in terms of domination and resistance, or of ritualistic and of hidden transcripts.

The performative shift may help explain the sudden shifts leading to the collapse of the Soviet Union; and yet, one should not equate the emergence of new meanings as inherently counter political. To give an example from contemporary China: these days, membership of the Chinese Communist Party among young Chinese is on the rise. On a performative level, this can be explained by the opportunities it gives for networking. The communist ideology attached to party membership – the constative level – is increasingly being pushed into the background. This, however, does not imply that new members do not feel any commitment to the ideological underpinnings. But the increased importance of the performative does help to produce new, unanticipated meanings, to de-territorialize the meaning or significance of party membership to new ideological terrains.

Welcome to Olympic Beijing

As we wrote earlier, the constative and the performative go hand in hand. For the sake of laying down our argument, we would like to first zoom in on what is being stated in these Olympic songs, both in terms of lyrics as well as of visual language, and then move on to their performative dimension. This division is artificial, as both dimensions occur simultaneously. Furthermore, following Yurchak, we also notice a similar development in China, namely that the performative dimension has been gaining importance at the expense of the constative. Let us begin with the introductory text as printed on the jacket of the official CD containing the Olympic songs:

> This is not an ordinary album; this is the heavenly (divine) sound of the Olympics. What is collected here is the human beauty, the silent strength, the joyful sentiments that human beings express through the Olympics. This is the bliss when all the hearts on earth meet.

> This is not an ordinary album, this is China's Olympic story. What is collected here is the unique understanding and interpretation, glory and pride, expectation and fulfilment of a dream that the Chinese (*zhongguoren*) give to the Olympics. This is the highest happiness of participation and dedication.

> This is not an ordinary album, this is Chinese (*huaren*) music-makers Olympic love. What is collected here is their whole-hearted participation and dedication to the Beijing Olympics, their heart's blood and sweat, their exploration and break through. Every note is infused with affect […]

> Music is the loudest existence of the Olympic Spirit outside the arena. Music writes the Olympic epic in beautiful melody and words. This album will be the latest and brilliant chapter of this epic! This chapter is written by all the Chinese (*huaren*) music-makers together with the world.

This text embodies the main thrust of the Olympic project for China. It is a divine moment for a secular country, a moment of cosmopolitanism, when all the hearts of the earth meet. At the same time, it is claimed to be a Chinese story, a Chinese dream. While at times the geopolitically defined mainland Chinese are being interpellated (*zhongguoren*), the national also smoothly glides into the ethnic/racial when the term *huaren* is mobilized. Lubricated by this linguistic gliding, the Olympics opens up its claim to be a celebration for *all* the ethnic/racial Chinese around the globe. The celebration of Chineseness is thus a conflation of both the national and the ethnic/racial. The imagery used is emotional and bodily; it is about blood, sweat and tears, used as proof of the commitment of the people to this project.

Our analysis of four songs – the lyrics and the accompanying MTV images – closely resembles this initial sketch of thematic patterns. The songs in our analysis are (1) 'We Are Ready', (2) 'I Am a Star/我是明星', (3) 'Beijing Welcomes You/北京歡迎你' and (4) 'Forever Friends/永遠朋友'. The context of production as well as its reception (and appropriation) are relevant here, which we consider to be part of the performative dimension. Before moving there, we want to map out the constative dimension of the songs under study. Our analysis of both lyrics as well as images revealed recurrent articulations of a (1) pastoral and traditional, (2) open and cosmopolitan, (3) high-tech futuristic, (4) multi-vocal yet united and harmonious and (5) divine China.

First, the articulation of a pastoral and traditional China: the clips show time and again Chinese traditional culture, ranging from Taichi exercises (*taichichuan*) and calligraphy, to kites, paper cuttings and Beijing opera as in, for instance, 'Beijing Welcomes You'. These traditions are seen being performed against a backdrop of traditional architecture such as temples and the Forbidden City. This mobilization and reiteration of China's idealized long history and assumed unique and rich culture strikes us as the most clichéd mode of representation, one that we also find in tourist brochures, and documentaries on travelling in China. The coupling of these images of the traditional with the pastoral is no coincidence, as it signifies purity and naturalness. Chinese tradition is thus stripped of all its violence and ugliness; what is left for the audience to witness, to indulge in, is a primitive, clean and sanitized version of the past, as symbolized by green forests, and yellow flowers in the meadow. In 'Beijing Welcomes You', we hear:

My home is growing a '10,000 year old green' (*wannianqing* – a kind of plant)
Blossoming legends, sowing seeds in traditional soils

Whereas in 'I Am a Star', we hear:

Endless sea and infinite sky, I am the wind
Blowing the flags of North, South, East and West

The fog above Beijing has vanished, as has the greyness of its cityscape. In their place we find the lush green of the forests around the Great Wall that are aligned to performances of what are assumed to be traditional Chinese cultural practices.

Second, in line with the Olympic ideology as formulated by Baron Pierre de Coubertin, considered to be the father of the modern Olympic Games, the songs contain ample references to an open and cosmopolitan China. If the old and glorious past must go through centuries of vicissitudes including warfare, chaos and bloodshed, the lyrics and images of the songs enable a swift and seamless transition to an open and cosmopolitan present. They do not only ignore the dynastic changes, but also conveniently skip over the tumultuous period between 1911 and 1989. The old makes a leap towards the present, no reference is made to communism, or to its previously celebrated leaders. Gone are Mao Zedong, Zhou Enlai or Deng Xiaoping. Instead, the songs are completely devoid of politics; we see, for instance in the MTV images of 'Forever Friends', smiling volunteers waiting for the foreign guests at the airport and later in the video we also see these foreigners join the Chinese with their Taichi exercises in the park.

Lyrically, here are but a few cosmopolitan excerpts:

Whether we know each other, you are my guest, don't be polite
The door of my home is always open, open to the world
However big the world is, we are friends, feel yourself at home
All the lovely atmosphere if filled with smiles, waiting for you

('Beijing Welcomes You')

We are ready, join sky and earth together
This race [*minzu*] is ready, smilingly, we come and ask: how are you?
Let the world focus its gaze

('We Are Ready')

Forever friends
In harmony
As the whole world joins and sees
Days of unity and peace [...]
Joy and laughter everywhere!
We're together there to share

('Forever Friends')

Even though we met as strangers
No one is ordinary
For all of us are heroes

('I Am a Star')

What is celebrated here is a cheerfully open and cosmopolitan China that welcomes the strangers from all over the world with a smile on its face, erasing what the same state sometimes alludes to as the century of national humiliation. In her study on the training of the Olympic volunteers, Gladys Pak Lei Chong observes a similar erasure, in the manual for volunteers, 'the past became almost "humiliation-free"' (Chong 2011: 42); it was only mentioned in passing.

Third, the articulation of a high-tech and futuristic China: these articulations are embedded particularly in the visuals in the clips; the new Olympic buildings like the Bird's Nest and the Watercube appear frequently in the clips, pushing the line that was already established between the past and the present, with a break of about one century, forward towards the future. Together with the previous articulations, we can see how at the constative level the songs are involved in a management of time, in the representation of a specific temporality that ties in neatly with authoritative discourse. As Callahan observes in his study on national humiliation day, while much attention is paid to the contingencies of the cultural and territorial construction of the nation, the use of time and temporality in nation-building projects is much less scrutinized (2006: 181). The temporal dimension of the Olympics is part and parcel of the Beijing Olympics. All over Beijing, massive clocks were indicating the number of days, hours, minutes and seconds left till the opening ceremony, reminding the citizens on a second-by-second basis about the upcoming arrival of this mega event. The new architecture presented a massive leap towards the future, one that also returned in the opening ceremony when the Taikonauts (the Chinese bastardization of the term 'astronauts') of China were celebrated. Interestingly, as a study shows, in the mediation of this opening ceremony in Taiwan and Hong Kong, the references to the old China were picked up with enthusiasm, whereas the references to today's China and its technological advancements were either ignored or frowned upon (Zeng forthcoming).

Fourth, the articulation of a multi-vocal yet united China: the involvement of children, minorities and stars from all over the Greater China region all feed into the discourse of multi-vocality. China is one, but one in many voices, seems to be the message here. The song 'We Are Ready' is strikingly similar to that of 'We Are the World'; we see a line up of Chinese artists in the studio who enthusiastically sing out loud that they are ready for the Olympic Games. But who exactly is this 'we'? Let us first explore the curious resemblance with 'We Are the World', a song that brought together numerous American artists in the joint 'USA for Africa' project in 1985. In his analysis of that song, Jaap Kooijman argues that '"We Are the World" is not merely a charity pop record to raise western awareness of the Ethiopian famine and to collect money for aid, but is most of all a showcase of American superstars who function as ideological ambassadors of American values such as freedom and democracy within a free market economy, using a language that is strikingly similar to the rhetoric of Pepsi and Coca-Cola commercials' (Kooijman 2008: 21). This performance of American values that are presented as universal values is part and parcel of a hegemonic project, 'pop stardom, and the commercial rhetoric of mass advertising ends up promoting an American conception of the world, thereby presenting the values of democracy, individual freedom, and choice through consumerism as seemingly universal and global ones' (Kooijman 2008: 22).

If we take a look at the title of the Beijing song, we can already observe a difference. 'We Are Ready' indicates a more humble attitude than 'We Are the World'. It assumes implicitly that people may wonder if China is ready for the Olympics, and answers this by a strong and affirmative: yes, we are ready. It does so through the inclusion of numerous stars who, enfusedly, sing out loud that 'we are ready'. The 'we' in this title refers to *all* the Chinese; it is an inclusive we, given the involvement of stars from mainland China, Hong Kong and Taiwan. In the extended clip that can easily be found on YouTube, we see first a parade of the stars, who all look directly into the camera and say out loud, in English, 'Beijing, we are ready!' The fact that it is said in English indicates that this message is not really meant for the Beijing citizens, despite the fact that they are addressed here, but to the world at large. With this statement, China wants to reaffirm that they are ready to host the Olympics, and by extension, that they are ready for the role of future global power. This articulation, in conjunction with the cosmopolitan one, evokes a strong sense of harmony; the rise of China is a harmonious one, and this comes as no surprise since the idea of harmony was not only one of the major themes of the Beijing Olympics (during the opening ceremony, the Chinese character for harmony (*he*) plays a central role); harmony is one of the key tropes of today's communist propaganda. In the words of Stephanie Hemelryk Donald, 'harmonious society is both declared as the aim of policy development but is also assumed to be already the condition of the Chinese state and people. Harmonization operates as a rhetorical description of class change in China, which yet immediately and retrospectively elides and occludes the problems of the underclass, the shifting value of working-class political capital, and the rise of the new rich elites' (Donald 2010: 128).

Fifth, and finally, is the articulation of a divine China, an articulation in which the divine intermingles with the bodily, both expressing a passionate devotion to the Olympic project. In addition to the general statement of the Olympic CD quoted earlier, where references were made to blood, sweat and love, here is a selection of other examples from the lyrics:

We use our sweat to nourish five colours.

('We Are Ready')

There's a dream, started by me, changing my sweat into a smile, endless sea and infinite sky, I am the wind.

('I Am a Star')

In terms of visualization, we see, for instance, Chinese people spreading their arms upwards to the sky, images that resemble the religious postcards in which the sun, as a signifier for god, embraces the people. The entry into the league of world powers is thus symbolized as a divine moment, one in which the people are, as it were, baptized by a god of wealth and prosperity, a moment of hope and belonging.

The five articulations we have traced are part and parcel of the constative meaning of these songs, resonating closely with the official framing of the Beijing Olympics. In that sense, they can be considered part of the authoritative discourse, in which the Olympics were promoted as a 'Green Olympics', a 'High-tech Olympics' and a 'People's Olympics'. According to the website of the Beijing Organizing Committee for the Games of the XXIX Olympiad (BOCOG), a 'Green Olympics' (*Luse Aoyun*) emphasized the use of environmental friendly technologies and measures to design and construct Olympic facilities and the promotion of environmental awareness to the general public; a 'High-tech Olympics' (*Keji Aoyun*) stressed the scientific innovativeness and high-tech achievements of the games and also their popular use in daily life; a 'People's Olympics' (*Renwen Aoyun*) aimed, on the one hand, to showcase Chinese culture, historical and cultural heritage and the population's positive support of the Games, and, on the other, to advance cultural exchanges and promote harmonious development between mankind and nature.[1] Given the omnipresence and repetition of these articulations since 2001, the authoritative discourses must have been hardened into a solidity that would hardly allow any space for new meanings to proliferate, or so it seems.

This overview of the constative meanings as articulated in the songs brings little new, as we are all aware of these promotional discourses through which China wants to promote itself. They are part of the soft power strategies mobilized by the nation-state. For that reason, we have refrained from giving a very close analysis of either lyrics or clips. We may even venture to propose that China was not that exceptional in such constructions and celebrations; other Olympic host countries would most likely present a similar rosy picture of themselves. In that sense, there is not much peculiarly Chinese about these songs. The overcoded language of the Olympic songs resonates with the posters, television announcements and all other promotion materials of the party; it makes one almost yawn with boredom.

But not quite, really. As there is more to these songs; there is more that moves beyond their constative meanings. Not only are the stars familiar to us, already triggering a more complex web of signification, the songs themselves are catchy, easy to sing along with; the sonic energy evoked by the music of the Olympic songs makes one sing along, and now, a few years later, the songs bring back memories of that summer in Beijing, when the air was filled with expectations about the biggest event yet to come. To grasp these complexities, and the inherent slippages of meanings, of affects, of associations, we need to scrutinize the performative dimensions of the Olympic songs.

Performing Olympic China from Hong Kong

While the opening ceremony of the Beijing Olympics was above all a transnational project that involved artists and producers from all over the world, the production of the Olympic songs too was anything but a purely mainland Chinese affair. The meanings analysed thus far can be considered part of the constative dimension of the Olympic songs. These are meanings that are reiterated, constantly constructing the Olympic nationalistic project that has kept China enchanted since Beijing's bid was awarded in 2001. These meanings constitute a strategic alliance between the Olympic ideals and the maintenance of the Chinese nation-state (see de Kloet et al. 2008). The hypernormalized language, or better, the hypernormalized or overcoded meanings conveyed through these songs are repetitions of countless other forms of propaganda, part and parcel of the Olympic nationalism that has permeated all discourse in China since 2001. Following Yurchak's observation, we argue that precisely because it was such a hypernormalized mode of communication, its constative meaning matters less and less. Listeners, for instance, are so used to the rhetoric of harmony, that operates in tandem with the discourse on nationalism, that it ceases to mean what it is supposed to; it may even provide the listeners with the symbolic tools to fiddle around with meaning, to deterritorialize the Chinese-socialist discourse.

One crucial part that allows for this slippage of meaning is the highly visible involvement of stars, lyric writers and music producers from Hong Kong. If we stick to the constative dimension, we may ask ourselves, how can they, whose alliance with Beijing is bound to be problematic or contested, align themselves with such a blatant celebration of the nation? Dovetailing to these questions is the question: *do* they actually perform a blatant and simplistic version of Chineseness? Let us look at three cases that may trouble the assumed univocality of the Olympic celebration: first, the discussions surrounding Lin Xi's participation in the Olympic celebration; second, the simultaneous involvement of Yiu Fai Chow in the production of an Olympic song as well as a song that unsettles the Olympic message; and, finally, an alternative version of 'Beijing Welcomes You' that emerged and circulated on the Internet as a political critique on the shrinking rights of Hong Kong in the midst of the grand national event.

Lin Xi is Hong Kong's most prolific lyricist, and lyric writer of the important Olympic promotional song 'Beijing Welcomes You'. Wang Dan, one of the leaders of the student movement of 1989, who now lives in Taiwan, launched a severe critique against Lin Xi in an article titled 'Olympic Games is a mirror to reflect the devils: Lin Xi lost himself in the mass hysteria' (2008).[2] In this piece, Wang expresses his disappointment at the lyricist he once adored; he particularly took issue with another Olympic song 'Red throughout the World', composed by Mark Lui and performed by Jacky Cheung, both based in Hong Kong. Wang Dan writes:

> Mainland China has collapsed into a collective Olympic hysteria. Everything must be about the Olympics; every bit of human and material resources must be dedicated to the Olympics; everybody must protect and celebrate the Olympics and China's nationalistic dignity. This is actually sick. Our only hope is to find some intellectuals with independent thinking, those cultured people who can stay alert and calm, never losing oneself even at the peak of nationalistic hysteria. But when we come across works like Lin Xi's, what can you say apart from lamenting?

Soon, the veteran mainland music critic Zhang Xiaozhou joined forces and wrote a blog piece on 30 July 2008 titled 'Lin Xi chooses to degrade himself.' In addition to Lin Xi, Zhang also denounced those from the music industry who were selling themselves out to the Olympic project, claiming it to be obnoxious to see so many people dedicating their music and time to such an event.

It should be noted that the engagement of these critics with Lin Xi's work is grounded in the constative meanings of the songs; they take the contents as literal markers of a blatant nationalistic project from which they want to distance themselves. The critique of Wang Dan clearly validates intellectual culture, and its primacy of the mind over the body, of thinking over emotions. Such a position generally focuses on the constative level, assuming that what counts in arguments and debates are the actual meanings being conveyed. In doing so, it glosses over the emotional, affective and above all performative dimensions of speech. The banal observation itself that the production team of these songs are from Hong Kong already complicates any univocal claim on Chineseness. The subsequent debate that raged over the Internet is part of the performative dimension of these songs, steering attention away from its constative meaning, to be replaced by discussions over nationalism, popular culture and the Beijing Olympics. The songs may thus enable discussions over nationalism rather than simply promote it, testifying the increased importance of the performative dimension. The necessity to foreground the performative dimension of Lin Xi's work would become even more apparent when we take a look at the contribution of his contemporary colleague to the Olympic celebration.

Yiu Fai Chow, co-author of this book, has been writing lyrics since 1988. While in Chapter 1 he examines his own writing tactics vis-à-vis hegemonic Chineseness during the re-nationalization of Hong Kong, we would like to discuss here his involvement in the Olympic project just a decade after the political handover. At the time of the Beijing Olympics, the Hong Kong-based record company EEG asked him to write a theme song for the equestrian events that were held in Hong Kong – that these particular Olympic events were 'outsourced' to Hong Kong was generally promoted as Beijing's favour to the Special Administrative Region. The resultant song, titled 'Decathlon', composed by Punk Chan, was, like many other Olympic songs, performed by various EEG artists, among whom were Jacky Chan, the former Olympic winner Tian Liang and the pop idol Nicholas Tse (see Chapter 1 for a detailed discussion of his career in mainland China). Part of the lyrics run like:

> Olympics, add oil, we show off with our equestrian skills
> Riding on thousand horsebacks, waving thousand arms, we try our best and big things will soon happen
> Don't let opportunities pass, all the miracles are possible
> Lift up your chin, straighten your back, winning the decathlon is possible.

The constative meaning itself already slips away, one could argue, from a Beijing-centred articulation of Chineseness, given that it is the Hong Kong side that is celebrated here. At exactly the same time that Chow wrote the Olympic song, he collaborated with Anthony Wong on another song uncannily titled 'One World' (see a discussion of Chow's collaboration with Wong in Chapter 1). In the politically engaging style Wong has established in his repertoire, the song offers an ironic twist to the central Olympic slogan 'One World, One Dream'. (Even more ironically, Wong, like Chow, also participated in the other Hong Kong Olympic song 'Decathlon'.) While the simple appropriation of the slogan itself would already constitute an act of desecration, Chow's lyrics pose fundamental questions concerning the cosmopolitan ideal as embodied in the Olympic Games. At the constative level, the song expresses angst about the world becoming increasingly one; it sighs over the forces of homogenization:

> One world, in one world
> Perhaps only one dream
> Every time I check into a new hotel room, I think of my old hometown
> Although I have clearly said goodbye to you.

More important, in our view, is how the release of this 'counter-Olympic song' corresponds to Chow's 'official' Olympic song and by extension to the whole Olympic chorus. Just like Anthony Wong's involvement in both songs complicates their respective constative meanings. The dialogue thus opened up also opens up the space for the performative, ultimately for slippages of meaning, disturbing any univocal claim on Chineseness. In Bakhtinian terms, the desired proliferation of the authoritative discourse of Chineseness runs amok; instead, what we witness, or hear, is a discursive and sonic heteroglossia.

If the creators of the Olympic songs, in our cases the lyric writers, are not to be contained by the constative, audiences are no less creative in their performance of the songs. We need to look at the creative appropriations of the Olympic songs both in Hong Kong as well as in China, in which people poke fun at, or play with, the Olympic project. Different alternative versions were released on the Internet; for example, one version appeared in 2008 in Hong Kong to support the local campaign for direct elections in 2012. Adopting the same melody and the same title, the rewritten lyrics refer to the city's readiness for full democracy. The refrain from the song 'We Are Ready', written by Lam Chi Kin, now runs, in Cantonese, as follows:

> 2012 (we are ready) hope to see the start of universal suffrage on that day
> 2012 (we are ready) determined to unite now
> The entire city, try our best and retrieve that lost history
> Everybody, get involved, be confident, we are ready.

The clip on youtube (http://www.youtube.com/watch?v=6XDHYNf5Lak) starts with the signing of the agreement between China and the United Kingdom by the then British Prime Minister Margaret Thatcher, to be followed by numerous other moments in the recent history of Hong Kong's tortuous pro-democracy movement. The clip continues with a parade of activists, time and again interrupted by imageries of the protests in Hong Kong for democracy.³ Following Yurchak, we argue that it is precisely when the constative meaning of the song matters less and less, such performative reinterpretations are made possible. In other words, the possibilities for the articulation of alternative discourses are ingrained in, and are a fundamental part of, the official, state-driven promotional campaigns. The intensive involvement of Hong Kong in the production of these songs is just a first step in the rearticulation of the assumed univocal message of Chineseness, eventually rendering this univocality inherently impossible to achieve. At the performative level, a heteroglossia of meaning unfolds, generating new constative meanings. And this mutation of meaning continues; it breeds in the numerous karaoke rooms, where people are infected and affected in numerous different ways by the Olympic songs, and sing along with them in their numerous own ways – just as it inspires bands in China to create their own Olympic songs.

Shanghai also welcomes you!

The creative appropriation of, and discussion of, the Olympic songs took place in mainland China in both online and offline realities. One example comes from the art-punk band Top Floor Circus. Humour, parody and irony are the building blocks of their performances. The vocalist Lu Chen delivers a parody on the Olympic Games in their version of the hit song 'Beijing Welcomes You'. He sings 'Shanghai Welcomes You' (see also de Kloet 2010: 128):

> Shanghai welcomes you, welcomes you to come shopping
> Don't forget to bring your RMB Shanghai welcomes you,
> What's so special about the Olympic Games?
> Shanghai Welcomes You [...] The pretty girls at Huaihai Road Are No.1 around the whole country [...]
> Shanghai welcomes you,
> What's so special about the Olympic Games?
> Let's get together at World Expo.

Lu Chen plays out the clichéd references to Shanghai in this song, exaggerates them, thus poking fun at the stereotypes people from Beijing generally employ when describing Shanghai. In his ridiculing of the games, he mocks the nationalism propagated by the officials and questions Beijing as the centre of Chinese culture.

Another example comes from the New Labour Art Troupe, a collective that emerged at the outskirts of Beijing as part of a cultural centre for migrant workers. The group performs at construction sites for migrant labourers, and tries to give a voice to them, the labourers who actually helped build Olympic Beijing, and, ironically, were forced to leave the city when the actual spectacle was taking place. The CD that they released after the Olympics (it would not be possible to launch it earlier due to censorship regulations) was aptly titled 'Our World, Our Dream.' Its cover (see Figure 6.1) shows the high-rise buildings of Beijing as well as the Bird's Nest, the ultimate architectural icon of the Beijing Olympics. The imageries as well as the slogan that were so ubiquitous during the Olympics are reconfigured to carve out a space for the migrant workers, who left their homes to build someone else's world, someone else's dream.

The songs on the CD express the feelings of alienation and loneliness, in conjunction with the dangers inherent to construction labour, for example in the title song 'Our World, Our Dream', they sing:

Figure 6.1: New Labour Art Troupe's 'Our World, Our Dream'.

> Our world is full of loneliness
> To make a living, I left my native place and wander around
> The city neon lights only shine into my emptiness [...]
> I live in a world full of discrimination [...]
> Industrial accident, occupational disease, pain and despair
> Our dreams are safety, health and security
> Our dream is to create a new world.

The hegemonic quasi-cosmopolitan illusion as encoded in the main official slogan 'One world, one dream', mutates towards an articulation of an alternative world with alternative dreams, in which migrant workers are not the second rate citizens as they are now in mainland China, in which working conditions are safe and health care is available for all workers – in short, a world far removed from today's harsh realities in China. By articulating these voices, by performing the Olympic slogan to their own tunes, the CD forces us to pay attention to the flip side of China's economic rise, a side that has so conveniently, yet not quite successfully, been silenced during the Beijing Olympics.

Finally, the Olympic songs triggered off many postings in the Chinese blogosphere, in which they were ridiculed, critiqued and altered. One such posting mentions, with reference to the song 'We Are Ready', that it is clear that when you have to repeat this time and again, only one conclusion is possible, that is, you are not ready at all. Others laughed at the English, claiming that what they heard is 'We are weady', not ready. Given the sheer size of the Chinese blogosphere, this list of performative de-territorializations of the constative meanings of the songs is endless. The citations here, however, are typical, attesting to the continuous slippages of meaning of authoritative discourse.

Criticality and popular culture

Neither the Adorno-ian claim that popular culture is supporting the ideological status quo of society nor its Fiske-ian inversion that popular culture provides the symbolic toolbox to subvert that status quo are particularly new or original. What we have tried to show in this chapter is that the opposition between compliance and resistance as articulated through such readings of popular culture is a false binary, one that often creeps back to the limelight in readings of communist-authoritarian regimes like mainland China. To escape from such binary socialism that is rooted in a Cold War rhetoric, inspired by the work of Yurchak, we have proposed to read popular culture as having both a constative as well as performative dimension. These two are not juxtaposed to each other; under the current conditions of late-socialism, we observe that the importance of the constative level has faded, whereas the performative dimension has gained importance. We opened this chapter with a quote from the French philosopher Jacques Rancière, who claims that 'an aesthetic politics always defines itself by a certain recasting of the distribution of the sensible, a reconfiguration of the given perceptual forms' (2004: 63). Olympic songs are part and parcel of the construction of a regime of the sensible. Their MTV images, the sounds, the lyrics, all constitute a regime of the Olympic sensibility, in which we can find the building blocks, the visual, auditory and linguistic tools, for a reconfiguration of their aesthetic principles. This reconfiguration takes place at the level of the performative, rather than constative.

Taking the Olympic songs as an entry point, we have shown how the direct involvement of Hong Kong lyricists, producers and stars already immediately renders any univocal claim on Chineseness impossible. It would be quite beside the point if we choose to lament Hong Kong's 'shameless', to quote Wang Dan, contribution to the chorus of official Olympic songs as a sell-out of one local person or the entire city. We have chosen not only to listen to the constative, but also to watch the performative. And if Hong Kong's (co-)production of the Olympic songs of official celebration is far from univocal, we have reasons to – we must – believe in the cacophony of the rest. Perhaps it is one of Hong Kong's contributions to the Olympic project: to pose the fundamental question of who has the authority to author (the constative), and ultimately to strip itself, and the rest, of the authority altogether (towards the performative). No matter what the constative meanings are from the songs – and we have traced the articulations of a pastoral and traditional, open and cosmopolitan, high-tech futuristic, multi-vocal yet united and harmonious and, finally, a divine China – the increased importance of the performative allows for continuous mutations of meaning, propelling the proliferation of new and different meanings, some clearly oppositional, others parodic, or simply funny and light-hearted. Popular culture is, like all forms of culture, a field of contestation, a struggle over meaning. Under the condition of late-socialism in China, the official, authoritative rhetoric of official discourse is increasingly losing its power, despite its packaging in catchy pop songs in which multiple stars are involved. Instead, the performative dimension of communication is gaining importance, and we have used Yurchak's work to delve into this shift. With him, it is our contention that, in the context of late socialism in China, 'when authoritative discourse became hyper-normalized, its performative dimension grew in importance and its constative dimension became unanchored from concrete core meanings and increasingly open to new interpretations' (Yurchak 2005: 285).

It is important not to read this as something unique to China or to late-socialism. Elsewhere, Yurchak argues, together with Dominic Boyer, that a similar situation can be traced in the United States under current conditions of late liberalism. In their words, 'late liberalism today operates increasingly under discursive and ideological conditions similar to those of late socialism, and we argue that these conditions are contributing to the development of certain analogous political and cultural effects' (Boyer and Yurchak 2010: 181). Our analysis of the hollowing-out of authoritative discourse, the continuous evaporation of meaning, that enables the unfolding of a heteroglossic discourse is thus also relevant outside its Chinese context.

When we go back to Hong Kong and its fraught relationship with the mainland, what we have shown in this chapter is how the meanings of the songs that are used to construct a new and prosperous China immediately de-territorialize, and how Hong Kong plays a key role in this process of de-territorialization. It is our hope that Hong Kong will continue to capitalize on this in-between position, that it will mobilize its ability to give a twist to the production of Chineseness, to read the discourse of nationalism against the grain, to fiddle around with authoritative discourse, not necessarily instead of, but perhaps while, paying (lip-)service to Beijing. As paradoxical as it may sound, this requires not only the creative production of alternative culture, but also a direct involvement in the production of authoritative discourse.

Notes

1   http://en.beijing2008.cn/bocog/concepts/index.shtml, accessed on 13 June 2011.
2   http://www.aboluowang.com/ent/print.php?articleid=13740, accessed on 20 July 2011.
3   Here, we would like to add that one should be careful in celebrating the agency and creativity of YouTube users and their clips. In the words of José van Dijck, 'Users like "you", as I will argue, have a rather limited potential to "wrest power from the few", let alone to "change the way the world changes"' (2009: 42).

Chapter 7

MUSIC, DESIRE AND THE TRANSNATIONAL POLITICS OF CHINESENESS: FOLLOWING DIANA

Figure 7.1: Diana Zhu.

Born and bred in the Netherlands, Diana Zhu, at 15, won a Chinese singing contest in Amsterdam in 2006. Subsequently, she got a contract first from Warner Music Hong Kong, then from Warner Taiwan. Relocated to Shanghai, her parents' 'home' city, Diana was working on her hope for a future in the Chinese pop market. Taking our cues from Lash and Lury's method of 'following the object', we followed one person. We followed Diana and started to see her entanglement – particularly over her language, music and body – not only with Warner Music, but more fundamentally with the wider dynamics that seeks to configure and maintain a sense of hopefulness in the same Chinese society where inequality, injustice and inhumanity are threatening the 'harmonious society' the political establishment has been campaigning for (see for instance Pun 2005; Qiu 2009).[1]

In this final chapter, we aim to do two things. First, we will focus on the empirical insights drawn from this journey with Diana, particularly on the complex relationship between the diasporic, the popular and the political in contemporary China. Second, we will take this particular case study as an occasion to reflect on its wider methodological implications for conducting research on contemporary popular culture. In other words, this final chapter will serve, if you like, as a general methodological endnote to the rest of the book. If the preceding chapters and studies have appeared to be methodologically eclectic, or promiscuous, such eclecticism, such promiscuity is embedded in the continuing interrogation of certain methods', or any method's, claim to know truth, to represent reality other than being messy, confusing and disorderly (Law 2004). Eventually, we are seeking, attempting, and proposing ways of telling 'better stories about what's going on' (Grossberg 2010: 241).

Following Diana

Diana had a hope, a hope that later relocated her to China, to the local music industry, to a series of market-oriented practices that sought to package her to a better-selling product and weave her hope to the weft of a complex of economic and political interests not necessarily hers, not ours. This was how her hope was articulated:

> **Diana:** Whenever I was in Shanghai, I was happy. I told my grandfather, in Shanghai there were so many tall buildings, so many bright lights. I told him, in Shanghai, it felt like New Year everyday. In the Netherlands, only during Christmas would there be more lights. In any case, I liked Shanghai very much. It started when I was a child. I went there all the time.
> **Yiu Fai:** You said, in Shanghai, it felt like New Year everyday.
> **Diana:** Yes, really, I was very happy. I like to have a lot of people around me. In the Netherlands, I only see very few people.
> **Yiu Fai:** It's quiet.
> **Diana:** Yes, like at 5pm, everyone would go home and make dinner. And there is nobody in the street any more. I like to see people. That was after my first visit to Shanghai. Back in the Netherlands, I did a drawing for my class. I drew a girl holding a microphone, singing. I was six, or perhaps five. And then I told them that was Asia, I liked Asia. And my dad and mom came from China, and I was Chinese. I wanted to go back. To sing, I like singing.

We wondered: How would a young girl growing up in the Netherlands imagine and anchor her career hope in a Chinese locality? How would the Chinese cultural industries make it possible for her to realize such a transnational hope?

When we started this project, we were tempted by two sets of discourse: the diasporic and the popular, or, to be more precise, we were tempted by the promises they were whispering, somewhere from the fringes of hegemony. Embedded in metaphors of scattering and displacement, diasporic experience has long been conceptualized as living between homeland and hostland, and valorized from such metaphors to an archetype of identity negotiation, community construction and potential resistance (see for instance, Ma 2003; Shi 2005). From here, it is not surprising that studies that situate diasporic studies in the field of popular culture, for all its appeal to, identification by and possibilities of resistance for the people (Fiske 1989), share two common features.[2] First, they are mostly concerned with the struggles of diaspora in their hostland; second, they tend to focus on how diasporic subjects use popular culture in realizing their political potentials (see for instance, Naficy 1999; Yue 2009).

The current inquiry is a departure from, and supplement to, the aforementioned line of studies on diaspora and popular culture; it is neither confined to hostland problematics, nor framed by typical popular culture use perspective. Rather, in this so-called China Century where China is predominantly perceived as an emerging global power and transnational nationalism has become increasingly threatening (Ong 1999), it is imperative, for us, to locate the politics of diaspora in its engagement with this imaginary but powerful centre of Chineseness. In other words, we will take Diana as one of the various agents in the political site of popular music where the popular and the political is anything but contingent and contested.

At the same time, we also have to stay sensitive not only to what Diana actually does, what makes her do what she does, and what does it mean to her. Perhaps even more critically, we have to salvage what she does not do, or, put differently, what other forces may have done in containing other practices and experiences in virtuality. And all the stories, real and virtual, spoken and embodied, created and co-written, by Diana are waiting to be recuperated from her continuing entanglement with transnational cultural industries characterized by movement and circulation.

Taking our cues from Lash and Lury's method of 'following the object' (2007: 16), we would like to follow one person, in this case, Diana Zhu. Without situating ourselves in the thrust of their project, we share their urge to go beyond (media) representation and the foregrounding of movement, dynamic constitution between agents in cultural production, and finally their method. To follow the object, for Lash and Lury, is 'to consider the markets of the global culture industry as neither pre-given nor static, as neither simply global nor as a merely local, but as dynamically constituted by the movements, the biographies, of objects' (2007: 18–19). We believe we can do the same with a person.

In our journey with Diana, we must admit we were not totally ductile, pliable tourists in her landscape. One of us was part of her landscape. Yiu Fai Chow met Diana the first time at the finals of the Chinese singing contest held in Amsterdam. He was a member of the jury, in his capacity not as a researcher, but as a lyric writer for Chinese language pop music. In fact, before Chow met Diana, he had already heard of her. An A&R Manager of

Warner Hong Kong, Evelyn Yang (who was interviewed later for this project) called him one day to ask him if he knew this Chinese girl from the Netherlands. She got a demo sung by Diana. In the end, Diana won the singing contest. She was also Chow's favourite. He told Yang afterwards that Diana was worth a contract, forming, later he realized, part of the beginning of this case study. Intrigued by Yang's interest in recruiting a diasporic member and Diana's eagerness to relocate herself to the Chinese market, he started this project. And we also want to acknowledge the possible complex dynamics Chow might have with Diana, her family as well as the music professionals he subsequently talked to. He told Diana and her parents, for instance, about his confidence in her talents, when they asked him. He also told the Warner people his views of how to 'produce' Diana, again when they pressed for his views. Chow found it impossible to re-erect his academic boundaries when he believed they took him more as an insider, their colleague than as an outsider, a researcher. Above all, he felt trust and rapport.

Diasporic hope: Rewriting migration narrative

> This has become a knot in my wife's and my hearts, that is, we hope that Diana will be able to do what she likes to. I told my daughter, you don't have to work for money. I also told the president of Warner [Taiwan …] I told him, my daughter comes to Taiwan for music, not for money.[3]

Zhu Jun, Diana's father, was talking to Chow in quiet Purmerend, Diana's hometown before she left for Shanghai in 2009. Zhu, his wife, Wang Lei, and Chow were sitting in a spacious, luxuriously decorated house overlooking an impressive expanse of water, a house that exuded credibility to the kind of parental support Zhu articulated to their daughter. There had been harder times. Zhu and Wang boarded the plane from Shanghai to Amsterdam in 1989, shortly after they finished their studies respectively in drama and Peking opera. It was Zhu's decision to continue his studies abroad. He was not alone; in fact, many of their contemporaries – both Zhu and Wang were born in late 1960s – were determined in continuing their tertiary studies somewhere outside China. They would stay abroad at least for a few years, if not for good. According to Wang, 'we were the generation of our time [...] people of our generation went abroad the most.'

But the cultural scene of Amsterdam did not open up for the couple. In 1996, the migration narrative of Zhu and Wang was increasingly scripted by the dominant modernity narrative of China itself: earning money. They decided that year to open a company and since then their Sino-European trading business has secured them a comfortable life and their daughter the possibility of her own hope. Talking to Diana at a hotel complex transformed from a group of colonial mansions in the heart of Shanghai, Chow learned of her first glimpse of a different life in the form of a childhood drawing quoted in the excerpt at the beginning of this chapter. Diana continued to talk enthusiastically about the Shanghai she visited frequently during her growing up. 'It felt like New Year every day', she said repeatedly. While Diana's diasporic experience was an intimate part of her personal biography, it was enabled by her parents' economic capital and the life of a burgeoning coastal Chinese metropolis, themselves constituted by the so-called rise of China when China has become the world's factory, not only of capitalistic commodities but also of economic opportunities and fantasies. This particular imaginary of China is compelling us to read the relationship between China and Chinese diaspora differently. While China might be experienced and understood as an imagined homeland, grounded in memory and the past, it is in the process of being reconfigured into a homeland of hope and the future for its diasporic subjects and a 'transnational Chinese imagination' (Sun 2005). The drawing of Diana, a diasporic Chinese born in 1990, was one of the testaments to that radical change. And again, the drawing and the testament would have remained in the realm of virtuality, had the reality or the perception of it, in the Netherlands, opened up more cultural space for its new citizens.

A generation later, Diana's hostland remains largely the same as her parents', where younger Dutch-born Chinese, despite their generally favourable socio-economic conditions and perceived high degree of integration, continue to suffer from cultural invisibility, everyday racism and symbolic marginalization (Chow 2009). While the latest global wave of singing contest-cum-reality show, such as *Idols* or *X-Factor*, has been attracting hordes of mostly young participants with hopes for an entrance ticket to the popular music industry, in a predominantly white locality such as the Netherlands, those hopes seem to be only available for the culturally central, white population, as well as the black ethnicity, which, according to popular construction, is blessed with musicality. In the Dutch version of *Idols*, all the winners were either white or black, while Asians were only occasionally featured in the televised montage of audition fragments, mostly, like other candidates, as object of ridicule.[4]

It came as no surprise that while both Diana and her parents articulated the possibility of joining the Dutch *Idols* or *X-Factor*, in the end the singing contest she joined was the *European Chinese New Talent Singing Contest*. Occupying a space opened up by the diasporic struggle against such symbolic marginalization, the singing contest was initiated in 2003 by OrienTouch Entertainment, an Amsterdam-based company run by third-generation Chinese. On why he came up with such an idea, Kevin Chow, Managing Director of OrienTouch, told Chow in his Chinatown office this simple reason: 'I love singing and I love pop music from Hong Kong.' But he was quick to articulate a sense of hopelessness to transform that diasporic love into some sort of career in the Dutch national music industry. 'I don't think it's racial discrimination or whatever, but since you are a Chinese, even if you sing well, they won't sign you', Kevin said. He chose to anchor his singing contest on transnational possibility. For the brief span of its existence – the contest was suspended in 2007 due to lack of sponsors – the contest aimed to select a European representative to join the global Chinese singing contest organized annually by Hong Kong-based media group Television Broadcast Ltd. (TVB). Diana won the 2006 contest and went to Hong Kong for the global event. She did not win any titles, but a contract.

Musical hope: Rewriting modernity narrative

It started with a family friend who happened to hear Diana sing during one of his visits to her parents when the Zhu family was in Shanghai. He was so impressed that he made a simple demo of Diana's singing and sent it to record companies he knew of. Warner Hong Kong responded and arranged an interview with Diana and her father, when she was in town for the global Chinese singing contest. The interview resulted in an initial agreement, but it was only three years later, in 2009, that a final contract was signed – not with Warner Hong Kong, but Taiwan. On the one hand, the considerations involved in this time lapse and transfer could be seen as part and parcel of the realignment of Chinese popular music industries, where Hong Kong has been gradually replaced by Taiwan as the centre of global Chinese cool as well as producer of global Chinese pop stars.[5] On the other hand, they could also explicate the complex dynamics and cultural politics between the three localities – Hong Kong, Taiwan and mainland China. Before we engage with the considerations of Warner and the dynamics they were embedded in, we want to note the readiness shared by both the Hong Kong and Taiwan offices to launch a diasporic member into Chinese stardom.

Following Diana, Chow went to Hong Kong to talk to Evelyn Yang, former A&R Director, and Gordon Lee, Deputy Managing Director of Warner Hong Kong. Yang was the one who responded to Diana's demo while Lee decided to propose transferring Diana to Taiwan. In Taipei, Chow talked to Terry Leung, Creative Director of Warner Taiwan, who was handling Diana's project at the moment of fieldwork. Alongside the particularities of Diana, all three of them referred, in rather sweeping terms, positively to Diana's diasporic background, whether as an alternative musical upbringing, or, to quote Leung, an 'added value' in marketing strategy. They also noted the relatively higher EQ, or emotional intelligence, and the degree of determination embodied in a diasporic Chinese when she or he decided to leave their regular place of residence and pursue their career, both of which were prerequisites, these professionals claimed, for a successful career in the demanding music industry. This emphasis on personality reminded Chow of the sense of sympathy, almost guilt, that several other colleagues shared with him when they saw the emotional duress – paparazzi, nasty game shows, busy schedule – a young artist has to endure. No wonder in the last years, quite a few diasporic members were co-opted to the Chinese popular music industries such as Leehom Wang, Khalil Fong and MC Jin.

More fundamentally, we also see the signing of Diana as a corollary of smooth correspondence – and the beginning of contestation – between her own narrative and the Chinese modernity narrative. So far, Diana's musical hope was largely hers. Cast onto the broader backdrop of transnational Chinese imagination, her personal, diasporic narrative offered a positive episode in the Chinese modernity narrative. Coming from a good hard-working migrant family, a young diasporic member favoured her homeland above her hostland as the locality to pursue her aspirations; in short, Diana's narrative would feed the necessary nutrients to the officially endorsed Chinese modernity narrative of progress, upward mobility and transnational but Sinocentric Chineseness – indeed, China would be the new homeland of hope and future. Conflated with her potentials, as a pop star candidate, to guide, mould and contain popular (youth) desires and fantasies, Diana might function as a powerful symbol for officially sanctioned hopes, of the kind of possible better future that will justify any present hardship, inequality and injustice. Given the imbricate relationship between the state and market in the Chinese context, and the important task for such partnership to manage popular culture to the advantage of the political and capitalistic elite (Fung 2007), it was not surprising that a young diasporic Chinese star would be welcome to join the construction force of China's modernity narrative. And the packaging and marketing tactics imposed on Diana may be driven economically, but they were deeply political as well. However, as much as her diasporic and potential pop star status might be 'constructive', it could also become subversive. And those subversive potentials must be contained, but not without contestations. In the following, we will focus on the contestations in containing Diana's subversive potentials, when international capital started making demands on her hope. While Diana's trajectory brought us to Warner Hong Kong and Taiwan, the contestations must be projected onto the context where musical stars from Hong Kong and Taiwan continue to carve their symbolic position in mainland China.

Language

After tentatively agreeing to sign Diana, Warner Hong Kong's first demand on her was to learn Cantonese, the version of Chinese dominant in Hong Kong. According to Yang, their plan was to release Diana's debut record first in Hong Kong and after attracting a certain degree of attention, they would launch her to the rest of the Greater China region, that is Taiwan and mainland China. Although Diana was expected to sing in Mandarin Chinese, the dominant language used in the Chinese region, also the language she was trained at home, Yang asked her to learn Cantonese primarily for her local promotional activities. Pragmatic as it might sound, this demand was also made in the cultural dynamics where Cantonese was being 'increasingly marginalized'. During its heyday in 1970s to arguably 1990s when Cantonese popular music from Hong Kong was considered to be 'the sound of Chinese cool' (Burpee in Chu 2007: 2), Cantonese Chinese was being circulated among Chinese around the world as the fashionable and desirable version of Chinese. It is no longer the case (Chu 2007). (See a full discussion on the marginalization of Hong Kong pop music in Chapter 3.)

For that particular while, Cantonese was the only 'dialect' to contest with Mandarin Chinese, officially sanctioned both in mainland China and Taiwan, as signifier of authentic Chineseness (Mattar 2009).[6] Yang's demand on Diana to learn Cantonese could be seen as a way to disrupt these affiliations, and recuperate some traces of that subversive potential, of the possibility to interrogate – through mobilizing a different Chinese language, a southern tongue – a monolithic construction of Chineseness.[7]

But even in Mandarin, the contestation as to which version and thus which locality would represent authentic Chineseness continues. Subsequent to Yang's plan, her superior Lee considered the start of Diana's project in Hong Kong, a different linguistic environment, might be 'too tough for her'; he decided to propose a transfer to Warner Taiwan. One of the demands Taiwan office came up with was, again: language. Leung, recalling his first meeting with Diana, mentioned her Shanghai background. 'Probably because of that, her vocabulary, her pronunciation is somewhat mainlandish. Her accent. At that point, we did raise the possibility of asking her to move to Taiwan, to undo her mainland Chinese vocabulary and her mainland accent.' Leung's comment was noteworthy particularly in the context of the Chinese music market where like Hong Kong, local Taiwanese sales were declining drastically, forcing local record companies to focus increasingly on the mainland market. Instead of giving his approval to Diana's mainland linguistic inflection, Leung was actually trying to maintain a Taiwanese-centred take on Chinese. His demand on Diana to speak Chinese the Taiwanese way was in turn embedded in the older, historical context where the Chinese Nationalists still considered themselves the guardian of Cultural China, not the Communists.

Amidst all these negotiations in linguistic and cultural politics, Diana, with the support by her family, decided to suspend her studies in the Netherlands and moved to Shanghai in 2009. Both Warner Taiwan and Hong Kong agreed that such a move would help her improve her Chinese, despite their different stands on Cantonese and Mandarin. In that sense, Diana's situation is not unlike Ien Ang's experience, in China and elsewhere, when she was supposed to be fluent in Chinese because she looked Chinese (Ang 2001). Despite, or precisely because of, her diasporic background, Diana must learn her Chinese properly. While Ang ponders the possibility of diasporic Chinese resisting the dominant expectations of Cultural China to which they are supposed to belong, Diana, in conjunction with her parents and the record company, yielded to those expectations. In doing so, and again in view of her potential star status, Diana, as a diasporic subject, is not only caught in the negotiations of which Chinese she should learn to speak (better) and which centres of Chineseness she should ally with (more); more fundamentally, she is being cleansed of her subversive diasporic potentials that may open up the freedom not to speak Chinese, or, in other words, to do Chineseness differently.

Music

We used the term 'cleanse' here in response to Kwai Cheung Lo's observation of China's modernity construction project. In his study on web marriage game in China, Lo understands the popularity of that game in the context of China's dreams of 'achieving modernity through a consistent, dependable, controlled, and "clean" path', which was 'not simply in contrast to the old-fashioned, "dirty" industrialization and mechanical production but vis-à-vis the "excess", such as liberty, chaos, antagonism, corrupted lifestyle, and capitalist malaise brought on by modernization' (Lo 2009: 395–396). Following Diana, we realized that in the battlefield of hope, she was being placed in a weird, symbolic process of ethnic cleansing, the diasporic kind. Her subversive potentials as a diasporic subject, ready to be multiplied by her popularizing potentials as a pop star, were being cleansed to make way for, to paraphrase Lo, the 'clean' modernity China aspires to. While the web marriage game under Lo's scrutiny offers 'a social imaginary in which contemporary Chinese people picture their social existence in the unstable transitional moment' (Lo 2009: 396), the star-producing exercise of transnational capital in our inquiry may be designed to regulate, control and cleanse the existence of a particularly salient contemporary Chinese: Diana. This exercise will ultimately, if not deliberately, help stabilize the same transitional moment. In short, if Diana remains modern, but not too modern or not too much of the western version of modernity (Oza 2001), her potential Chinese fans will be more likely to hope for the desired modernity, for instance, the success logic, without aspiring for the undesirable modern and western values to start asking questions on that very logic. Next to language, Diana's music becomes another site of this hegemonic struggle.[8]

Recalling one of the reasons why she was interested in signing Diana, Yang highlighted her cultural background. 'I think her Dutch background, plus her Shanghai background, I think it's very compatible with the music and culture of this new era [...] Her thinking is Westernized, European. I think such background exudes a certain exotic touch in our Chinese market.' When Yang envisaged the musical direction of Diana, she was thinking of Diana's own preference for 'black music', and Yang would like to have more 'Western feeling' in her project. Indeed when Diana started going to singing lessons at the age of 13, she was learning gospel music from a 'black teacher' and her musical taste leaned towards black genres such as soul, R&B, hip-hop and jazz.

Now, when she was preparing for her debut in the transnational Chinese music industry, Diana started writing music that surprised even her own parents. 'When I checked my older compositions, they were all very European or American, also very black. I am afraid I have become too western', she said. And that fear might have been generated by her increasingly frequent encounters with Warner Taiwan. While Yang, of Warner's Hong Kong office, preferred to build on that western and black musical and cultural background of Diana's, Leung, of Taiwan office, was thinking quite differently: he believed her musical style needs to be 'rectified'. 'Because in the Chinese market, whether in Taiwan or mainland China, no way we can accept someone so Westernized, whether in appearance or musical style [...] People don't want to listen to someone with Westernized looks and vocals to sing Chinese songs.' In fact, since it was confirmed that Diana should be handled by Taiwan office, she was 'stopped' from singing western songs any more, as part of the effort to de-westernize Diana and her musical style.

Grounded in the capitalistic discourse of the music industry, this process of de-westernization, or what we called earlier diasporic cleansing, is in our view deeply political. On a more immediate level, this process seeks to disentangle Diana from any affiliation and therefore alliance with black music genres and their dominant imaginary of political struggles and revolt. While the empowering appeal of black genres to both ethnic youth in Europe (Solomon 2009) as well as to indigenous groups around the world (Alvarez 2008) suggests a shared sense of marginalization, de-territorialization and struggles for a better world, Diana, once inserted in the circuits of Chinese music industry, must keep a greater distance from such solidarity, and her music stripped of the potential of such solidarity. On a more fundamental level, this idea that Diana cannot be too westernized in her looks and music is both an acknowledgement of her diasporic background and, at the same time, prevention of its disruption to China's modernity narrative.

As a diasporic subject traversing here and there, Diana and her migration narrative insinuate the possibility of a Chinese subject be(com)ing modern and western at the same time. In that sense, she has the potential to collapse not only space, but also time: if the imagination of Chineseness is to include the diasporic, that is, not to be confined by the geographical delineation of China itself, the narrative of Chinese modernity, by extension, must be liberated from its reified uniqueness whether in spatial or temporal terms. A diasporic subject poses questions and ultimately threats to fixated ways of treating space and time, opening up to fluidity and circulation, and thus the necessity to see the relationship between China and the rest of the world in ways different from a temporal continuum or spatial distinction. Seen from this perspective, Diana and her future function as cultural icon can be understood as a battleground for different versions of modernity. If Diana and her migration narrative may become part of what Wagner calls 'modernity offensives from below', Warner Taiwan, by asking her not to look western or sing in a westernized manner, is realigning her more to 'modernity offensives from above' (Wagner 1994). If in language, Diana is being cleansed of her subversive diasporic potentials to do Chineseness differently, here in the process of reconfiguring her musical style and personae, she is pre-empted from doing modernity differently.

Body

Finally, following Diana in the pursuit of her hope brought us to another battlefield: her body. When Chow met her in Shanghai for an interview, it was the second time he saw her. What struck Chow was her loss of weight; compared to the first time when he saw her during the Chinese singing contest in summer 2006, less than three years ago, she looked categorically thinner. According to Diana, to slim down was the 'most important request' by Warner if she was to realize her music career in the Chinese market. During their first round of discussions, back in 2006, Diana, at 1.64 metres, weighed between '60 to 70 kg', she recalled. After putting herself in a strict dieting regime roughly a year and a half ago, Diana weighed 48 kg when Chow met her in Shanghai. Her target? '41 to 42 kg', she said.

Whatever the exact target weight was, that Diana must slim down was clear to everybody who was concerned with her music career. Kevin Chow, organizer of the Chinese singing contest in the Netherlands, was of the opinion if Diana wanted to go further, she needed to reduce weight. Summarizing the common view of Warner Taiwan and Hong Kong, Evelyn Yang noted, simply: 'In our business, you can't be fat.' While such comment may be generally applicable to aspiring stars, the negotiation on Diana's body is underwritten by a specific gendered paradox. On the one hand, a female, much more than a male, body is always conceived to be passive and malleable, something to be worked on, rather than to work with; on the other hand, a woman's body is always seen as the major, if not only, resource she can and should mobilize to realize her career, music or otherwise.

This gendered dimension becomes apparent if we take into account another, but male, diasporic music-maker, Khalil Fong. Born in Hawaii, Khalil followed his father, a professional drummer, around the world. After spending some time in Shanghai and Guangzhou, Khalil moved to Hong Kong in 1998, at the age of 15. In 2005, he released his debut album, a series of soul and R&B compositions performed in Mandarin, under Warner Hong Kong, and subsequently, similar to Diana, his production base was shifted to Taiwan. Partly because they were signed to the same label and partly because of their similar diasporic and musical backgrounds, all the Warner professionals Chow talked to mentioned Khalil as reference point – in fact, Evelyn Yang was one of the Khalil's producers in Hong Kong. However, for all the similarities between them, Khalil was launched radically different from Diana. If Diana's body has become hypervisible under all the disciplining gazes, Khalil's was rendered, literally, invisible. Warner Hong Kong decided to plug his songs without allowing the audience any glimpse of the performer – a highly unusual practice in the current music industry, which is deeply embedded in visual culture. Instead, all the attention was being diverted to Khalil's musical upbringing and talent.

Khalil's reference was probably the most extreme, but by no means atypical, of the marketing of diasporic male singers. While their bodies (face, figure, sartorial style etc.) remain important components in their show business, the more popular ones, such as Khalil and Leehom Wang, seem to owe their commercial and critical acclaim to their unusually rich musical upbringing and talent (see for instance Fung 2006). That a diasporic woman, Diana, must transform and conform her body to the dominant desirable versions of Chinese femininity in order to realize her musical hope, foregrounds, we will argue, the so-called crisis of Chinese men in contemporary China (Yi 2007), which can also be seen as a crisis of Chinese modernity, at least in two ways. On the one hand, in this globalizing era where Chinese men (and women) are exposed to greater flows of western cultural products, they are being subjected increasingly to struggles with western hegemonic masculinity (Chow 2008). On the other hand, the perceived threat of losing their masculinity creeps from the disjuncture where Chinese men are losing their physical advantages as labourer, and thus socio-economic edges, to women in this more globalized, modern time while clinging onto a presumably Chinese, patriarchal order of the pre-modern era.

Seen from this vantage point, Diana's weight management, taken in the more general obsession with idealized female body in contemporary Chinese societies,[9] seeks, not unlike the web marriage game in Kwai Cheung Lo's study, to 're-constitute shattered Chinese masculinity in a cushioned and imaginary yet virtual configuration' (Lo 2009: 396). As a diasporic subject, supposedly more rebellious, more independent, more modern, Diana offers added value to this salvage attempt; if a woman from the fringes of Chineseness is able and willing to surrender to the traditional order, there is no reason why Chinese women in the centre should resist. It is not only a control of the female body, but also the female will. In the final analysis, the disciplining of a potential female star to her physicality (body) is to place her outside Culture (mind), disenfranchizing her of the right to orthodox cultural articulation and construction, and in that sense, as we argue in Chapter 3, part of the masculinist attempt to rewrite culture without woman (Chow 1995).[10]

This empirical inquiry saw us follow Diana, from her sweet childhood dream to a battlefield of hopes, from how her aspirations were formed to how they were reformed. In between we realized we need to understand Diana's trajectory of hope as a correspondence between her migration narrative and China's modernity narrative. At the same time, we believe more research needs to be done on the site of hope management if we are to have a better grasp of what is going on in China and engage with its cultural politics. We need to understand how different social agents are negotiating and giving shape to dominant hopes in contemporary China. More specifically, the complex entanglement between Hong Kong and Taiwan; the gendering of hope; the consumption of hope; and in a general sense the correspondence between the migration and modernity narratives in the site of hope management, will all be urgent inquiries to be conducted in diasporic and cultural studies. So far, what we have witnessed was primarily an exercise of collaboration between the market and state ideology, to cleanse the subversive potentials of a diasporic subject, a woman and a candidate star. We need to continue. We need to continue following Diana because her narrative continues.

Methodological endnote

At the same time, we also want to take a pause, to have a moment of methodological reflection. As a supplement, or an endnote, to the empirical insights drawn from our method of 'following the person', we want to see what this journey has to offer to research methodology in studies of Hong Kong popular music in particular, and contemporary popular culture in general. Although our reflection is primarily based on this last study on Diana Zhu, we will revisit and retrieve examples from previous chapters to present and substantiate our appeal. In other words, we want to turn this book project into a process. Such a knowledge-making process, or what we would like to call a raw chronology of intellectual activities – done individually and specifically, undone as a whole – is to lay down a sort of raw text for potential readers to read between the activities, to draw attention to the nature of knowledge and knowledge production itself, and at least realize how contingent, incomplete and undone knowledge production is. It is our 'research narrative', our own account of how these pieces of research came to be the way they are (Lawler 2008: 47). After all, the act of knowing may be as messy as the reality it is supposed to know (Law 2004).

While our insights are drawn from this particular research narrative weaving from Hong Kong popular music, our appeal is more general: to reconfigure and study popular culture in its interface with these four dimensions – the flow, the bodily, the political and the personal. Before we go further, we want to insert two supplements. First, we find it imperative to put forward this suggestion not so much because it is new, but more because many inquiries on popular culture are still framed otherwise. Second, such reconfiguration is meant to interrogate and mess up the boundaries of the field rather than to clarify new ones.

The flow

Revisiting the studies included in this book, we have observed in our fieldwork and our own experience an increasing insertion of links, flows and networks across cultural contexts (Kim-Puri 2005). While the pop venue study (Chapter 5) was framed in a largely static manner by focusing the experience on Hong Kong, the comparative perspective assumed in the Dutch and Hong Kong fans study as well as in the China Wind study (Chapters 2 and 3) has gradually morphed through the sex photo scandal study and the Olympic songs study to its most explicit articulation in the Diana Zhu study, which was guided by movement and characterized by us as a journey, a trajectory. Whatever 'origin' the research objects might appear to have – sex photos by a Hong Kong-based star Edison Chen, theme songs created by Hong Kong-based music industry workers, or new talents handpicked by Hong Kong-based record labels – they travel, geographically, virtually and symbolically; and they travel for, through or with popular culture. They mutate and differentiate, in the process, till the next round of mutation and differentiation. To confine the studies with the marker 'Hong Kong' and thus align the scope of study according to the geographical boundaries of Hong Kong will be inadequate, if we are to understand how popular culture functions in our time. Commenting on globalization and area studies, Arjun Appadurai points to the 'world of flows' and its disjunctures with more stable social forms such as the nation-states (2000: 5).

Translating this understanding to the study of popular culture, we believe one urgent need is to go beyond not only nationally but also locally framed or centred studies. Such framing does not only run the danger of privileging, if not reifying the 'local'; more fundamentally it seeks to congeal and squeeze the more fluid cultural experience and identification under monolithic, weighty, freezing imaginaries, such as the Chinese. Following scholars on Chinese transnationalism (for instance, Ang 2003; Ong and Nonini 1997; Ma 2003; Sun 2005), we argue that insofar as popular culture is a manifestation and effect of globalization, it should best be understood in terms of flows and movements between here and there, and attention must be given to all the concomitant mutations and differentiations during such flows and movements. To extrapolate Lash and Lury's thinking on 'things' and contemporary cultural industry, this is to consider the use of popular culture as 'neither pre-given or static, as neither simply global nor as a mere local, but as dynamically constituted by the movements, the biographies' (2007: 18–19). We argue for the same dynamic constitution of the study of Hong Kong, or any 'local', popular culture.

The bodily

Connecting the studies in previous chapters to the last study on Diana Zhu and transnational Chinese popular music, we were compelled to notice our own inadequate attention to the bodily. While issues of visual representation as well as gender performance were covered in, for instance, our studies concerning the Hong Kong and Dutch pop stars Leon Lai and Marco Borsato (Chapter 2), the women in the Hong Kong China Wind video clips (Chapter 3) and the sex photo scandal (Chapter 4), they were not particularly examined in the context of the bodily. Our journey with Diana Zhu finally interpellated us to the embodied dimension of popular culture production. And from there we believe it would be illuminating if the bodily would have been inserted to our other studies in this book: say the tactile, sensory experience of audience in the pop venues studied in Chapter 5, or the collective singing sensation offered by the Olympic songs studied in Chapter 6. Although we maintain the value of the studies as they now stand, we would propose at this juncture the bodily as an important interface in our other studies on diaspora and popular culture, particularly in connection with gender. In explaining her use of stories, Donna Haraway expresses her wish to tell 'what I think is the truth – a located, *embodied*, contingent and therefore real truth' (Haraway 1997: 230, our italics).

The elision of the bodily is perhaps not that surprising if we take into account the fact that popular culture at large is seldom conceptualized and examined (also) as something embodied. It may even be understandable, given that theorizations and thus research methods on popular culture are overdetermined by concerns of identification, which are often articulated and constructed as structures of feelings, at most the affective, the experiential, not exactly the bodily. To flag up the bodily is of course not to suggest any non-ambiguous distinction between the bodily and other analytic categories – the affective, the experiential, the gendered, the classed, the aged and the virtual; rather, it is to draw attention to the importance of the bodily in its entanglement with the other analytic categories, and perhaps more.

The political

Studies of popular culture, for all its appeal to, identification by and possibilities of resistance for the people, often concern themselves with the possibilities of popular culture to realize its political potentials. Various chapters in this book, likewise, were intended to recuperate and reiterate that alliance of the popular and the political. We think it is an urgent and necessary project not only concerning Hong Kong popular culture, but popular culture at large, given the (symbolic) inequality, disenfranchisement and struggles many of us are living in. At the same time, the studies we conducted also show us the complicated developments of the resistance narrative, namely how popular culture can and does become the accomplice of the oppressive powers, the co-producer of hegemonic discourses and imaginaries. In Chapter 1, for instance, we have reflected, and cast doubt, on the tactics of Yiu Fai Chow's pop lyric writing to trouble dominant versions of Chineseness. In Chapters 3 and 6, we have examined how the popular music genre China Wind and how popular music professionals help construct and maintain dominant understandings of Chineseness. In the current case of Diana Zhu, we witness how the subversive potentials of a diasporic subject, a potential star, are being cleansed by the popular music industry in collaboration with the Chinese state.

These instances resonate with debates on popular culture and popular music, where the 'naïve assumption that the popular could "overcome" the nastiness of politics' is severely interrogated (Tsai 2007). In the more immediate sense, we believe there is a need to see popular culture not only as potential agents of resistance, but also of oppression. More structurally, we find it important to dismantle the default link of popular culture with resistance, relocating it, at least potentially, as part of a web of ideological control. To quote the Diana Zhu study again, a diasporic member is being disciplined to embody a particular version of hope that may be deployed to discipline the people of her perceived homeland. As Michel Foucault argues, 'with government it is a question not of imposing law on men, but of disposing things: that is to say, of employing tactics rather than laws, and even of using laws themselves as tactics – to arrange things in such a way that, through a certain number of means, such and such ends may be achieved' (1991: 95). Taking this notion of governmentality, it is necessary, we think, to ground the understanding of popular culture in what Toby Miller calls, in a different context, 'a longstanding issue of management – how to control populations' (2009: 90). In other words, the political question is not only about the resistance potentials of popular culture, but also about the collaboration of popular culture in the management system; or more concretely, how is popular culture being controlled, to control other populations? It is urgent, we believe, to see how popular culture may have contributed to the current conjuncture, where economic liberalism and (transnational) nationalism has become hegemonic in the Chinese one (Ong 1999; Lo 2009).

The personal

The last point we want to make is also an attempt to connect the three aforementioned points. Put simply, we find it increasingly useful, if not necessary, to take a person not only as the object but also the subject of study on popular culture. What we embarked on in Chapter 1 of this book, an autobiographical approach to examine Yiu Fai Chow's pop lyric-writing experience resumed in the biography-centred experiment we conducted in following Diana Zhu in this final chapter: we follow the person. In this final study, we argue, if a diasporic member can be understood as a subject inserted in geopolitics (Langellier 2010), it is also possible and necessary to see him or her as geopolitics inserted in a subject. If diasporic subjects are nomads, they are also monads. Without intending to engage with the whole philosophical discussion surrounding monadology (see, for instance, Leibniz 2008 [1714] or Taoist thinking), we venture here to assert the need to take not only diaspora but any user of popular culture in this globalized time as a monad, that is a unit, a single entity, a person, to index the plural, the population. In a more general sense, we argue for the need to think of the person as connecting the flow, the bodily and the political.

To follow a person is to concentrate on cultural flows embodied and converged, and locate the politics actualized in the person under research. As a method, it may have the benefit of sidestepping arbitrary and essentially static constructions such as local, national or regional confines, normally taken as the research field. Imagine we had done the Diana Zhu case differently, that we had taken the young Dutch-Chinese diaspora as a collectivity. We might then have chosen to study the diasporic cultural production in the form of a Dutch-Chinese singing contest. We might have focused on the geopolitical construction called the Netherlands and have drawn my insights in that context. We might have missed the geopolitics as inserted in the person of Diana. We might have missed the connection with, for instance, her and her parents' migration narrative. In a similar way, to follow a person may have the benefit of sidestepping other arbitrary conventions or research paradigms. In particular if we zoom in to the domain of popular culture, a monadic approach is also to address the critique towards studies on media and culture, namely that they run the risk of reifying their own importance, their centrality in people's lives (see, for instance, Couldry 2006). If one sets out to investigate the meaning of popular culture to its consumers, it is easy to exclude, perhaps unconsciously, the other aspects of their lives that may also be important in configuring their identities. A shift towards the person is also to open up the space, or some would call ecology or cosmology, to examine practices not necessarily or primarily linked to media or popular culture, such as, in this particular inquiry of Diana, language and body.

Driven by our biographies, by our engagements, by our understanding of the world we are living in, we want to insist on sustaining Hong Kong and its popular culture – whether on the levels of production, representation or consumption – in the research agenda of scholars concerned with Hong Kong, Chinese, Asian and global popular culture. Particularly in the post-1997 era where Hong Kong has been increasingly erased by the geographical-historical-political conflation of the Middle Kingdom and the People's Republic of China not only in terms of popular culture but also as sites of academic inquiry and knowledge production. However paradoxical it may sound, we want to keep on studying Hong Kong not as a unique site, but rather, as a site not essentially different from other localities. In short, we propose to study Hong Kong and its popular culture always and already in its entanglement in a complex transnational cultural web, in its dynamic interface with the flow, the bodily, the political and the personal.

Notes

1. 'Harmonious society' (*hexie shehui*), and the urgency to build a harmonious socialist society, was proposed by the Chinese President Hu Jintao when he became general secretary of the Communist Party in 2002. Since then, the term has been gaining currency both in political and popular discourses. While members of political elite often mobilize the term and its 'advantages' to silence dissident voices, it has become an almost vacuous or even satirical expression in popular discourses.
2. As if to underwrite the continuing thrust of thinking popular culture as resistance, a new Chinese-language book was just published detailing the protesting tradition in western popular music. See Chang 2010.
3. All our interviews were conducted in the language the interviewees preferred, either in Cantonese or Mandarin Chinese. They were recorded and transcribed verbatim. Translations to English were ours. Interviewees gave their explicit consent to recording and using their real names for this inquiry.
4. It is interesting to note that even in the United States, a nation proud of its democracy, of the American dream and melting pot multiculturalism, the single Chinese (and Asian, for that matter) candidate who managed to use the American version of *Idols* to launch a career in popular music was William Hung. Commenting on Hung's nerdishness, bad teeth and 'fresh-off-the-boat' accent, a number of observers have argued that his career was a sign of mockery, and that the media exploited him as a joke rather than as a musical talent (see for instance http://www.sfgate.com/cgi-bin/article.cgi?file=/gate/archive/2004/04/06/eguillermo.DTL).
5. For a more detailed account of the fall and rise of Hong Kong and Taiwanese pop, see Fung (2007).
6. The shift towards the use of Mandarin is also noticeable among diasporic Chinese communities, for instance, in Southeast Asia. Particularly indicative was the introduction of Speak Mandarin Campaign as early as 1979 by the Singaporean state, where other Chinese 'dialects' including Cantonese were officially disapproved (Bockhorst-Heng 1999).
7. We know of at least one pop radio station in Hong Kong adopting a (subtle) policy not to promote mandarin songs. For a discussion on Yiu Fai Chow's attempt as a lyric writer to interrupt the powerful totality of Chineseness by inserting a 'Southern' identification, see Chapter 1.
8. While drafting this chapter, Chow heard that the mainland censors have requested to change the title of a Mandarin Chinese song he penned himself, 'Go Downstream/下流'. The song, performed by the Hong Kong star Anthony Wong, invokes an image of going downstream, instead of upstream, proposing thereby a counter-narrative to the success logic of upward mobility. Go downstream, or *xialiu*, in Chinese, also suggests something indecent. The song was eventually released under a different title in mainland China.

9 To underline this obsession, a term 'career line' was recently coined and has been gaining currency in Chinese societies. Referring to the cleavage of woman's breasts, the term suggests, simply, the bigger the breasts, the deeper the cleavage, and the stronger the line, the more successful a woman's career.

10 One of the possible rewriting projects, we suspect, is to flatten diasporic experience to feed into the transnational Chinese nationalism. For instance, Leehom Wang, in his remix of 'Descendants of the Dragon', invoked the biography of his parents who moved from Taiwan to the United States and conflated their nostalgia with nationalistic sentiments embedded in this classic number. See a discussion on this particular song in Chapter 1.

Bibliography

Abbas, Ackbar (1997), *Hong Kong: Culture and the Politics of Disappearance*. Hong Kong: Hong Kong University Press.

—— (2001), '(H)Edge City: A Response to "Becoming (Postcolonial) Hong Kong"', *Cultural Studies*, 15:3–4, pp. 621–626.

Ali, Suki (2002), 'Friendship and Fandom: Ethnicity, Power and Gendering Readings of the Popular', *Discourse*, 23:2, pp. 153–165.

Alvarez, Luis (2008), 'Reggae Rhythms in Dignity's Diaspora: Globalization, Indigenous Identity, and the Circulation of Cultural Struggle', *Popular Music and Society*, 31:5, pp. 575–597.

Ang, Ien (2001), *On Not Speaking Chinese: Living between Asia and the West*. London and New York: Routledge.

—— (2003), 'Together-in-difference: Beyond Diaspora, into Hybridity', *Asian Studies Review*, 27:2, pp. 141–154.

Anthias, Floya (1998), 'Evaluating "Diaspora": Beyond Ethnicity', *Sociology*, 32:3, pp. 557–580.

Appadurai, Arjun (1996), *Modernity at Large*. Minnesota: University of Minnesota.

Arendt, Hannah (1958), *The Human Condition*. Chicago: University of Chicago Press.

Baranovitch, Nimrod (2003), *China's New Voices – Popular Music, Ethnicity, Gender, and Politics, 1978–1997*. Berkeley: University of California Press.

Barmé, Geremie (1999), *In the Red – on Contemporary Chinese Culture*. New York: Columbia University Press.

Baym, Nancy (2000), *Tune in, Log on: Soap, Fandom and Online Community*. London: Sage.

Berry, Chris (2000), 'If China Can Say No, Can China Make Movies? Or Do Movies Make China? Rethinking National Cinema and National Agency', in Rey Chow (ed.), *Modern Chinese Literary and Cultural Studies in the Age of Theory: Reimagining a Field*. Durham: Duke University Press, pp. 159–180.

Boomkens, Rene (2000), *$ign of the Times*. Amsterdam: Amsterdam University Press.

Bloch, Ernst (1988), *The Utopian Function of Art and Literature*. Cambridge, MA: MIT Press.

Bockhorst-Heng, Wendy (1999), 'Singapore's Speak Mandarin Campaign: Language Ideological Debates in the Imagining of the Nation', in J. Blommaert (ed.), *Language Ideological Debates*. Berlin and New York: Mouton de Gruyter, pp. 235–266.

Boyer, Dominic and Alexi Yurchak (2010), 'American Stoib: Or, What Late-Socialist Aesthetics of Parody Reveal about Contemporary Political Culture in the West', *Cultural Anthopology*, 25:2, pp 179–221.

Brown, Adam (ed.) (1998), *Fanatics! Power, Identity and Fandom in Football*. London: Routledge.

Brown, Jeffrey (1997), 'Comic Book Fandom and Cultural Capital', *Journal of Popular Culture*, 30:4, pp. 13–31.

Bryson, Bethany (1996), 'Anything but Heavy Metal: Symbolic Exclusion and Musical Dislikes', *American Sociological Review*, 61:5, pp. 884–899.

Buck-Morss, Susan (2004), 'Visual Studies and Global Imagination', *Papers of Surrealism*, 2.

Bull, Michael (2000), *Sounding Out the City – Personal Stereos and the Management of Everyday Life*. Oxford: Berg.

Butler, Judith (1990), *Gender Trouble: Feminism and the Subversion of Identity*. New York: Routledge.

Butler, Jeremy (1991), 'Introduction', in Jeremy Butler (ed.), *Star Texts: Image and Performance in Film and Television*. Detroit: Wayne State University, pp. 1–19.

Callahan, William A. (2005), 'Nationalism, Civilization and Transnational Relations: The Discourse of Greater China', *Journal of Contemporary China*, 14:43, pp. 269–289.

———. (2006), 'History, Identity, and Security: Producing and Consuming Nationalism in China', *Critical Asian Studies*, 38:2, pp. 179–208.

Cao, Hongpei (2006), 'Youshi Zhongguofeng Qishi'/'China Wind Blows Again', *Zhongguo Xinwen Zhoukan (China News Weekly)*, pp. 68–69.

Chan, Kwok Bun (2005), 'The Stranger's Plight, and Delight', *Social Transformations in Chinese Societies*, 1, pp. 191–219.

Chang, Tie Zhi (2010), *Shidai di zaoyin: cong dilun dao U2 de dikang zhiyin/Noise of the Times: The Protesting Sound from Dylan to U2*. Guilin: Guangxi Normal University Press.

Chen, Kuan-Hsing (2006), *Qu di Guo: Ya zhou de zuo wei fang fa/Towards De-Imperialization: Asia as Method*. Taipei: Xing ren.

Chen, Xin (2007), 'Huayu Yuetan Zhongguofeng Dapandian'/'China Wind in Chinese Language Pop World', *Guangbo Gexuan (Broadcast Music Choice)*, 25.

Cheung, Esther Mei-kwan (1997), 'Hui Gui Zhi Lu: ba shi nian dai yi lai xiang gang liu xing qu zhong de jia guo qing/The Return Trip: Sentiments of Home and Nation in Hong Kong Pop Music Since 1980s', in Stephen C. K. Chan (ed.), *Qing Gan De Shi jian: xiang gang liu xing ge ci yan jiu/The Practice of Affect: Studies in Hong Kong Popular Song Lyrics*. Hong Kong: Oxford University Press, pp. 45–74.

Chew, Matthew M. (2008). 'Reading Hong Kong Entertainment's Decline from the Bottom-up.' Paper presented at the First International Conference on Education and Popular Culture, Hong Kong Institute of Education, Hong Kong, 11–13 December.

Chi, Ching (1990), 'Tian wen', *Ci Hui/Lyrics Interflow* [No official English name. this is the name suggested by the editor], March: 2.

Chong, Gladys Pak Lei (2011), 'Volunteers as the "New" Model Citizens: Governing Citizens through Soft Power', *China Information*, 25:1, pp. 33–59.

Chow, Rey (1993), *Writing Diaspora: Tactics of Intervention in Contemporary Cultural Studies*. Bloomington: Indiana University Press.

—— (1995), *Primitive Passions: Visuality, Sexuality, Ethnography, and Contemporary Chinese Cinema*. New York: Columbia University Press.

—— (1998), *Ethics After Idealism: Theory, Culture, Ethnicity, Reading*, Bloomington. Indiana University Press.

—— (2000), 'Introduction: On Chineseness as a Theoretical Problem', in Rey Chow (ed.), *Modern Chinese Literature and Cultural Studies in the Age of Theory: Reimagining a Field*. Durham: Duke University Press, pp. 1–25.

Chow, Wah-shan (1990), *Consuming Culture: Image, Words and Music*. Hong Kong: Youth Literary Book Store.

Chow, Yiu Fai (2008), 'Martial Arts Films and Dutch-Chinese Masculinities: Smaller is Better', *China Information*, 22:2, pp. 331–359.

—— (2009a), 'Multicultural Schizophrenia: "You Are Different, You Are Chinese"', *Amsterdam Social Science*, 1:4, pp. 45–52.

—— (2009b), 'Me and the Dragon: A Lyrical Engagement with the Politics of Chineseness', *Inter-Asia Cultural Studies*, 10:4, pp. 544–564.

Chow, Yiu Fai and de Kloet, Jeroen (2008), 'Building Memories – a Study of Pop Venues in Hong Kong', *Berliner-China Hefte/Chinese History and Society*, 34, pp. 53–62.

—— (2011), 'Blowing in the China Wind: Engagements with Chineseness in Hong Kong's zhongguofeng Music Videos', *Visual Anthropology*, 24:1–2, pp. 59–76.

Chu, Stephen Yiu-Wai (1998), *A Study of Hong Kong Popular Lyrics: From the Mid-70s to the Mid-90s*. Hong Kong: Hong Kong Popular Lyrics Studies, 1997. Revised version. Hong Kong: Joint Publishing Co, 1998.

—— (2000), *Glorious Days: A Study of Hong Kong Popular Bands (1984–1990)*. Hong Kong: Infolink.

—— (2001), *A Study of the 'Chinese Songs Campaign' in Hong Kong*. Hong Kong: Infolink.

—— (2004), *A Study of the 'Original Songs Campaign' in Hong Kong*. Hong Kong: Bestever.

—— (2007), 'Before and After the Fall: Mapping Hong Kong Cantopop in the Global Era', *LEWI Working Paper Series*, 63. Hong Kong: David C. Lam Institute of East-West Study.

Chu, Stephen Yiu-Wai and Leung, Wai Sze (2011), *A Study of Post-1997 Hong Kong Popular Lyrics*. Hong Kong: Enlighten & Fish.

Chua, Beng Huat (2003), *Life is Not Complete Without Shopping*. Singapore: Singapore University Press.

Chun, Allen (1996), 'Fuck Chineseness: On the Ambiguities of Ethnicity as Culture as Identity', *boundary 2*, 23:2, pp. 111–138.

Ciecko, Anne (2011), 'Contemporary Meta-Chinese Film Stardom and Transnational Transmedia Celebrity', in S. H. Lim and J. Ward (eds), *The Chinese Cinema Book*. London, BFI: Palgrave Macmillan.

Cline, Cheryl (1992), 'Essays from Bitch: The Women's Rock Newsletter with Bite', in Lisa A. Lewis (ed.), *The Adoring Audience – Fan Culture and Popular Media*. London: Routledge, pp. 69–83.

Cohen, Stanley (1972), *Folk Devils and Moral Panics*. London: MacGibbon and Kee.

Couldry, Nick (2006), *Listening Beyond the Echoes: Media, Ethics, and Agency in an Uncertain World.* Boulder, CO: Paradigm Publishers.

Dai, Jinhua (2001), 'Behind Global Spectacle and National Image Making', *Positions*, 9:1, pp. 161–186.

Debord, Guy (1995 [1967]), *The Society of the Spectacle.* New York: Zone Books.

de Certeau, Michel (1984), *The Practice of Everyday Life.* Berkeley and Los Angeles: University of California Press.

de Kloet, Jeroen (2005a), *China with a Cut – Globalisation, Urban Youth and Popular Music.* Amsterdam: Amsterdam University Press.

—— (2005b), 'Sonic Sturdiness – The Globalization of "Chinese" Pop and Rock', *Critical Studies in Media Communication*, 22:4, pp. 321–338.

—— (2010), *China with a Cut: Globalization, Urban Youth and Popular Music.* Amsterdam: Amsterdam University Press.

de Kloet, Jeroen, Chong, Gladys Pak Lei and Wei, Liu (2008), 'The Beijing Olympics and the Art of Nation-State Maintenance', *China Aktuell – Journal of Current Chinese Affairs*, 2, pp. 6–36.

de Kloet, Jeroen and Chow, Yiu Fai (2000), 'Born on the First of July', in Third Crossroads Conference (the University of Birmingham), Birmingham, 21–25 June.

Dikötter, Frank (2003), 'The Discourse of Race in Modern China', in John Stone and Dennis Rutledge (eds), *Race and Ethnicity: Comparative and Theoretical Approaches.* Malden: Blackwell, pp. 125–135.

Dirlik, Arif and Zhang, Xudong (eds) (2000), *Postmodernism and China.* Durham: Duke University Press.

Donald, Stephanie Hemelryk (2010), 'Global Beijing – "the World" is a Violent Place', in Christoph Lindner (ed.), *Globalization, Violence, and the Visual Culture of Cities.* London: Routledge, pp. 122–134.

Duara, Prasenjit (1999), 'On Theories of Nationalism for India and China', in Tan Chung (ed.), *In the Footsteps of Xuanzang: Tan Yun-Shan and India.* New Delhi: Indira Gandhi National Center for the Arts, pp. 131–146.

Duits, Linda and Van Zoonen, Liesbet (2006), 'Headscarves and Porno-Chic', *European Journal of Women's Studies*, 13, pp. 103–117.

Dyer, Richard (1982), *Stars.* London: Routledge.

Edwards, Louise and Jeffreys, Elaine (eds) (2010), *Celebrity in China.* Hong Kong: Hong Kong University Press.

Ehrenreich, Barbara, Hess, Elizabeth and Jacobs, Gloria (1992), 'Beatlemania: Girls Jut Want to Have Fun', in Lisa A. Lewis (ed.), *The Adoring Audience – Fan Culture and Popular Media.* London: Routledge, pp. 84–106.

Eperjesi, John R. (2004), 'Crouching Tiger, Hidden Dragon: Kung Fu Diplomacy and the Dream of Cultural China', *Asian Studies Review*, 28, pp. 25–39.

Erni, John Nguyet (2001), 'Like a Postcolonial Culture: Hong Kong Re-Imagined', *Cultural Studies*, 15:3–4, pp. 389–418.

—— (2007), 'Gender and Everyday Evasions: Moving with Cantopop', *Inter-Asia Cultural Studies*, 8:1, pp. 86–105.

Fang, Wenshan (2008), *Zhongguofeng: Gecilide Wenzi Youxi/China Wind: Word Games in Lyrics*. Taipei: Firstman Group.

Farmer, Brett (2009), 'Crossing the Line: Reading the Edison Chen Scandal', *Journal of Chinese Cinemas*, 3, pp. 73–77.

Fast, Susan (2006), 'Popular Music Performance and Cultural Memory. Queen: Live Aid, Wembley Stadium, July 13, 1985', in Ian Inglis (ed.), *Performance and Popular Music: History, Place, and Time*. London: Ashgate, pp. 138–154.

Fiske, John (1989), *Understanding Popular Culture*. Boston, MA: Unwin Hyman.

—— (1992), 'The Cultural Economy of Fandom', in Lisa A. Lewis (ed.), *The Adoring Audience – Fan Culture and Popular Media*. London: Routledge, pp. 30–49.

Foucault, Michel (1979), *Discipline and Punish: The Birth of the Prison*. New York: Vintage.

—— (1991), 'Governmentality', in G. Burchell, C. Gordon and P. Miller (eds), *The Foucault Effect: Studies in Governmentality*. Chicago: University of Chicago Press, pp. 87–104.

—— (2000[1982]), 'The Subject and Power', in James D. Faubion (ed.), *Michel Foucault – Power*. New York: The New Press, pp. 326–348.

Frith, Simon (1998), *Performing Rites: On the Value of Popular Music*. Cambridge: Harvard University Press.

Fung, Anthony (2001), 'What Makes the Local? A Brief Consideration of the Rejuvenation of Hong Kong Identity', *Cultural Studies*, 15:3–4, pp. 591–601.

—— (2007), 'The Emerging (National) Popular Music Culture in China', *Inter-Asia Cultural Studies*, 8:3, pp. 425–437.

—— (2008), 'Western Style, Chinese Pop: Jay Chou's Rap and Hip-Hop in China', *Asian Music*, 39:1, 69–80.

—— (2009a), 'Fandom, Youth and Consumption in China', *European Journal of Cultural Studies*, 12:3, pp. 285–303.

—— (ed.) (2009b), *Riding a Melodic Tide: The Development of Cantopop in Hong Kong*. Hong Kong: Subculture Press.

Fung, Anthony, and Curtin, Michael (2002), 'The Anomalies of Being Faye (Wong): Gender Politics in Chinese Popular Music', *International Journal of Cultural Studies*, 5:3, pp. 263–290.

Fung, Lai Chi (2006), 'Huayu liuxingqu yunniang di xinfengbao/New Storm Brewing Up in Chinese-langauge Pop', *Cashflow*, pp. 2–5.

Gaonkar, Dilip P. (ed.) (2001), *Alternative Modernities*. Durham, NC: Duke University Press.

Giles, David (2002), 'Parasocial Interaction: A Review of the Literature and a Model for Future Research', *Media Psychology*, 4, pp. 279–305.

Goode, Erich and Ben-Yehuda, Nachman (1994), *Moral Panics: The Social Construction of Deviance*. Oxford: Blackwell.

Gries, Peter Hays (2004), *China's New Nationalism: Pride, Politics, and Diplomacy.* Berkeley: University of California Press.

Groenewegen, Jeroen (2011), 'The Performance of Identity in Chinese Popular Music'. Unpublished Ph.D. Dissertation. Leiden University Institute for Area Studies, Faculty of Humanities, Leiden University.

Grossberg, Lawrence (1991), 'Is There a Fan in the House?: The Affective Sensibility of Fandom', in Lisa A. Lewis (ed.), *The Adoring Audience: Fan Culture and Popular Media.* London and New York: Routledge, pp. 50–67.

—— (2010), 'On the Political Responsibilities of Cultural Studies', *Inter-Asia Cultural Studies*, 11:2, pp. 241–247.

Hage, Ghassan (2003), *Against Paranoid Nationalism: Searching for Hope in a Shrinking Society.* Annandale: Pluto Press.

Hall, Stuart (1992), 'The Question of Cultural Identity', in Stuart Hall, David Held and Tony McGrew (eds), *Modernity and Its Futures.* Cambridge: Polity Press, pp. 273–316.

—— (1996), 'Cultural Studies and Its Theoretical Legacies', in David Morley and Chen Kuan-Hsing (eds), *Critical Dialogues in Cultural Studies.* New York and London: Routledge, pp. 262–275.

Hall, Stuart, Critcher, Chas, Jefferson, Tony, Clarke, John and Roberts, Brian (eds) (1978), *Policing the Crisis – Mugging, the State, and Law and Order.* New York: Holmes and Meier Publishers.

Hannerz, Ulf (1987), 'The World in Creolisation', *Africa*, 57:4, pp. 546–559.

Haraway, Donna (1997), *Modest_Witness@Second_Millennium. FemaleMan©_Meets_ OncoMouse™.* New York: Routledge.

Harootunian, Harry D. (2000), *History's Disquiet: Modernity, Cultural Practice, and the Question of Everyday Life.* New York: Columbia University Press.

Hardt, Michael and Negri, Antonio (2000), *Empire.* Cambridge: Harvard University Press.

Harvey, David (2000), *Spaces of Hope.* Edinburgh: Edinburgh University Press.

He, Wenzhao (2008), 'Excerpts from an Interview with Ai Weiwei: Proving Itself Amidst Absurdity', in Rui Huang (ed.), *Beijing 798 – Reflections on 'Factory' of Art.* Chengdu: Sichuan Fine Arts Publishing House, pp. 38–41.

Hebdige, Dick (1979), *Subculture: The Meaning of Style.* London: Methuen.

Hershatter, Gail (2007), *Women in China's Long Twentieth Century.* Berkeley: University of California Press.

Hesmondhalgh, David (2002), *The Cultural Industries.* Thousand Oaks: Sage.

Hesmondhalgh, David, and Baker, Sarah (2011), *Creative Labour: Media Work in Three Cultural Industries.* London: Routledge.

Hills, Matt (2002), *Fan Cultures.* London: Routledge.

Hinerman, Stephen (ed.) (1992), 'I'll Be Here With You: Fans, Fantasy and the Figure of Elvis', in Liza A. Lewis (ed.), *The Adoring Audience – Fan Culture and Popular Media.* London: Routledge, pp. 107–134.

Ho, Josephine C.J. et al. (2008), 'Edison Chen's Sex Photos and Internet Policing: "Society Must Be Defended?"', *Taiwan: A Radical Quarterly in Social Studies*, 70, pp. 335–378.

Ho, Wai-chung (2000), 'The Political Meaning of Hong Kong Popular Music: A Review of Sociopolitical Relations between Hong Kong and the People's Republic of China since the 1980s', *Popular Music*, 19:3, pp. 341–353.

―――― (2003), 'Between Globalisation and Localisation: A Study of Hong Kong Popular Music', *Popular Music*, 22:2, pp. 143–157.

Hodkinson, Paul (2002), *Goth – Identity, Style and Subculture*. Oxford: Berg Publishers Ltd.

Hou, Dejian (1983), 'Look at Chinese People's Tomorrow', *Youth Weekly*, 13:16.

Hughes, Christopher R. (2006), *Chinese Nationalism in the Global Era*. London: Routledge.

Jacobs, Katrien (2009), 'Sex Scandal Science in Hong Kong', *Sexualities*, 12, pp. 605–612.

Jancovich, Mark (2002), 'Cult Fictions: Cult Movies, Subcultural Capital and the Production of Cultural Distinctions', *Cultural Studies*, 16:2, pp. 306–322.

Jenkins, Henry (1992), *Textual Poachers: Television Fans and Participatory Culture*. New York: Routledge.

Jenson, Joli (1992), 'Fandom as Pathology: The Consequence of Characterisation', in Liza A. Lewis (ed.), *The Adoring Audience: Fan Culture and Popular Media*. London: Routledge, pp. 9–29.

Kagan, Alan L. (1963), 'Music and the Hundred Flowers Movement'. *Musical Quarterly*, 49, pp. 417–430.

Khiun, Liew Kai (2003), 'Limited Pidgin-Type Patois? Policy, Language, Technology, Identity and the Experience of Cantopop in Singapore', *Popular Music*, 22:2, pp. 217–233.

Kim, Hyun Mee (2004), 'Feminization of the 2002 World Cup and Women's Fandom', *Inter-Asia Cultural Studies*, 5:1, pp. 42–51.

Kim-Puri, H. J. (2005), 'Conceptualizing Gender-Sexuality-State-Nation: An Introduction.' *Gender & Society*, 19:2, pp. 137–159.

Killingbeck, Donna (2001), 'The Role of Television News in the Construction of School Violence as a "Moral Panic"', *Journal of Criminal Justice and Popular Culture*, 8, pp. 186–202.

Kooijman, Jaap (2008), *Fabricating the Absolute Fake – America in Contemporary Pop Culture*. Amsterdam: Amsterdam University Press.

Kouwenhoven, Frank (1997), 'Barbarian Pipes Forever: Some Thoughts on Chinese Culture and Nationalism', *Chime, Newsletter of the European Foundation for Chinese Music Research*, pp. 3–7.

Lacourse, Eric, Claes, Michel and Villeneuve, Martine (2001), 'Heavy Metal Music and Adolescent Suicidal Risk', *Journal of Youth and Adolescence*, 30:3, pp. 321–332.

Lan, Wei (2007), 'Zhongguofeng Jingyan Taiwan Nanyang Liuxingqu Zhongguo Yuanxu Juqi'/'China Wind Sweeps through Taiwan and Nanyang, the Rise of Chinese Elements', *Yazhou Zhoukan/Asiaweek*, 22 July 2007.

Lancaster, Kurt and Jenkins, Henry (2001), *Interacting with 'Babylon 5': Fan Performances in a Media Universe*. Austin: University of Texas Press.

Landsberger, Stefan (2009), 'Harmony, Olympic Manners and Morals – Chinese Television and the "New Propaganda" of Public Service Advertising', *European Journal of East Asian Studies*, 8:2, pp. 329–353.

Langellier, Kristin M. (2010), 'Performing Somali Identity in the Diaspora: "Wherever I go I know who I am"', *Cultural Studies*, 24:1, pp. 66–94.

Lash, Scott and Lury, Celia (2007), *Global Culture Industry: The Mediation of Things*. Cambridge: Polity Press.

Law, John (2004), *After Method: Mess in Social Science Research*. Abington, New York: Routledge.

Lawler, Steph (2008), 'Stories and the Social World', in M. Pickering (ed.), *Research Methods for Cultural Studies*. Edinburgh: Edinburgh University press, pp. 32–49.

Lee, Gregory B. (2002), *China Unlimited: Making the Imaginaries of China and Chineseness*. London and New York: Routledge.

Lee, Samuel (2002), 'East Asia is Crazy over Taiwanese Pop Stars Such as Jay Chou as Cantopop Fades Fades Away', in *The Strait Times Interactive*, http://www.asiawind.com/forums/read.php?f=2&i=1482&t=1482&v=t., accessed 8 June 2008.

Leibniz, Gottfried (2008 [1714]), *The Monadology*, translated from French by R. Latta, Forgotten Books.

Leung, Helen Hok-Sze (2001), 'Queerscapes in Hong Kong Cinema', *Positions*, 9:2, pp. 423–448.

Leung, Maggi Wai-Han (2004), *Chinese Migration in German: Making Home in Transnational Space*. London and Frankfurt am Main.

Leung, Helen Hok-sze (2008), *Undercurrents – Queer Culture and Postcolonial Hong Kong*. Vancouver: University of British Columbia Press.

Lewis, Lisa (ed.) (1992), *The Adoring Audience – Fan Culture and Popular Media*. London: Routledge.

Li, Siu Leung (2003), *Cross-Dressing in Chinese Opera*. Hong Kong: Hong Kong University Press.

Lim, Song-hwee (2006), 'Celluloid Comrades: Representations of Male Homsexuality', in *Contemporary Chinese Cinemas*. Honolulu, HI: University of Hawai'i Press.

Ling, Sihua (2005), 'Listen to Tatming's Song and Feel the Handover Pain', *Epoch Times*, http://www.epochtimes.com/b5/5/12/11/n1150061.htm, accessed on 6 February 2007.

Lo, Kwai-Cheung (2009), 'The Web Marriage Game, the Gendered Self, and Chinese Modernity', *Cultural Studies*, 23:3, pp. 381–403.

Lok, Fung (1995), *The Fin de Siecle City: A Study of Hong Kong Pop Lyrics*. Hong Kong: Oxford University Press.

Ma, Eric Kit-wai (2012), *Desiring Hong Kong, Consuming South China – Transborder Cultural Politics, 1970–2010*. Hong Kong: Hong Kong University Press.

Ma, Laurence J. C. (2003), 'Space, Place and Transnationalism in the Chinese Diaspora', in L. J. C. Ma and C. Cartier (eds), *The Chinese Diaspora: Place, Space, Mobility and Identity*. Landham, MD: Rowman and Littlefield.

Ma, Laurence J. C. and Cartier, Carolyn L. (eds) (2003) *The Chinese Diaspora: Space, Place, Mobility, and Identity*. Lanham, MD: Rowman and Littlefield Publishers.

Mattar, Yasser (2009), 'Popular Cultural Cringe: Language as Signifier of Authenticity and Quality in the Singaporean Popular Music Market', *Popular Music*, 28:2, pp. 179–195.

McIntyre, Bryce. T., Sum, Christine C. W. and Weiyu, Zhang (2002), 'Cantopop: The Voice of Hong Kong', *Journal of Asian Pacific Communication*, 12:2, pp. 217–243.

McRobbie, Angela (1997), 'The Es and the Anti-Es: New Questions for Feminism and Cultural Studies', in M. Ferguson and P. Golding (eds), *Cultural Studies in Question*. London: Sage.

Mendelsohn, Andrew L. (2007), 'On the Function of the United States Paparazzi: Mosquito Swarm or Watchdogs of Celebrity Image Control and Power', *Visual Studies*, 22, pp. 169–183.

Miller, Toby (2009), 'From Creative to Cultural Industries', *Cultural Studies*, 23:1, pp. 88–99.

Miyazaki, Hirokazu (2004), *The Method of Hope*. Stanford, CA: Stanford University Press.

Morley, David (2001), 'Belongings – Place, Space and Identity in a Mediated World', *European Journal of Cultural Studies*, 4:4, pp. 425–448.

Morris, Meaghan (1997), 'A Question of Cultural Studies', in Angela McRobbie (ed.), *Back to Reality? Social Experience and Cultural Studies*. Manchester: Manchester University Press, pp. 36–57.

Morris, Meaghan and Wright, Handel K. (2009) 'Introduction: Transnationalism and Cultural Studies', *Cultural Studies*, 23:5–6, pp. 689–693.

Moskowitz, Marc L. (2010), *Cries of Joy, Songs of Sorrow: Chinese Pop Music and Its Cultural Connotations*. Honolulu: University of Hawaii Press.

Naficy, Hamid (ed.) (1999), *Home, Exile, Homeland: Film, Media, and the Politics of Place*. New York: Routledge.

Nash, Rex (2001), 'English Football Fan Groups in the 1990s: Class, Representation and Fan Power', *Soccer and Society*, 2:1, pp. 39–58.

Negus, Keith (1999), *Music Genres and Corporate Cultures*. London: Routledge.

Nyiri, Pal, Zhang, Juan and Varral, Merriden (2010), 'China's Cosmopolitan Nationalists: Heroes and "Traitors" of the 2008 Olympics', *The China Journal*, 63, pp. 25–55.

Nora, Pierre (1989), 'Between Memory and History: Les Lieux de Memoire' (trans. Marc Roudebush), *Representations*, 26, pp. 7–25.

Ong, Aihwa (1999), *Flexible Citizenship: The Cultural Logics of Transnationalism*. Durham, NC: Duke University Press.

Ong, Aihwa and Nonini, Donald M. (1997), *Ungrounded Empires: The Cultural Politics of Modern Chinese Transnationalism*. London: Routledge.

Oza, Rupal (2001), 'Showcasing India: Gender, Geography, and Globalization', *Signs: Journal of Women in Culture and Society*, 26:4, pp. 1067–1095.

Pickering, Michael (2008), 'Introduction', in Michael Pickering (ed.), *Research Methods for Cultural Studies*. Edingburgh: Edinburgh University Press, pp. 1–14.

Pieke, Frank N. and Benton, Gregor (1995), 'Chinese in the Netherlands', *Leeds East Asia Papers*, 27, Leeds, Department of East Asian Studies, University of Leeds.

Pink, Sarah (2008), 'Analysing Visual Experience', in Michael Pickering (ed.), *Research Methods for Cultural Studies*. Edinburgh: Edinburgh University Press, 2008, pp. 125–149.

Pollock, Della (1998), 'Introduction: Making History Go', in D. Pollock (ed.), *Exceptional Spaces: Essays in Performance and History*. Chapel Hill: UNC Press, pp. 1–47.

Pun, Ngai (2005), *Made in China: Women Factory Workers in a Global Workplace*. North Carolina: Duke University Press.

Qiu, Jack Linchuan (2009), *Working-Class Network Society: Communication Technology and the Information Have-less in Urban China*. Cambridge, MA: MIT Press.

Rancière, Jacques (2004), *The Politics of Aesthetics*. London: Continuum.

Rijkschroeff, Boudewijn (1998), *Etnisch Ondermemerschap. De Chinese Horecasector in Nederland en de Verenigde Staten van Amerika/Ethnic Entrepreneurship: The Chinese Hotel, Restaurant and Catering Sector in the Netherlands and USA*. Capelle a/d Ljssel: Labyrinth.

Ritzer, George (2000), *The McDonalidisation of Society*. Thousand Oaks: Pine Forge Press.

Rorty, Richard (1999), *Philosophy and Social Hope*. London: Penguin Books.

Sandig, Barbara and Selting, Margret (1997), 'Discourse Styles', in T. van Dijk (ed.), *Discourse as Structure and Process*. London: Sage, pp. 138–156.

Sassen, Saskia (2001), *The Global City – New York*. London, Tokyo, Princeton: Princeton University Press.

—— (2006), *Territory – Authority – Rights – from Medieval to Global. Assemblages*, Princeton: Princeton University Press.

Scheel, Karen R. and Westeveld, John S. (1999), 'Heavy Metal Music and Adolescent Suicidality: An Empirical Observation', *Adolescence*, 34:134, pp. 253–273.

Scott, James C. (1990), *Domination and the Arts of Resistance – Hidden Transcripts*. New Haven: Yale University Press.

Shi, Yu (2005), 'Identity Construction of the Chinese Diaspora, Ethnic Media Use, Community Formation, and the Possibility of Social Activism', *Continuum*, 19:1, pp. 55–72.

Solomon, Thomas (2009), 'Berlin-Frankfurt-Istanbul: Turkish Hip-Hop in Motion', *European Journal of Cultural Studies*, 12:5, pp. 505–527.

Stack, Steven (2000), 'Blues Fans and Suicide Acceptability', *Death Studies*, 24:3, pp. 223–231.

Steedman, Carolyn Kay (1986), *Landscape for a Good Woman: A Story of Two Lives*. New Brunswick, NJ: Rutgers University Press.

Steinberg, Michael P. (1996), *Walter Benjamin and the Demands of History*. New York: Cornell University Press.

Stenger, Josh (2006), 'The Clothes Make the Fan: Fashion and Online Fandom when Buffy the Vampire Slayer Goes to eBay', *Cinema Journal*, 45:4, pp. 26–44.

Stokes, Martin (2004), 'Music and the Global Order', *Annual Review of Anthropology*, 33, pp. 47–72.

Sun, Wanning (2005), 'Media and the Chinese Diaspora Community, Consumption, and Transnational Imagination', *Journal of Chinese Overseas*, 1:1, pp. 65–86.

Szeto, Wah (2005), 'Don't Twist Any History', *Apple Daily*, 19 April: E13.

Tsai, Eva (2007), 'Caught in the Terrains: An Inter-Referential Inquiry of Trans-Border Stardom and Fandom', *Inter-Asia Cultural Studies*, 8:1, pp. 137–156.

Tu, Weiming (1994), 'Cultural China: The Periphery as the Centre', in Weiming Tu (ed.), *The Living Tree: The Changing Meaning of Being Chinese Today*. Stanford, CA: Stanford University Press, pp. 1–30.

Tuohy, Sue (2001), 'The Sonic Dimensions of Nationalism in Modern China: Musical Representation and Transformation', *Ethnomusicology*, 45:1, pp. 107–131.

Upton, Janet (2002), 'The Politics and Poetics of Sister Drum: "Tibetan" Music in the Global Market Place', in Timothy C. Craig and Richard King (eds), *Global Goes Local: Popular Culture in Asia*. Vancouver and Toronto: University of British Columbia Press, pp. 99–119.

van Dijck, José (2009), 'Users Like You? Theorizing Agency in User-Generated Content', *Media, Culture and Society*, 31:1, pp. 41–58.

Van Zoonen, Liesbet (1994), *Feminist Media Studies*. London: Sage.

Visser, Robin (forthcoming), 'Coming of Age in RMB City', in Jereon de Kloet and L. Scheen (eds), *Spectacle and the City – Urbanity in Popular Culture and Art in East Asia*. Amsterdam: Amsterdam University Press.

Wagner, Peter (1994), *A Sociology of Modernity. Liberty and Discipline*. London, New York: Routledge.

Wang, Chi-ming (2004), 'Capitalizing the Big Man: Yao Ming, Asian America, and the China Global', *Inter-Asia Cultural Studies*, 5:2, pp. 263–278.

Wang, Dan (2008), 'Ouyunhui Shi Zhouyaojing: Mishi Zai Jiti Kuangrezhong de Lin Xi'/'Olympic Games Is a Magic Mirror: Lin Xi Lost in the Collective Hysteria', http://www.aboluowang.com/ent/print.php?articleid=13740, accessed 20 July 2011.

Wang, Jing (1996), *High Culture Fever – Politics, Aesthetics, and Ideology in Deng's China*. Berkeley: University of California Press.

Wang, Peiwen (2007), 'Fang Wenshan Zhongguofeng Geci Chuangzuode Fugu Yu Chuanxin'/'Restoration and Innovation in Fang Wenshan's China Wind Lyrics', *Jiaoyu yanjiu/Educational Study*, 2:2, pp. 50–53.

Watson, Sophie (2006), *City Publics: The (Dis) Enchantments of Urban Encounters*. London: Routledge.

Williamson, Milly (2005), *The Lure of the Vampire: Gender, Fiction and Fandom From Bram Stoker to Buffy*. London: Wallflower Press.

Witzleben, Lawrence J. (1999), 'Cantopop and Mandopop in Pre-postcolonial Hong Kong: Identity Negotiation in the Performances of Anita Mui Yim-fong', *Popular Music*, 18:2, pp. 241–258.

Wolf, Eric R. (1990), 'Distinguished Lecture: Facing Power – Old Insights, New Questions', *American Anthropologist*, 92, pp. 586–596.

Wong Chi Wah (2006[1990]), *Four Decades of Cantopop*. Hong Kong: Joint Publishing Co.

Wong, Chi Wah, Chu, Stephen Yiu-Wai and Leung, Wai Sze (2010), *The Way of the Hong Kong Lyricists*. Hong Kong: Infolink.

Wong, Elvin Chi Chung (1989), 'Emergence of Post-June 4th Culture: Ask "Tian Wen"', *Contemporary Affairs Weekly*, 5, 23 December, p. 35.

—— (2007), *Liu Sheng*. Hong Kong: Home Affairs Department.

Wong, Isabel K. F. (1984), 'Geming Gequ: Songs for the Education of the Masses', in Bonnie S. McDougall (ed.), *Popular Chinese Literature and Performing Arts in the People's Republic of China*. Berkeley: University of California Press, pp. 112–143.

Wong, James (2003), 'The Rise and Decline of Cantopop: A Study of Hong Kong Popular Music', Ph.D. Thesis, University of Hong Kong.

Wright, Handel Kashope (2003), 'Cultural Studies as Praxis: (Making) an Autobiographical Case', *Cultural Studies*, 17:6, pp. 805–822.

Yang, Ruiqing (2000), '100 Years of Songs with Minzu Character', *The New Voice of Yue-fu*, pp. 32–34.

Yarar, Betul (2008), 'Politics of/and Popular Music: An Analysis of the History of Arabesk Music from the 1960s to the 1990s in Turkey', *Cultural Studies*, 22:1, pp. 35–79.

Yi, Zhong-tian (2007), *Zhongguo de Nanren he Nuran/China's Men and Women*. Hong Kong: Joint Publishing.

Yue, Ming-Bao (2009), 'Beyond Ethnicity, Into Equality', *Cultural Studies*, 23:5, pp. 775–794.

Yurchak, Alexei (2005), *Everything Was Forever, until It Was No More*. Princeton and Oxford: Princeton University Press.

Zeng, Guohua (forthcoming), 'The Making of China: The Construction of Chineseness during the Beijing Olympics and its Discontents', Ph.D. Thesis, Amsterdam: University of Amsterdam.

Zhang, Chaowei (2003), *Shuizai Nabian Chang Zijide Ge: Taiwan Xiandai Minge Yundongshi/ Who Are Singing Their Songs There – A History of Modern Taiwanese Folk Song Movement*. Taipei: Rock Culture.

Zhang, Liqiang (2006), 'Sing "Chinese songs" Aloud on the Five-Starred Stage, Take up the Inheritance of a People with Huaxia Characteritics', http://big5.cctv.com/qgds/20060729/100132.shtml, accessed 2 October 2006.

Zournazi, Mary (2002), *Hope: New Philosophies for Change*. Annandale: Pluto Press.

Index

Note: page numbers in italics refer to illustrations.

A
Abbas, Ackbar, 6, 29, 103
Academic Community Hall, 109, *110*, 114
Ai, Weiwei, 5
Americanization, 43, 56
Appadurai, Arjun, 42
areas studies, 5, 7, 8, 9, 151
Asia World Arena, 112
Asian Crisis, 28

B
Bai Xuexian, 75
Bakhtin, Mikhail, 121
'Ballroom of the South', 28–9
Baranovich, Nimrod, 4
Beatles, the, 44
Beijing Olympics *see* Olympic Games, Beijing, 2008
Beijing rock, 4
'Beijing Welcomes You' (Olympic song), 119, 123, 124, 128, 131
Ben-Yehuda, Nachman, 84
Berry, Chris, 21
'Big Red Robe', 68–70, *74*, 75, *75*, *76*
binaries, cultural
  and socialism, 133
  in Soviet Union, 120–2
'A Black Moon in Gusty Wind', 27
black music genres, 143, 147–8
Black, Sir Robert, 108
body image and weight, 148–50
Borsato, Marco, 9, 41, 44–6
character, and fan culture, 52–4
charitable work, 46–7, 48, 51–2
Boyer, Dominic, 134
Buddha, 65
Butler, Judith, 33

C
Cai Guoqiang, 119
Callahan, William A., 18
Cantopop, 3, 6, 18, 19, 46
  decline/disappearance of, 103–5
CCTV Youth Singing Contest 2006, 17
celebrities
  commercial branding, 93–8
  body image and weight, 148–50
celebrity culture, 87, 88, 92, 94
celebrity status, 53, 89
censorship, 33–4, 92, 93, 132
Certeau, Michel de, 36
Chan, Bobo, 83, 98
Chan, Jacky, 119, 129
Chan, Jolland, 20
Chan, Punk, 129
Chan Siu Kei, 106, 119
'Charged up' (World Cup 2002 theme song), 30–1
charitable work, of pop stars, 46–8, 51–2
Chen, Edison, 7, 10, 83, 89
  artwork and shows, 95–7
  public apologies, 88–91
  scandal, 84–98
Chen Kaige, 70

Cheng, Sammi, 70
Cheung, Celia, 83, 92, 98
Cheung, Jacky, 128
Cheung, Leslie, 4, 104, 115
Cheung, Mei-kwun, 17
Cheung, Ming-min, 21, 22
Chew, Matthew, 87
Chi Ching, 25
'China century', 7
China, images of
   cosmopolitan, 124–5
   multivocal yet united, 125–6
   pastoral and traditional, 123–4
China Newsweek, 62
China Wind (*zhongguofeng*), 10
   defining, 61
   entries to Commercia Radio
      pop chart, 64–5
   feminizing Chineseness, 70–7
   lyrics, 61–2
   music videos, China Wind, 65–77
   singles, 61
China with a Cut (de Kloet), 4
China's New Voices (Baranovich), 4
Chineseness
   celebrations of, 16, 25, 29, 30, 31, 123
   claiming and disclaiming, 30, 33
   critical understanding of, 17
   defining, 18
   discourses on, 36
   feminizing, 70–7
   language alternatives, 145–6
   narratives of, 33
   as performance, 15, 17–18, 33, 34
   pervasive ideology, 4
   questioning, 21, 25, 30
   sounds as markers of, 8
   versions of, 16, 18–19, 21, 29, 31
   see also China Wind (*zhongguofeng*);
      nationalistis songs (*minzu gequ*)
Chou, Jay, 61, 62, 70, 72
Chow, Kevin, 143, 144
Chow, Rey, 70, 104, 116

Chow, Yiu Fai, 128, 129–30, 141, 153
   interview with Diana Zhu, 140
Christian hymns, 19
'Chrysanthemum Terrace', 71, 72
Chu, Stephen, 4, 104
Chua, Beng Huat, 19, 116
Chun, Allen, 36
Chung, Gillian, 83, 91, 98
Ciecko, Anne, 87
Cline, Cheryl, 44
Cohen, Stanley, 84
Coliseum, Hong Kong *see* Hong Kong
   Coliseum
collective memory, 107–8
Communist Party, Chinese, 16, 122, 155
'Compendium of Materia Medica', 62
concerts
   and fan culture, 49–50
   reunion and comeback, 107
   see also pop music venues
'A Country Trail', 21
Cries of Joy, Songs of Sorrow (Moscowitz), 4
Crouching Tiger, Hidden Dragon, 65
cultural icons, global, 43
cultural indeterminacy of Hong Kong, 5
cultural studies, 7, 8–9, 15–16, 19, 42,
   84, 150
Curse of the Golden Flower (Zhang), 72
Curtin, Michael, 104

D

Dai Jinhua, 23
'Daiyu Smiles', 68, 71, *71*, *72*
Dawei, Jiang, 17
'de-Sinification' (*qu zhongguohua*) policy, 62
Debord, Guy, 88, 93
'Decathlon' (Olympic Song), 129, 130
Deng, Xiaoping, 20
'Descendants of the Dragon', 15, 20
diasporic narratives, 141–2, 144, 148–9
Dirlik, Arif, 115
Donald, Stephanie Hemelryk, 126
'Don't Question the Heaven', 24, 25, 26, 29

Dream of the Red Chamber, 68
Duara, Prasenjit, 25

E
EEG, 129
Ehrenreich, Barbara, 44
emigration, from Hong Kong, 23
Eperjesi, John, 65
Erni, John, 28
'Error in a Flower Field', 76–7
European Chinese New Talent Singing Contest, 143
Everything Was Forever Until It Was No More (Yurchak), 120–1

F
fan culture, 41–57
   and character of stars, 52–6
   and charitable work of stars, 46–8, 51–2
   and community, 49–50
   concerts, 49–50
   and homecoming of stars, 48–9
   and local stars/heroes, 44, 46–8
   studies of, 44–6
Fang, Wenshan, 62, *72*
Farmer, Brett, 85
Fast, Susan, 107
'Father's Straw Shoes', 22, 26
Fiske, John, 36, 44
folk devils, 84, 92
Fong, Khalil, 148–50
'Forever Friends' (Olympic song), 24, 123
Foucault, Michel, 87, 94, 153
'Fragrance of Rice', 70
Fung, Anthony, 20, 62, 104

G
gender, performing, 75, 76–7
'General's Decree', 68, 71
globalization, 5, 10, 42, 43, 47, 56, 84, 104, 151
'Goddess of Mercy', 65, *65*
Goode, Erich, 84

Grossberg, Larry, 9
guoxue (study of Chinese classics), 62

H
Hall, Stuart, 84
Hardt, Michael, 98
heimat (feeling of home), 43, 47
heroes, local, pop stars as, 46–8
Hess, Elizabeth, 44
Hills, Matt, 44
Hinerman, Stephen, 44
Ho, Denise, 68–70, 75, 76
Ho, Josephine, 87
Ho, Wai-chung, 17
homecoming narratives, 21, 47, 48–9
'Hong Kong Always Has You', 105–6
Hong Kong City Hall, 108, *109*, 110
Hong Kong Coliseum, 10, 103, 107–8, 111–12, 114–15, 116
Hong Kong: Culture and Politics of Disappearance (Abbas), 6
Hong Kong Exhibition and Convention Centre, 112, *113*
Hong Kong Special Administration Region Government, 28
Hou, Deijan, 37n8
'How Great Thou Art', 26
Huatiancuo, 77
Hui, Sam, 7, 107
'Hurry up!' 31–2

I
'I Am A Star' (Olympic song), 123–4, 126
'I Am Chinese', 21, 22
Idols (Dutch), 143

J
Jacobs, Gloria, 44
Jacobs, Katrien, 86, 87
Japanese imperialism, 23
Jenkins, Henry, 44
Jenson, Joli, 44
Juno, 91

K
Kaneshiro, Takeshi, 48
karaoke, 104
King of the Children (Chen), 70
Kloet, Jeroen de, 4
Kooijman, Jaap, 125
Ku, Ivy, 20
Kwok, Aaron, 45

L
'Lady', 61
Lai, Leon, 7, 9–10, 30, 31, 41, 44–6
   character, and fan culture, 54–6
   charitable work, 47–8, 51–2
Lam, Chi Kin, 130
language
   alternatives, 145–6
   linguistic boundaries, 46
Lash, Scott, 4, 11
'Latin face and sound', popularity of, 43
Lau, Andy, 65
Lee, Gordon, 144
'Let's Play Again When the New Century Comes', 26–7
Leung, Helen Hok-sze, 5, 116
Leung, Terry, 144
Liang, Tian, 129
Lin, Xi, 119, 128
Liu Jiachang, 22
Live Aid, London, 107
Lo, Kwai Cheung, 146, 147
Lu, Chen, 131
Lui, Mark, 128
Lury, Celia, 4, 11
lyrics
   censorship, 33–4
   China Wind (*zhongguofeng*), 61–2
   see also under song titles

M
Madeln Company, 95
Mandopop, 4, 104
marriage game, web, 146–7
McRobbie, Angela, 8
Mendelsohn, 98
methodology, endnote on, 150–5
migration narratives, 28, 142–3, 148, 150, 154
Miller, Toby, 153
modernity
   Chinese aspirations, 146–7
   narratives, 144–5, 150
moral panics, 83–4, 87, 92
Morley, David, 42, 47
Morris, Meaghan, 19
Moscowitz, Marc L., 4
Mui, Anita, 4, 104, 115
music videos, China Wind, 62–3, 65–77
   'Big Red Robe', 68–70, 74, 75, *75*, 76
   'Chrysanthemum Terrace', 71, *72*
   'Daiyu Smiles', 68, 71, *71*, *72*
   'Error in a Flower Field', 76–7
   'Fragrance of Rice', 70
   'General's Decree', 68, 71
   'Goddess of Mercy', 65, *65*
   'Small', 65, *67*, 71, 72
   'Sweet Dumplings', 68, *69*
   'Sword and Snow', 68, 70, 72, *73*

N
nationalistis songs (*minzu gequ*), 9, 17–18, 20, 22, 24, 33
Negri, Anthony, 98
New Labour Art Troupe, 131–2
Nora, Pierre, 108

O
Olympic Games, Beijing, 2008, 7, 10, 16, 119–20, 122–35
Olympic songs, 122–33
   CD jacket notes, 122
   performative aspects, 127–31
opera, Cantonese, 6, 65, 68–70, 75
Oriental Sunday magazine, 88, *89*
Orientalist paradigm, 7–8
Orientouch Entertainment, 143

'Our World, Our Dream' (New Labour Art
    Troupe), 132–3

P
Pearl River Delta project, 28
Pickering, Michael, 9
Pink, Sarah, 62
Pixel Toy, 107
pop music venues, 103
    Academic Community Hall, 109, *110*, 114
    Asia World Arena, 112
    development of, 108–13
    Hong Kong City Hall, 108, *109*, 110
    Hong Kong Coliseum, 107–8, 111–12,
        114–15, 116
    Hong Kong Exhibition and Convention
        Centre, 112, *113*
    outdoor, 114
    Queen Elizabeth Stadium, 109, 111,
        111, 114
    Queen's Pier, 106
    Sheung Wan Civic Centre, 107
    Star Hall, 112
popular music studies, 4, 5, 7, 8, 9
post-colonial identity of Hong Kong, 6
postmodernity, 115
Postmodernism and China (Dirlik and
    Xudong), 115
Presley, Elvis, 44

Q
Qu, Yuan, 24–5
Queen, 107
Queen Elizabeth Stadium, 109, 111, *111*, 114
Queen's Pier, 106

R
racism, 143
Radio Television Hong Kong (RTHK)
    Best Chinese Pop Song of 1990, 25
    Top 10 Chinese Pop Songs of the Year, 24
Rancière, Jacques, 133–4
record companies, local, 20

'Red Throughout the World' (Olympic
    song), 128
Ren, Jianhui, 75
resistance, political, 24, 36, 42
'Rood/Red', 41

S
Sandig, Barbara, 46
Sassen, Saskia, 42, 107, 114
school anthems, 19
Selting, Margret, 46
Seventh National University Games, theme
    song, 32–3
'Sex Photo Gate', 10
sexuality, society's unease with, 94
'Sexy Photos gate', 85
'Shanghai Welcomes You', 131
S.H.E., 61, 70
Sheung Wan Civic Centre, 107
Sino-British Joing Declaration, 24
Sit, Fiona, 68
'Small', 65, *67*, 71, 72
Solomon, Tom, 8
Soong, Roland, 93, 98
South China Morning Post, 114
'Speak Mandarin Campaigne', 46
Star Hall, 112
stars, local, 43, 44
Steedman, Carolyn, 16
Strait Times, 95
'Sweet Dumplings', 68, *69*
'Sword and Snow', 68, 70, 72, *73*
swordsmanship genre, Chinese, 70
Sze, Ho-Chun, 86

T
Taiwanese pop, 7
TANK, 61
Tao, David, 61
Tatming Pair, 24, 25, *26*, 27, 28, 30
Television Broadcast Ltd (TVB), 143
television drama series, theme songs,
    19, 23

'The Best of Youth' (Seventh National
    University Games theme song), 32–3
theme songs
    Seventh National University Games, 32–3
    television drama, 19, 23
    World Cup 2002, 30–1
Tiananmen Square demonstrations, 24
Tianya forum, 92–3
Top 10 Chinese Pop Songs of the Year
    (RTHK), 24
Top Floor Circus, 131
Tse, Nicholas, 30, 31, 32, 33, 35, 129

U
'USA for Africa' project, 125

V
Vincy, 68, 71, 75

W
Wang, Chi-ming, 28
Wang, Dan, 128, 134
Wang, Leehom, 61, 77, 148–50
Wang, Lei, 142
Wang, Peiwen, 62
War Child charity, 46–7
Warner Music, 139, 144, 147, 148–50
Watson, Sophie, 106
'We Are Ready' (Olympic song), 123, 124,
    125, 126, 130, 132–3
'We Are The World', 125
Weber, Max, 84
West Kowloon Cultural District project,
    112, *113*

Wolf, Eric, 62
Wong, Anthony, 25, 27, 30, 130
Wong, Elvin, 25
Wong, James, 3
World Cup 2002, theme song, 30–1
Wright, Handel Kashope, 18
Wu, Daniel, 87
Wu, Ken, 61, 68, 71

X
Xie, Xuexin, 75
Xu, Wenwei, 62

Y
Yang, Evelyn, 144, 147, 148–50
Yang Liwei, 31
Yazhou Zhoukan/Asiaweek, 61, 62, 77
Ye, Jieshou, 21
'Yellow People', 34–5
Yung, Joey, 65, 71, 72, 75
Yurchak, Alexei, 120, 128, 134

Z
Zhang, Liqiang, 17
Zhang, Xiaozhou, 128
Zhang, Xudong, 115
Zhang, Yimou, 72, 119
zhongguofeng see China Wind
    (*zhongguofeng*)
'Zhongguohua/Chinese Language', 70
Zhou, Fengwu, 77
Zhu, Diana, 10–11, 139–50

www.ingramcontent.com/pod-product-compliance
Ingram Content Group UK Ltd.
Pitfield, Milton Keynes, MK11 3LW, UK
UKHW050522150426
5217IPUK00026B/1756